I0795651

IMAGES
of America

PAWTUCKET

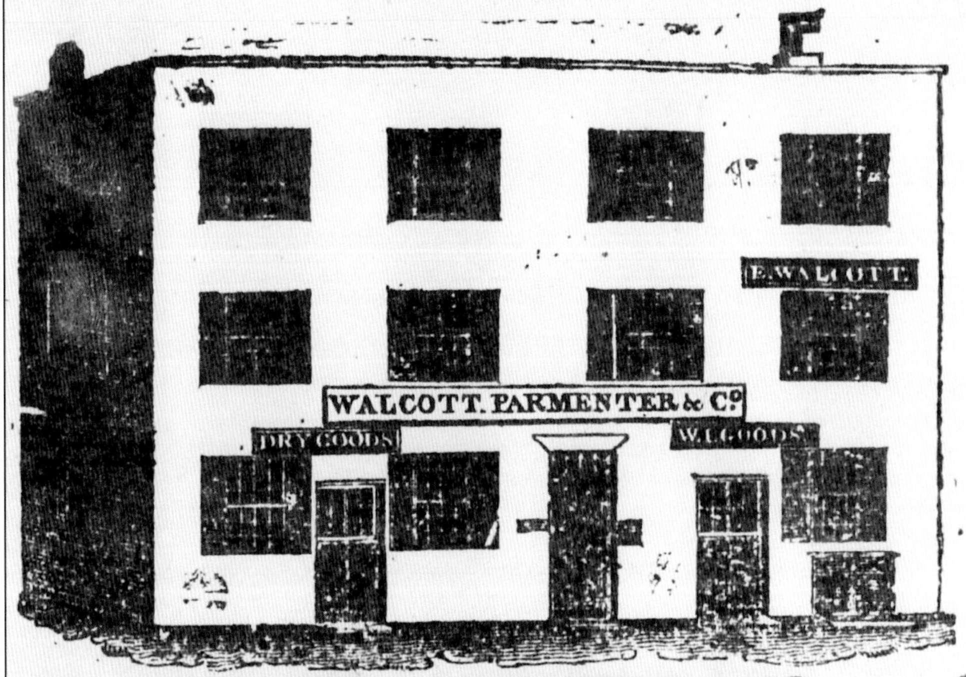

WALCOTT, PARMENTER & CO.

KEEP constantly on hand, at their Stores, directly opposite the Pawtucket Bank, and adjoining Pawtucket Bridge, (East Side,)

A General Assortment of
ENGLISH,
FRENCH,
INDIA,
AND
DOMESTIC
GOODS.

ALSO,
In their West-India Goods Department,
A constant supply of
GENUINE GROCERIES
AND
CROCKERY.

The Room directly over the Dry Goods Store will be devoted exclusively to the sale of LOOKING-GLASSES and CARPETING, all of which they will sell at small advance.

An advertisement from the December 3, 1825 edition of the *Pawtucket Chronicle*, showing the first illustration ever printed by that newspaper.

IMAGES
of America

PAWTUCKET

Elizabeth J. Johnson, James L. Wheaton, and Susan L.Reed

ARCADIA
PUBLISHING

ISBN 978-0-7385-1287-7

Published by Arcadia Publishing
Charleston, South Carolina

Printed in the United States of America

Library of Congress Catalog Card Number: 0752402439

For all general information contact Arcadia Publishing at:
Telephone 843-853-2070
Fax 843-853-0044
E-mail sales@arcadiapublishing.com
For customer service and orders:
Toll-Free 1-888-313-2665

Visit us on the Internet at www.arcadiapublishing.com

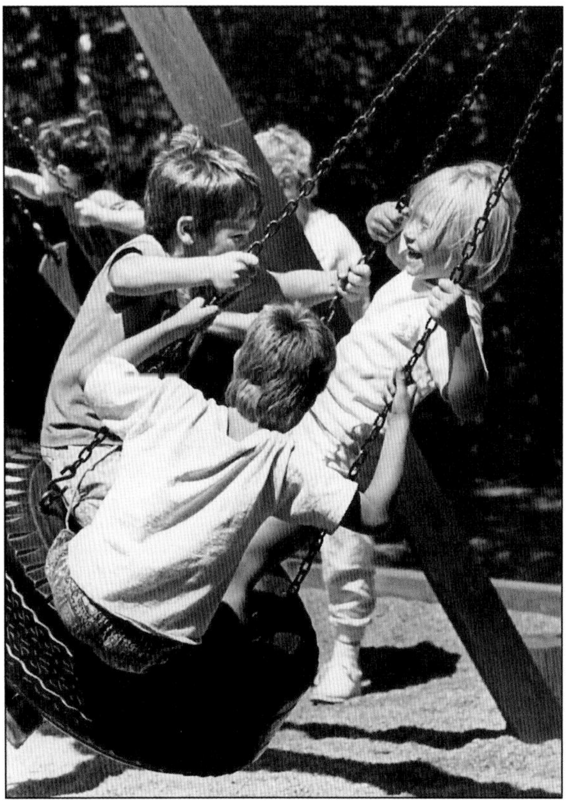

Dedicated to the children—the future of Pawtucket. Pictured are, from left to right, Joshua Birchall, Joshua Gomes, and Chantelle Rogers. This photograph was taken in 1992. (*Times*.)

Contents

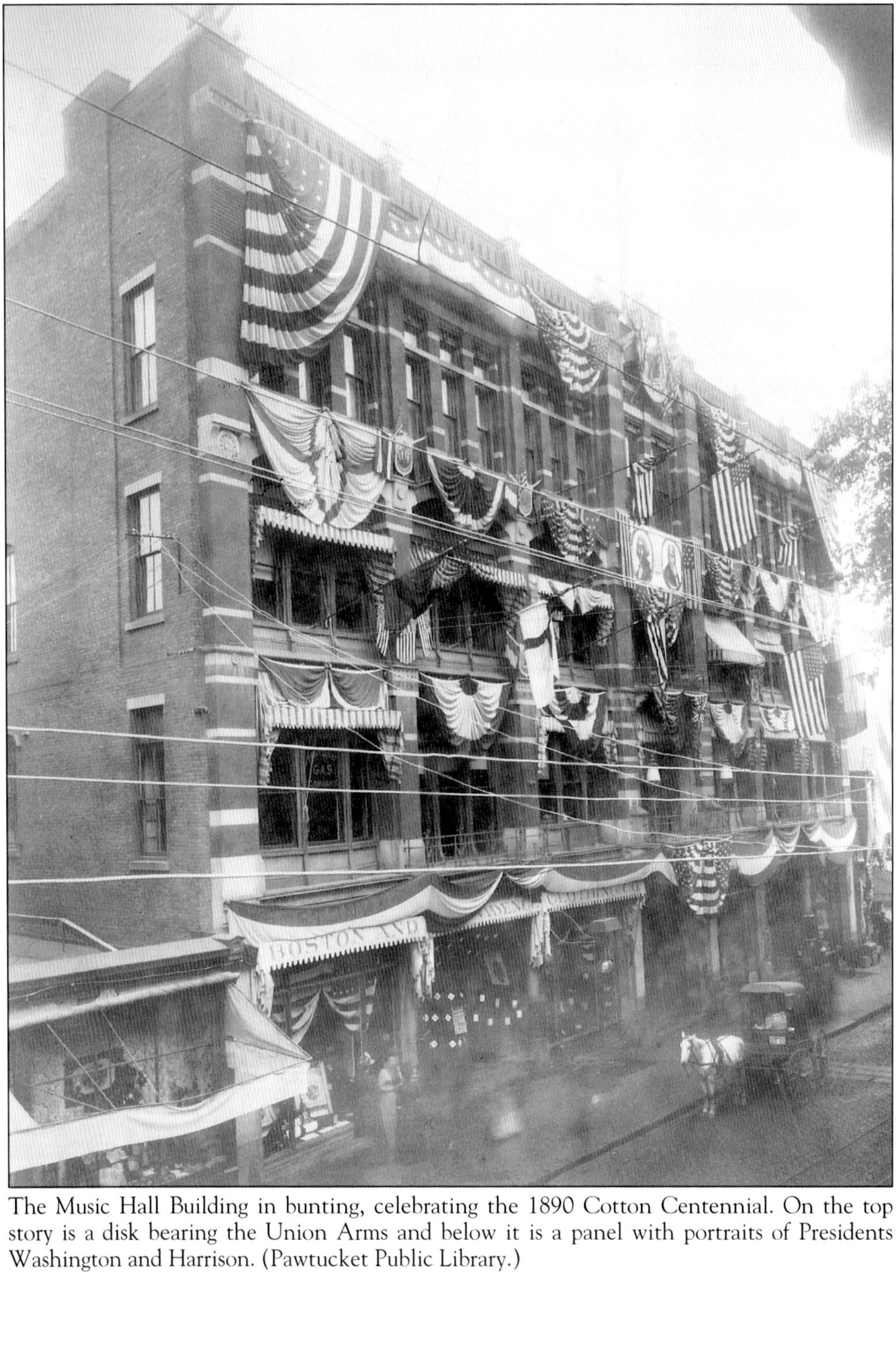

The Music Hall Building in bunting, celebrating the 1890 Cotton Centennial. On the top story is a disk bearing the Union Arms and below it is a panel with portraits of Presidents Washington and Harrison. (Pawtucket Public Library.)

INTRODUCTION

A city's very nature is the summary result of the life experiences and enterprise of its people over time. Who we are and how we react to the future are directly related. The preservation of knowledge about the facets of the whole picture of our past is not only pleasurable and gratifying nostalgia, but also essential to our understanding of ourselves.

The words of historians are relied upon to communicate the past, but, as reliable as they are, they describe only what historians perceive to have occurred. As the axiom goes, a picture is worth a thousand words. The past communicated through photography is not a perception but the truth.

The importance of the preservation of photographic history has been recognized at the Spaulding House Research Library, which specializes in Pawtucket and its past, and at the Pawtucket Public Library. Each maintains a photographic collection of volume and importance.

The publication of this book has provided a fortunate avenue for sharing our photographs of Pawtucket with you by allowing us to move our collections from dusty archives to a media that is readily available to a wide audience.

The work of making this book a reality has been an enjoyable and rewarding experience. It is our hope that it brings meaning and pleasure to you.

Elizabeth Jackson Johnson
James Lucas Wheaton, IV
The Spaulding House Research Library
30 Fruit Street, Pawtucket, RI 02860

Susan Leach Reed, Director
The Pawtucket Public Library
13 Summer Street, Pawtucket, RI 02860

One

Going Downtown

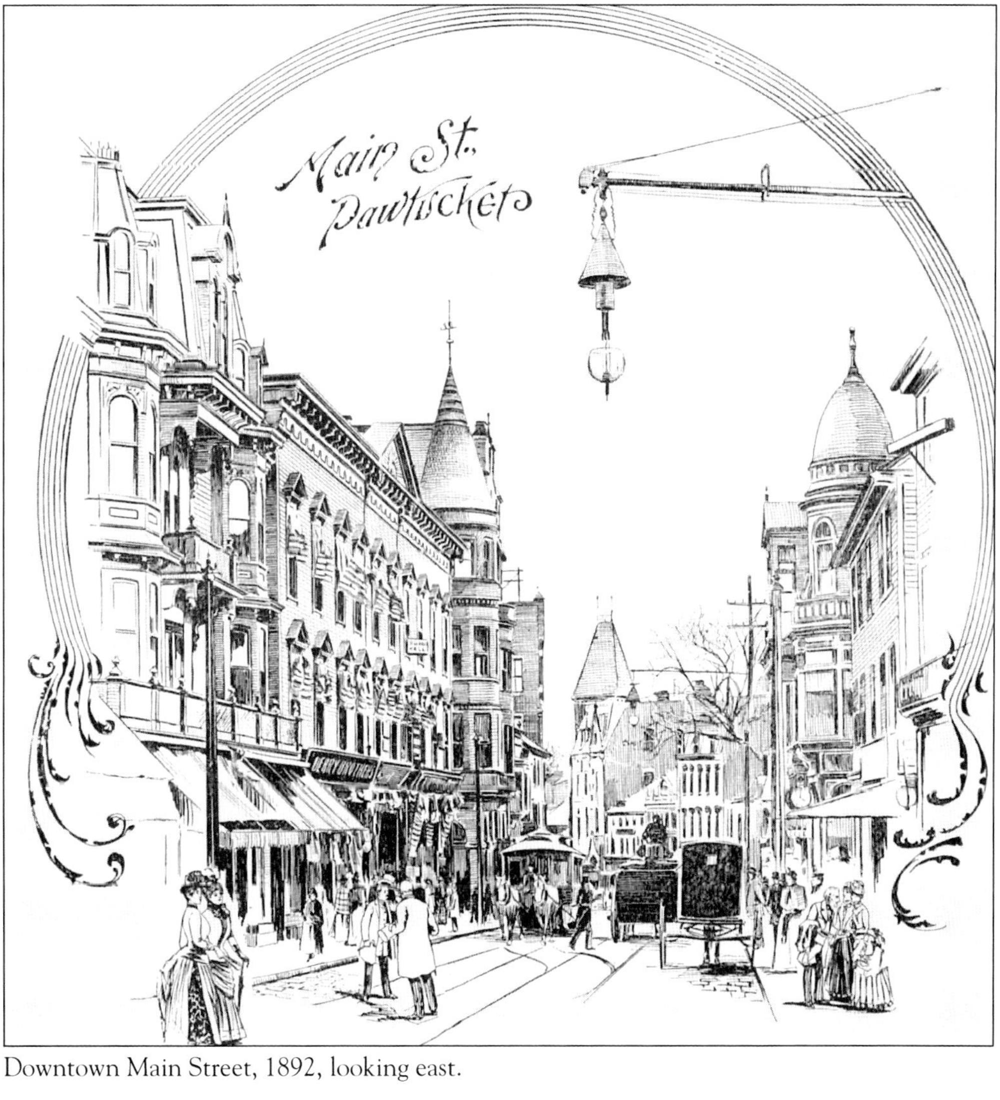

Downtown Main Street, 1892, looking east.

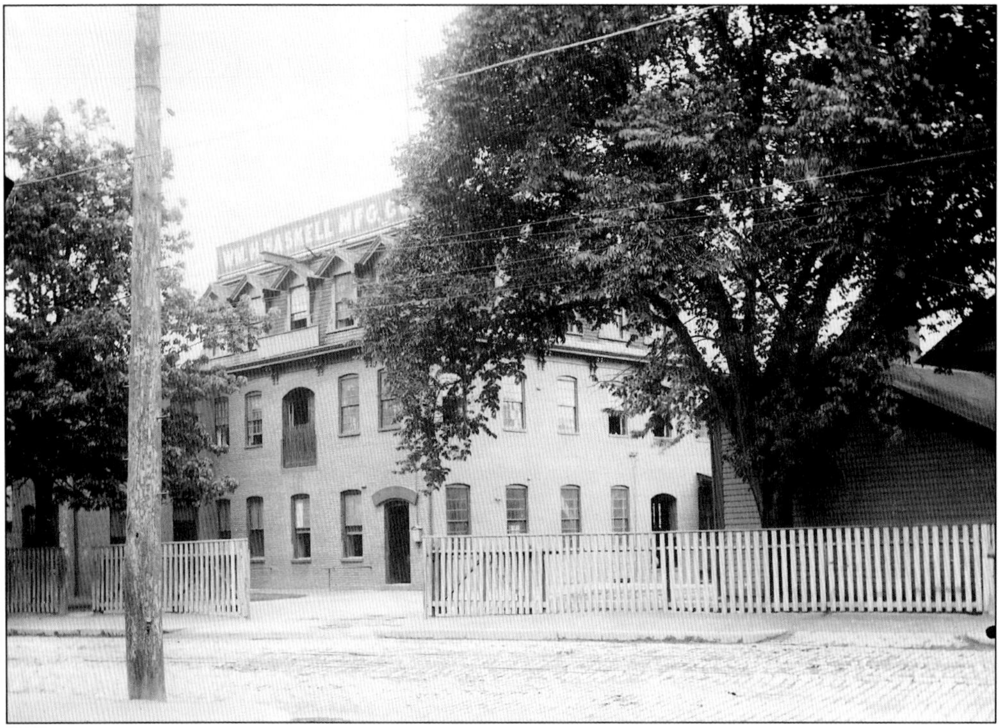

An 1879 photograph of the William H. Haskell Company, a manufacturer of nuts and bolts from 1860 to 1984 at 453 Main Street. This building is still standing.

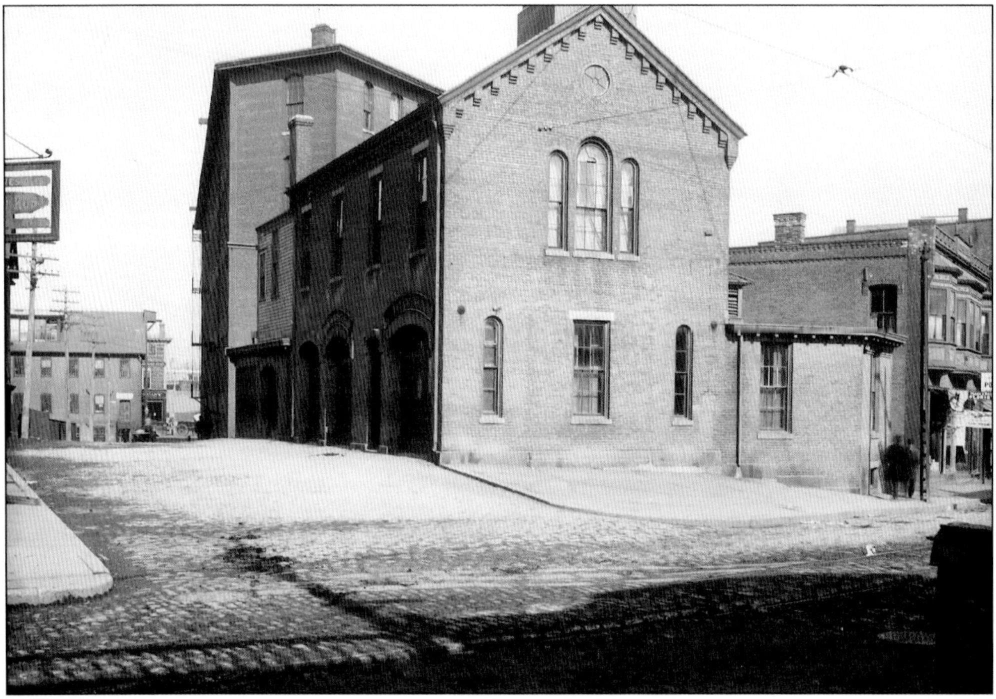

The Steam Fire Engine Company No. 2, the "Rough and Ready Station," located at the corner of Main and Commerce Streets. This photograph was taken in 1895.

G.W. Easterbrooks, Saddlery Goods, was located at 214 Main Street, opposite the Odd Fellow Building. This 1878 view shows Giles W. Easterbrooks (left) and Abraham Lassard. Easterbrooks was mayor of Pawtucket from 1911 to 1918. (Pawtucket Public Library.)

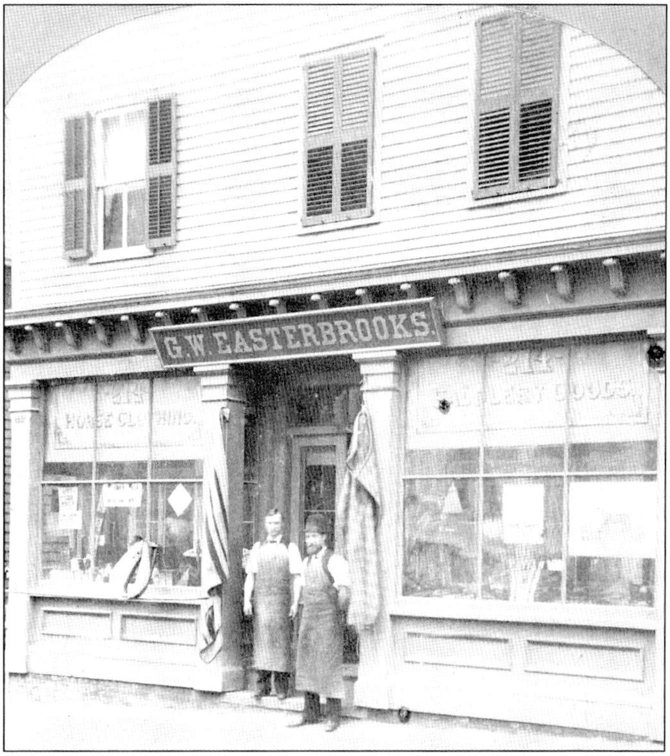

This was originally the M.J. Gallagher Building, built in 1921 at the corner of Main and Bayley Streets. Purchased by the Old Colony Bank in 1935, the building later housed the Bank of New England (see p. 42). This photograph was taken in May 1989. (*Times*.)

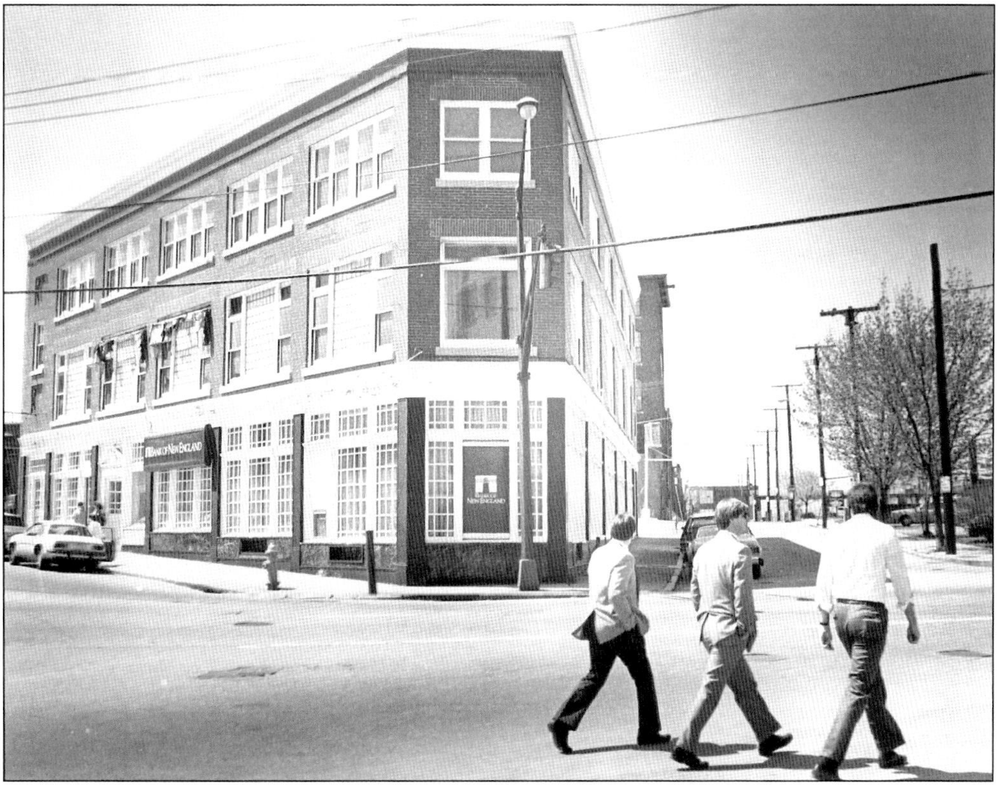

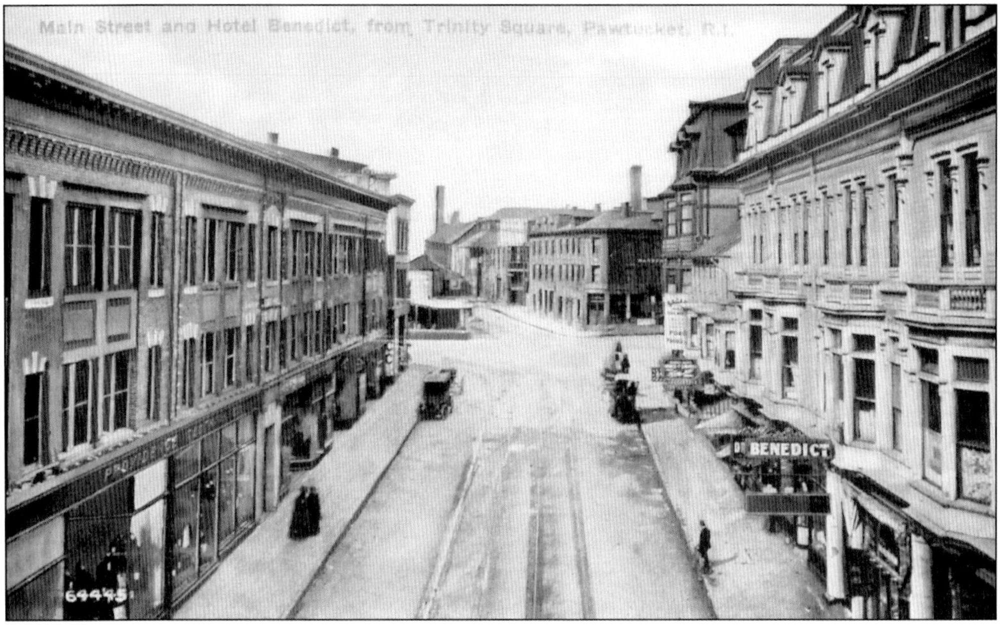

A 1908 view of upper Main Street, looking toward the junction with Dexter and Bayley Streets.

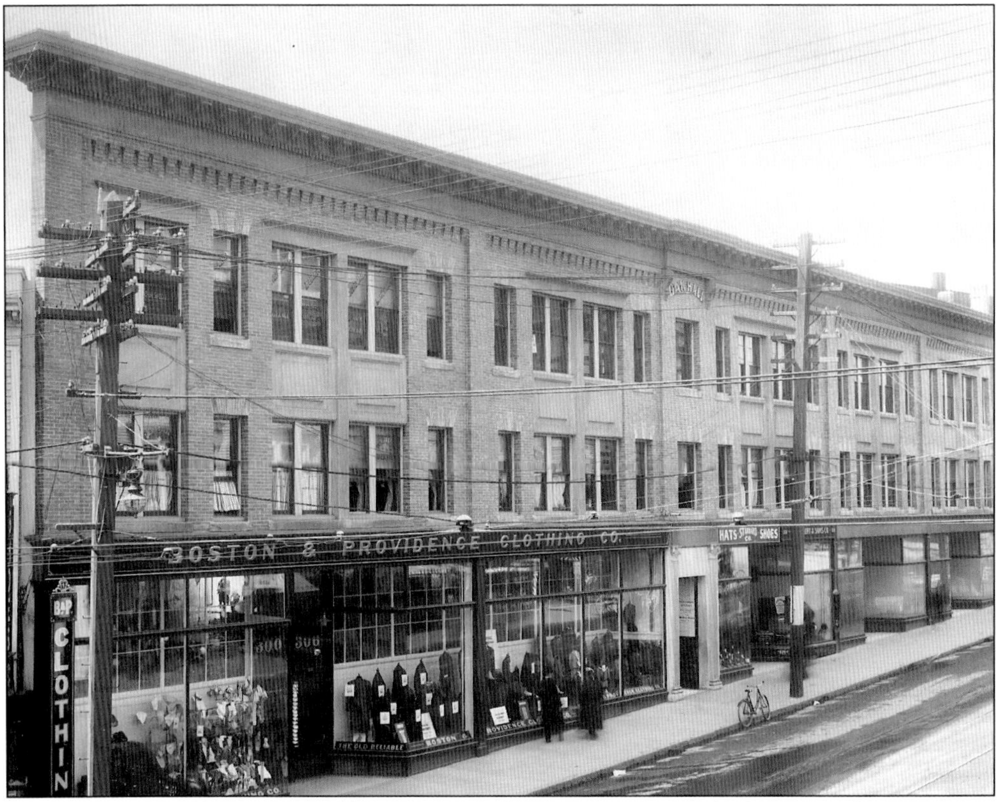

The Oak Hall Building, designed by architect Albert H. Humes, was built in 1906 for Forrest W. Taylor of Worcester, Massachusetts. It was demolished in 1975 to make way for the Pawtucket Institution for Savings/Pawtucket Trust Company. This photograph was taken in 1908.

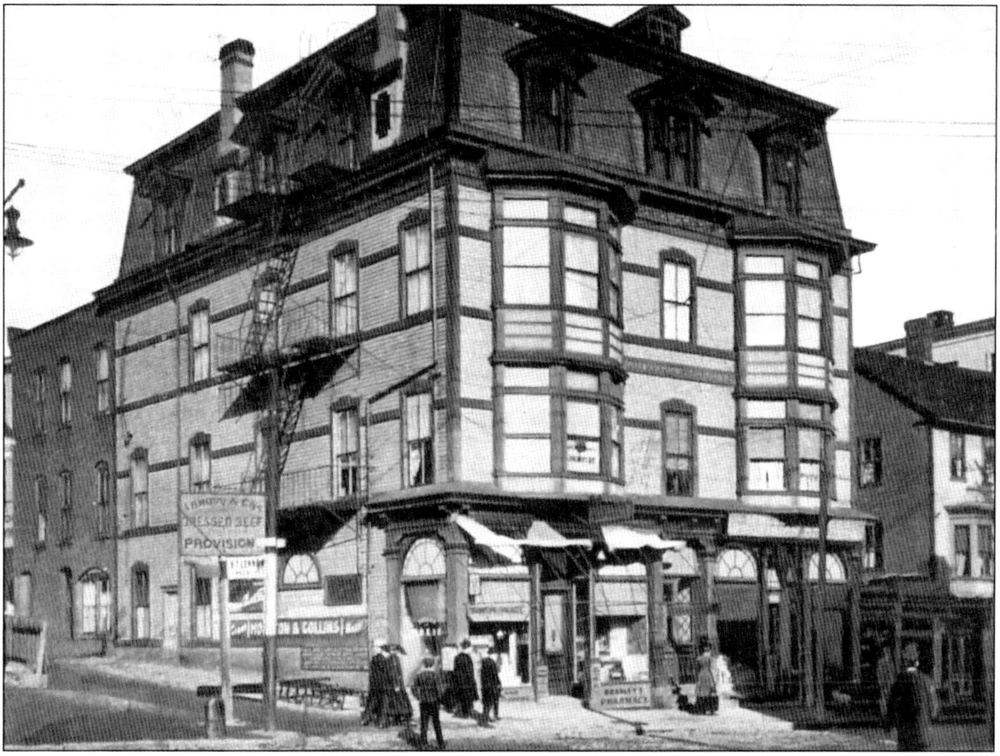

The Odd Fellow Building was built in 1874 by Isaac Straus, a clothier, on Main Street at the corner of Dexter Street and Maiden Lane. It was purchased by the Odd Fellows in 1876. The building was demolished in 1979 to make way for the Northern Plaza development. This photograph was taken in 1908.

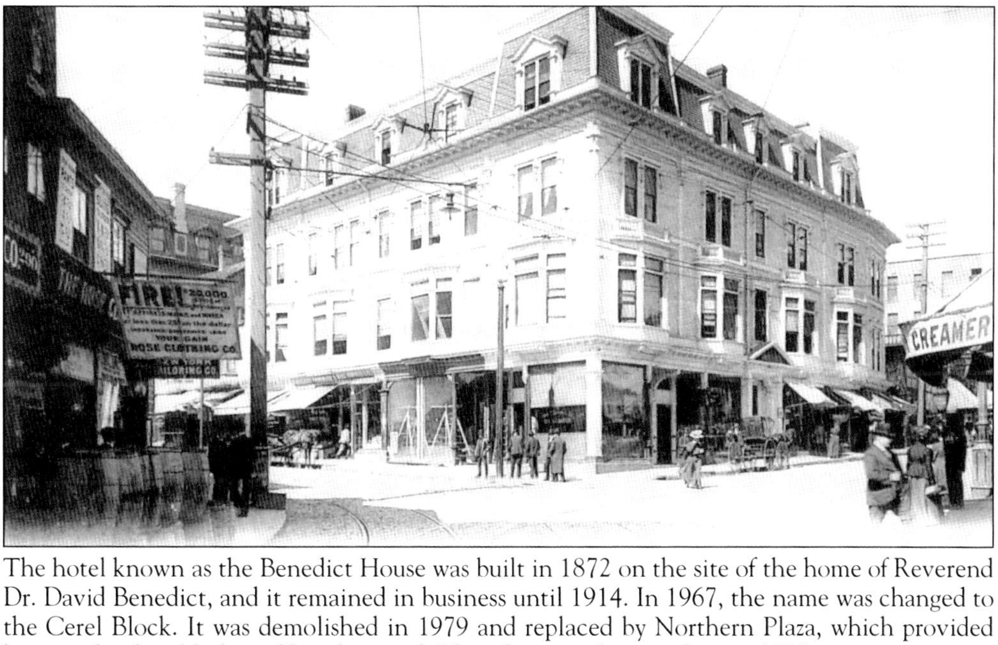

The hotel known as the Benedict House was built in 1872 on the site of the home of Reverend Dr. David Benedict, and it remained in business until 1914. In 1967, the name was changed to the Cerel Block. It was demolished in 1979 and replaced by Northern Plaza, which provided housing for the elderly and handicapped. This photograph was taken in 1908.

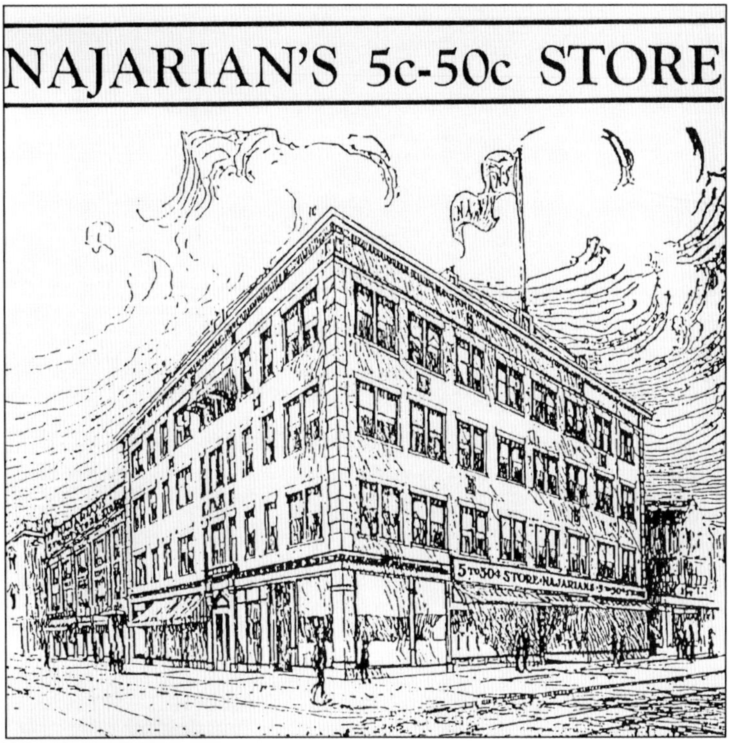

This April 1929 drawing announces the first anniversary of the opening of Najarian's Main Street store. It connected through with their Broad Street store, thus establishing "the largest and most up-to-date popular priced store in this community." The business opened in 1915 and closed in 1959.

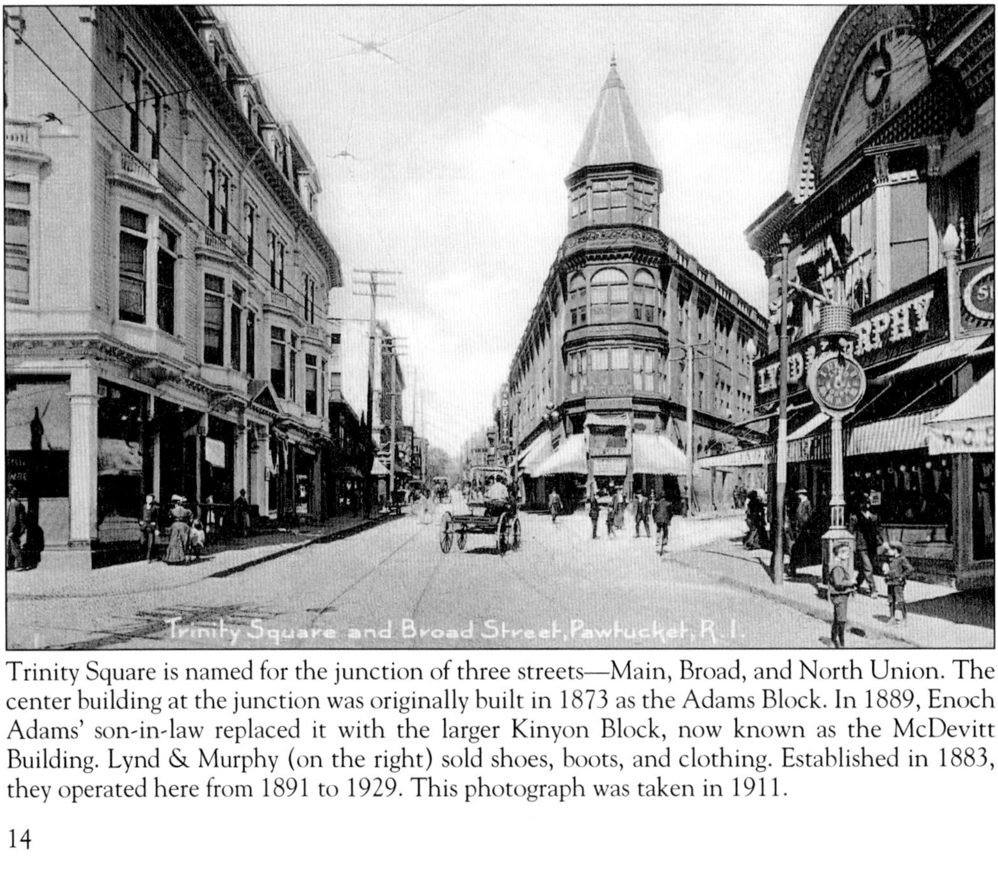

Trinity Square is named for the junction of three streets—Main, Broad, and North Union. The center building at the junction was originally built in 1873 as the Adams Block. In 1889, Enoch Adams' son-in-law replaced it with the larger Kinyon Block, now known as the McDevitt Building. Lynd & Murphy (on the right) sold shoes, boots, and clothing. Established in 1883, they operated here from 1891 to 1929. This photograph was taken in 1911.

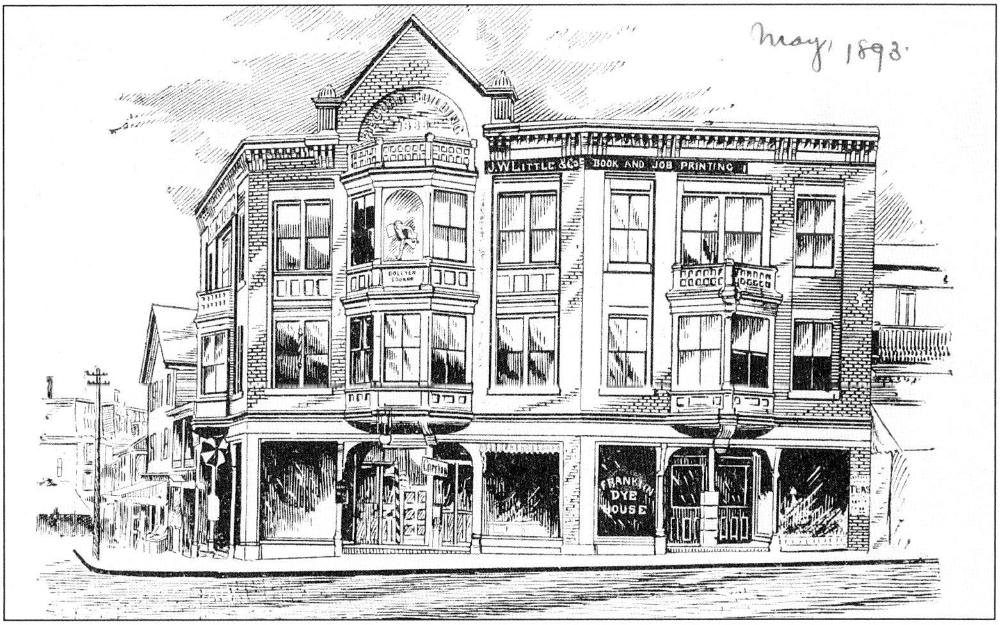

The Record Building, in what was then Collyer Square, was built in 1888 by Henry Herbert Sheldon for his new *Pawtucket Record* newspaper. In 1889, Martin Murray's *Pawtucket Tribune* and the printers John W. Little & Co. rented offices in Sheldon's building. In the niche on the exterior of the third floor is a statue of a "newsie" (newspaper boy), hawking a copy of the *Pawtucket Record* held high in his hand. The "newsie" is now owned by the Milwaukee Art Museum. This photograph was taken in 1893.

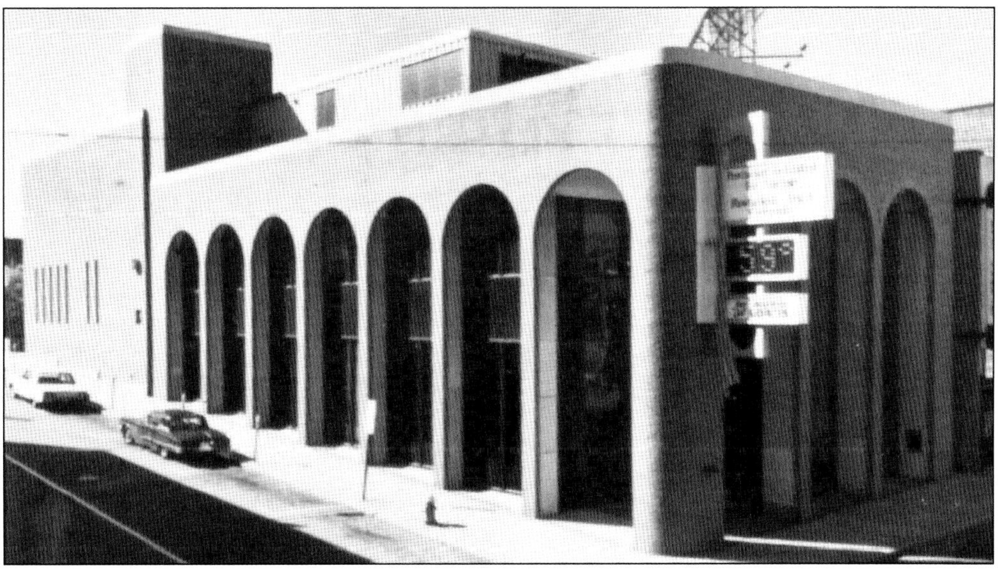

The Pawtucket Institution for Savings/Pawtucket Trust Company was established in the village of Pawtucket, North Providence, in 1836. The present building, seen here in 1971, was built at the corner of Main Street and Park Place in 1964 and enlarged in 1976. In 1987, it became the Attleboro-Pawtucket Savings Bank, and in 1992, a branch of the New Bedford Institution for Savings. Restauranteur Louis Yipp purchased the empty building in 1993. Its current tenant is the Rhode Island Registry of Motor Vehicles.

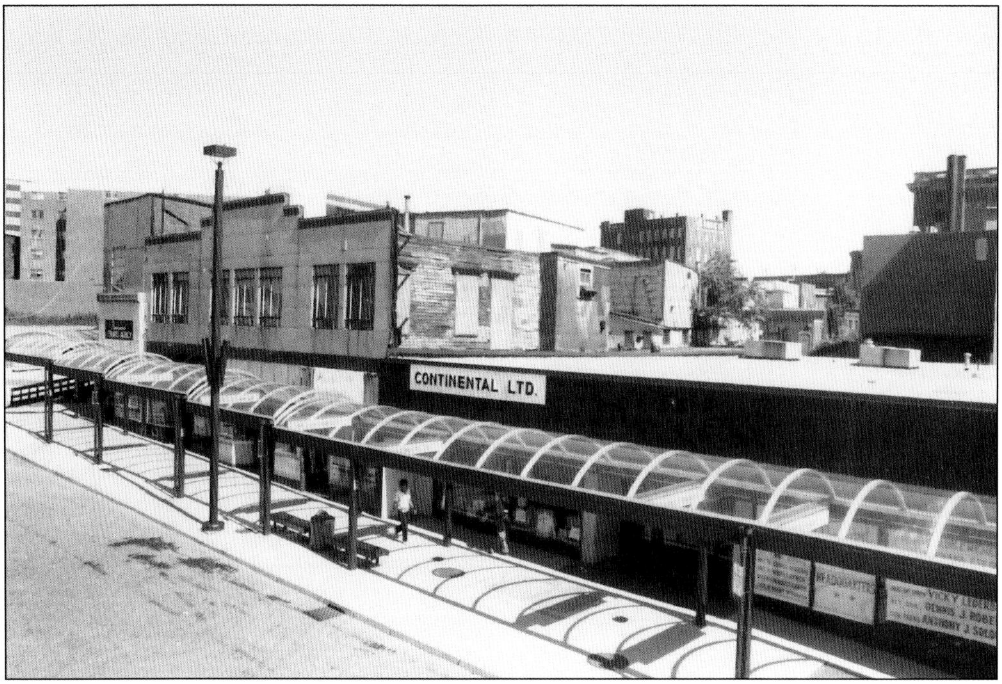

The installation of sidewalk canopies for the Downtown Pedestrian Mall, along Main Street, in 1982. The canopies were later removed, and one-way traffic was returned to Main Street.

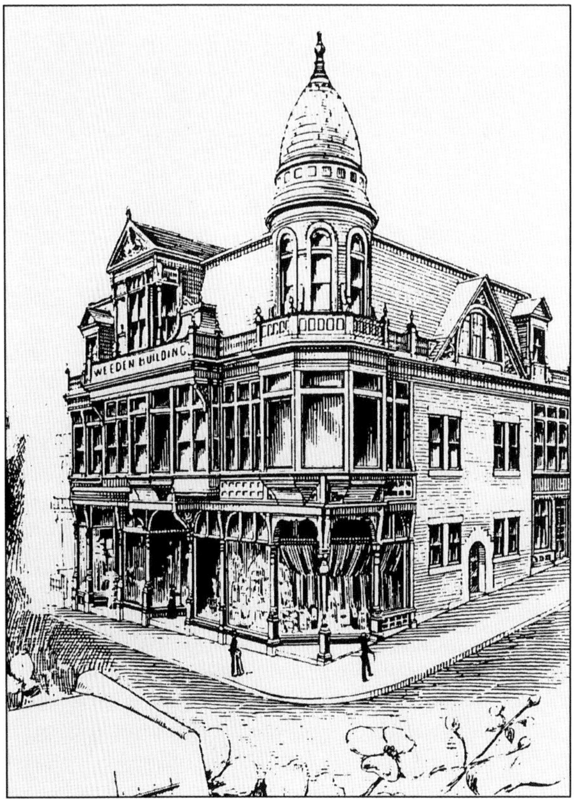

The Weeden (alias Moulton) Building was built in 1887 at the corner of Main Street and Park Place. Shartenberg and Robinson's New Idea Store immediately moved into this new building. They expanded by building the New Idea Building to its left, in 1900. By 1906, they had remodeled the Weeden Building with a new facade. Shartenberg's Department Store eventually occupied both buildings, until they were razed in late 1973 and replaced by the Downtown Parking Garage (see pp. 52 and 53).

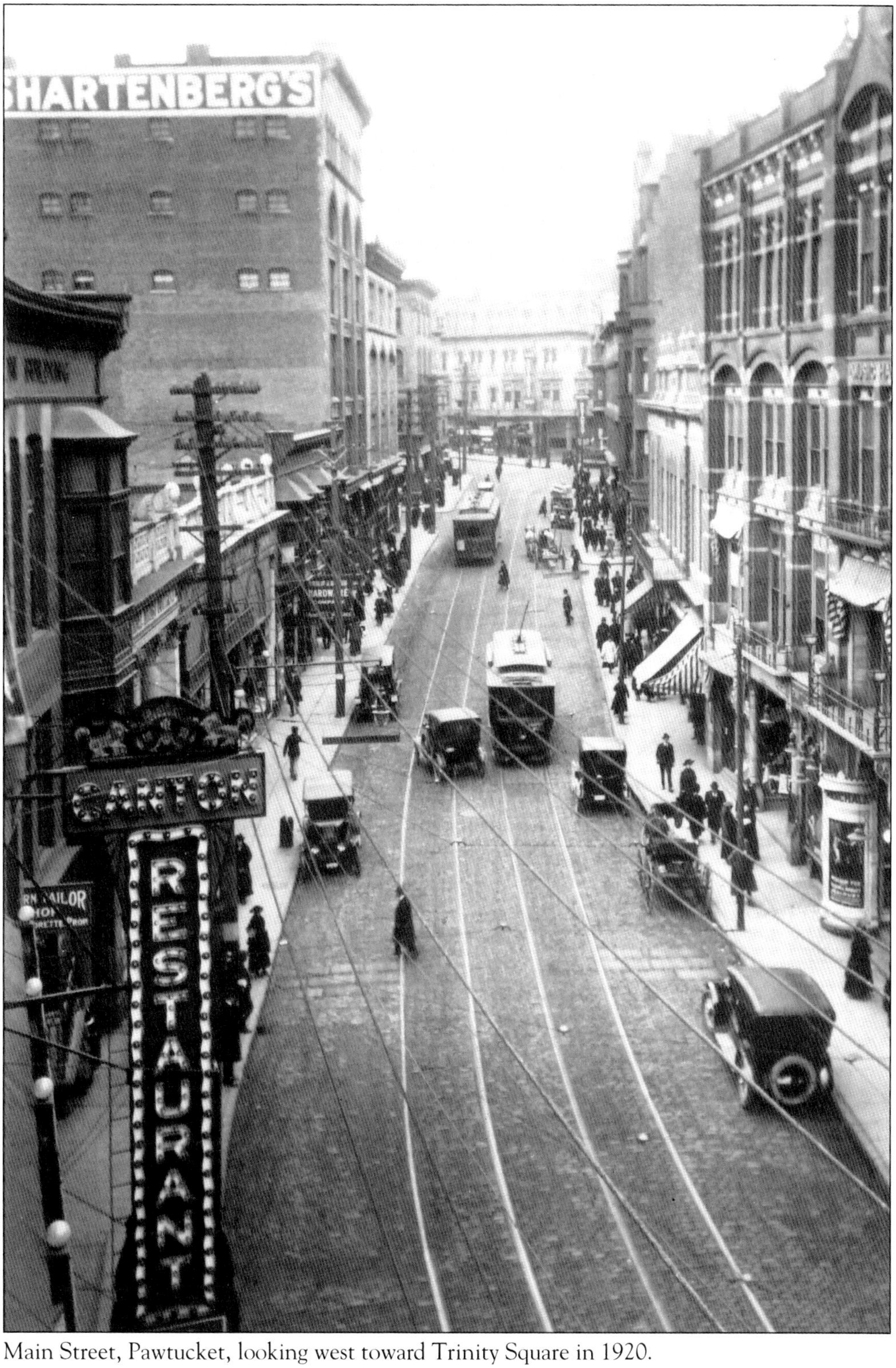

Main Street, Pawtucket, looking west toward Trinity Square in 1920.

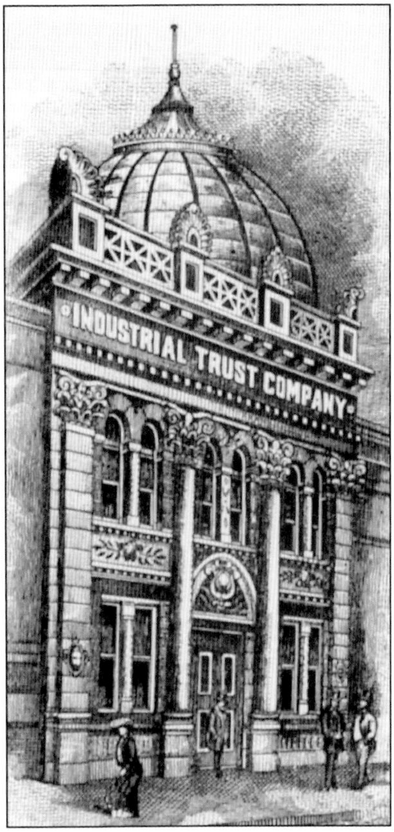

Plans for the Industrial Trust Company's Pawtucket Branch, at 238 Main Street, were drawn in 1900. The architect was William R. Walker & Son. The builder was the Sheldon Construction Company. Both architect and builder were Pawtucket residents. The floors were marble, the teller cages were shining mahogany and brass, and the vaulted dome was two-and-a-half stories above the floor. The bank left Pawtucket in 1950, and a modern facade now hides the original architecture. It was renovated to become Saco's fruit store. (*Times.*)

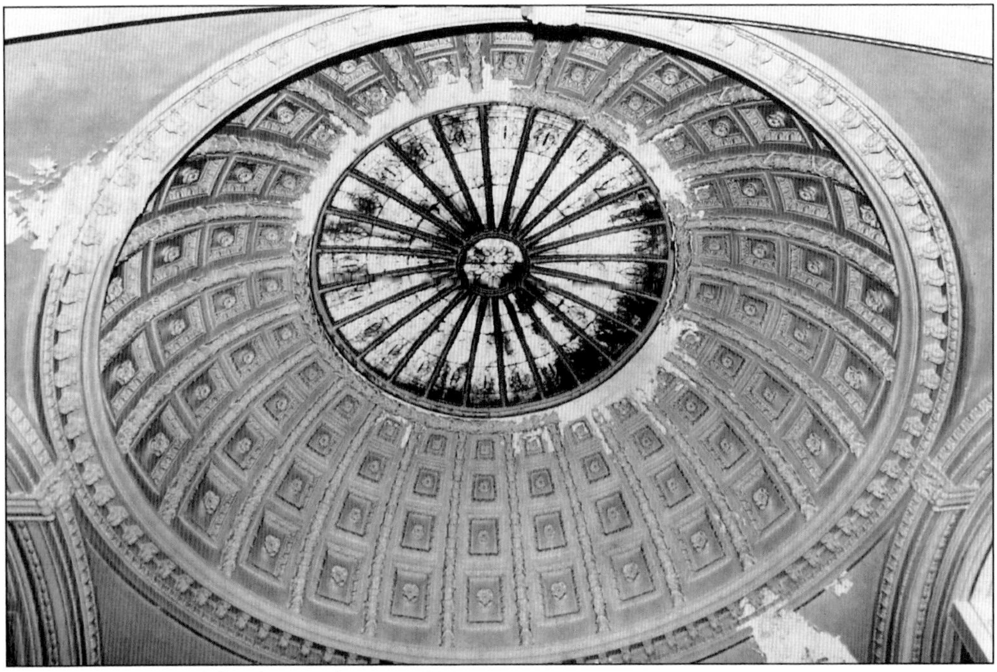

An interior view of the dome taken in 1980.

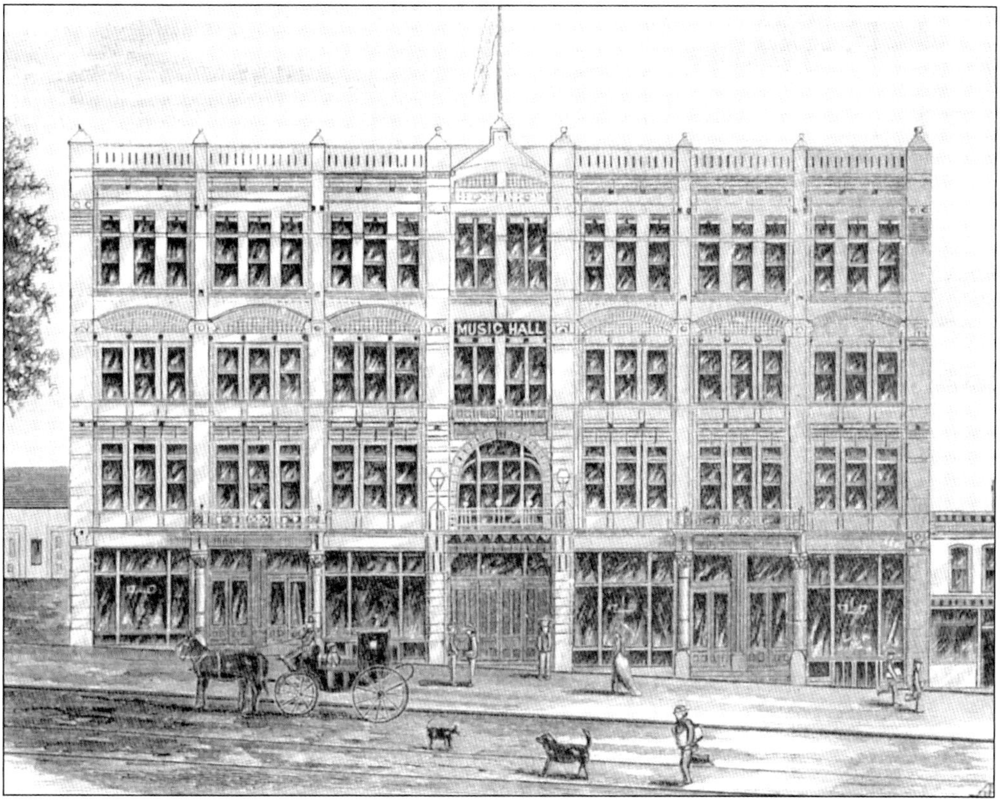

The Music Hall Building was built in 1880 for Lucius Bowles Darling, in the heart of the downtown area. It was considered the finest building in the city at the time, and was the center of entertainment. In 1936, the Music Hall was renovated with an Art Deco facade. Its new tenants were the Modern Shoe Store and the Peerless Company. The building disappeared in the early 1970s with urban renewal. The lithograph above was taken in 1880; the bottom photograph, in 1951.

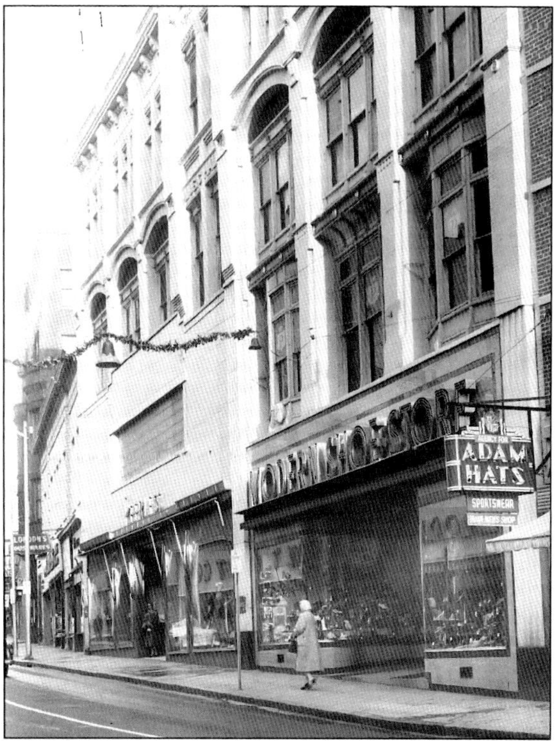

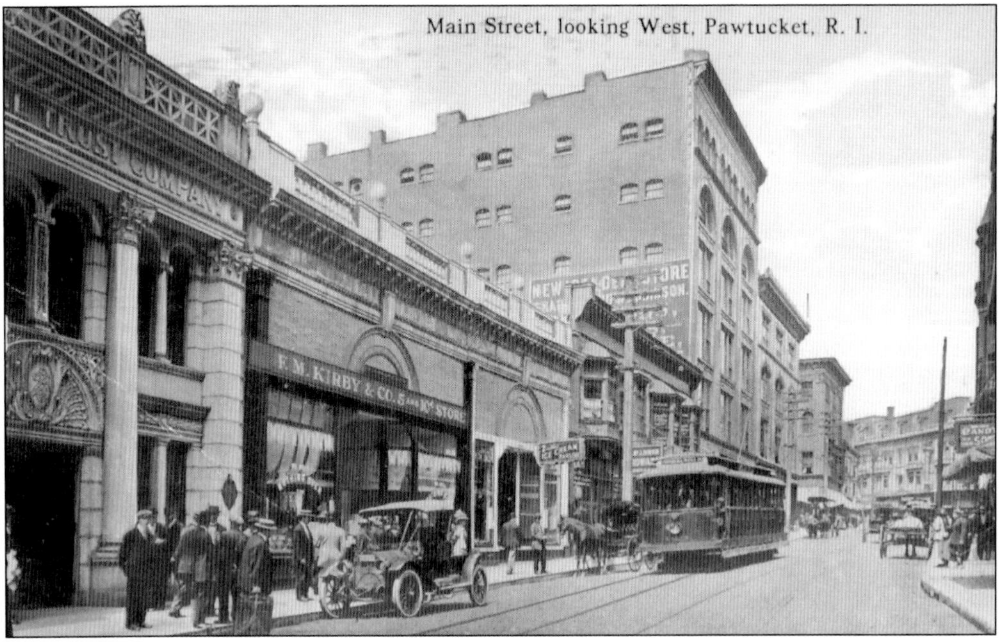

A street-level view of Main Street, captured on camera in 1913.

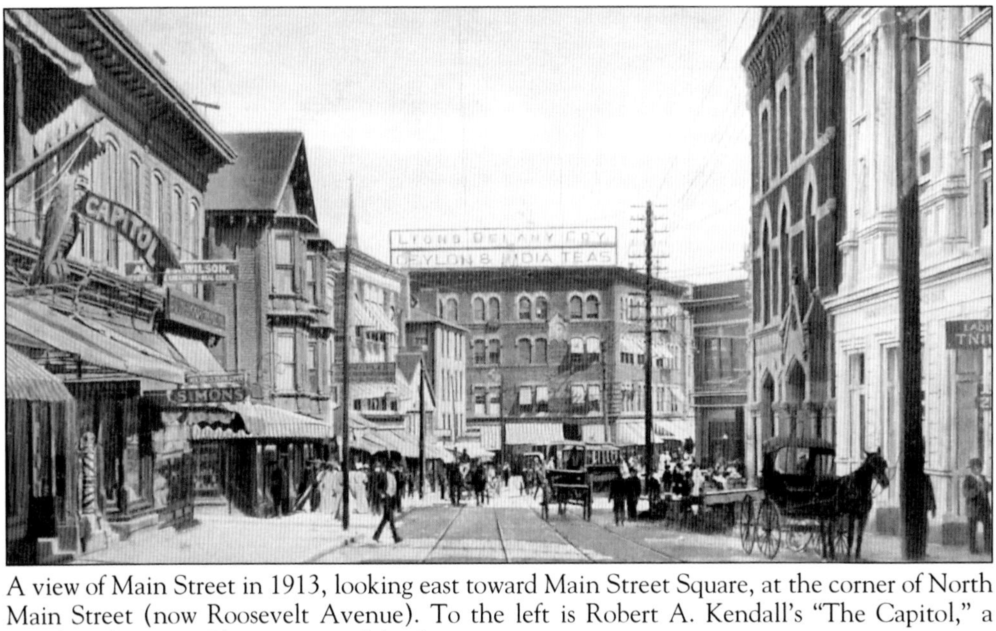

A view of Main Street in 1913, looking east toward Main Street Square, at the corner of North Main Street (now Roosevelt Avenue). To the left is Robert A. Kendall's "The Capitol," a popular tobacco and liquor store of the day.

James L. Wheaton (great-grandfather of the author) and the Wheaton-Toole Building. In 1892 Dr. James L. Wheaton, MD, razed the Walker House—where he had lived since 1864—to erect a handsome, three-story brick and iron building, with the Alcazar Hall located on the top floor. It was sold to William K. Toole in 1922, who had the architects Monahan & Meikle of Pawtucket add two more stories to the structure. (*Times*.)

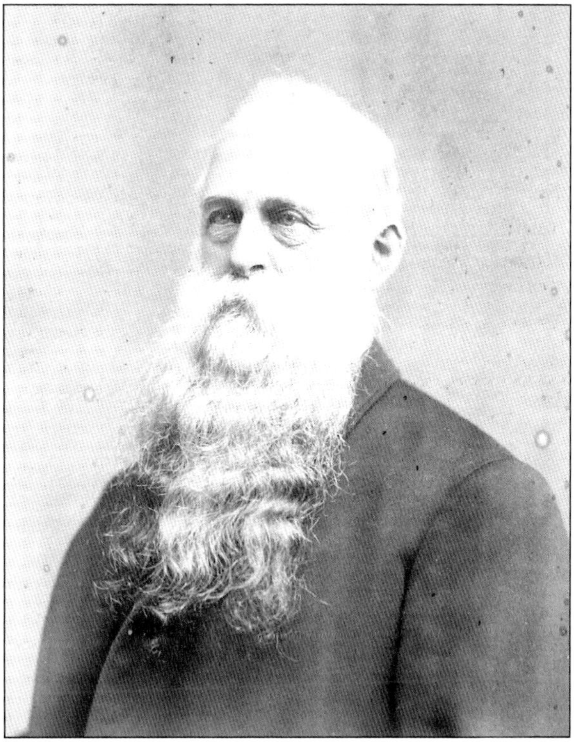

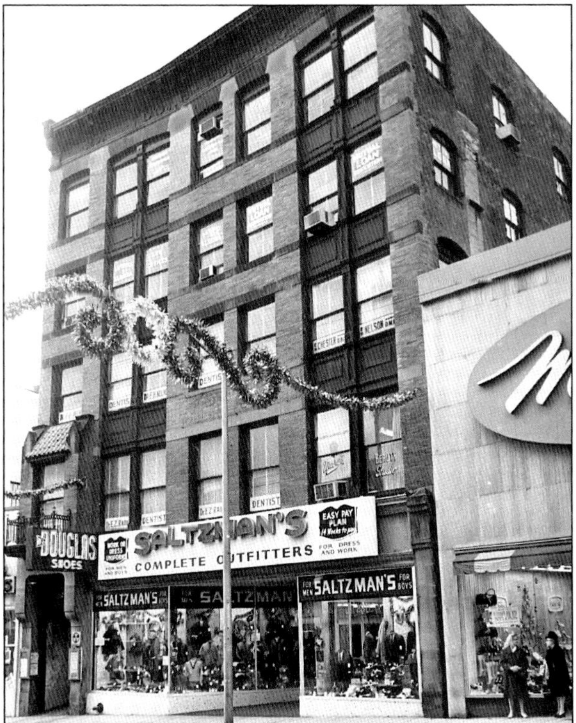

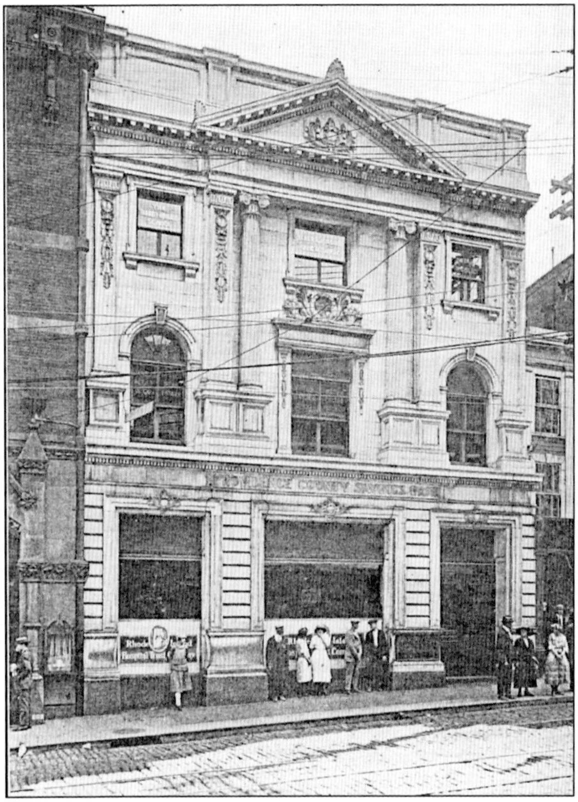

The Providence County Savings Bank, incorporated in 1853, opened for business in this marble-fronted building at 222 Main Street in April 1901. The Hospital Trust Company acquired the Providence County Savings Bank in May 1922, and served Pawtucket from this location until moving to their present quarters in 1977. This photograph was taken in 1901.

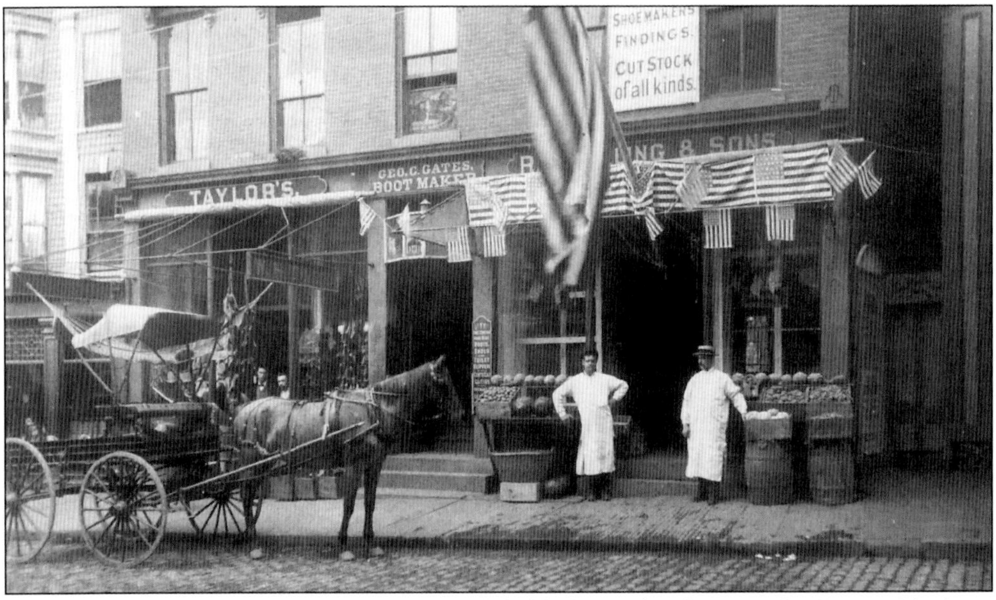

This 1884 picture, by photographer C.L. Littlefield, shows the shops in the Dexter Block, at what was then 138-142 Main Street, next to the Wheaton-Toole Building. The Dexter Block was built by Pawtucket's Nathaniel G.B. Dexter in 1865. William H. Taylor sold boots, shoes, hats, and caps, next to George C. Gates, the boot maker. On the right was Ruel S. Darling & Sons, a grocery and meat market.

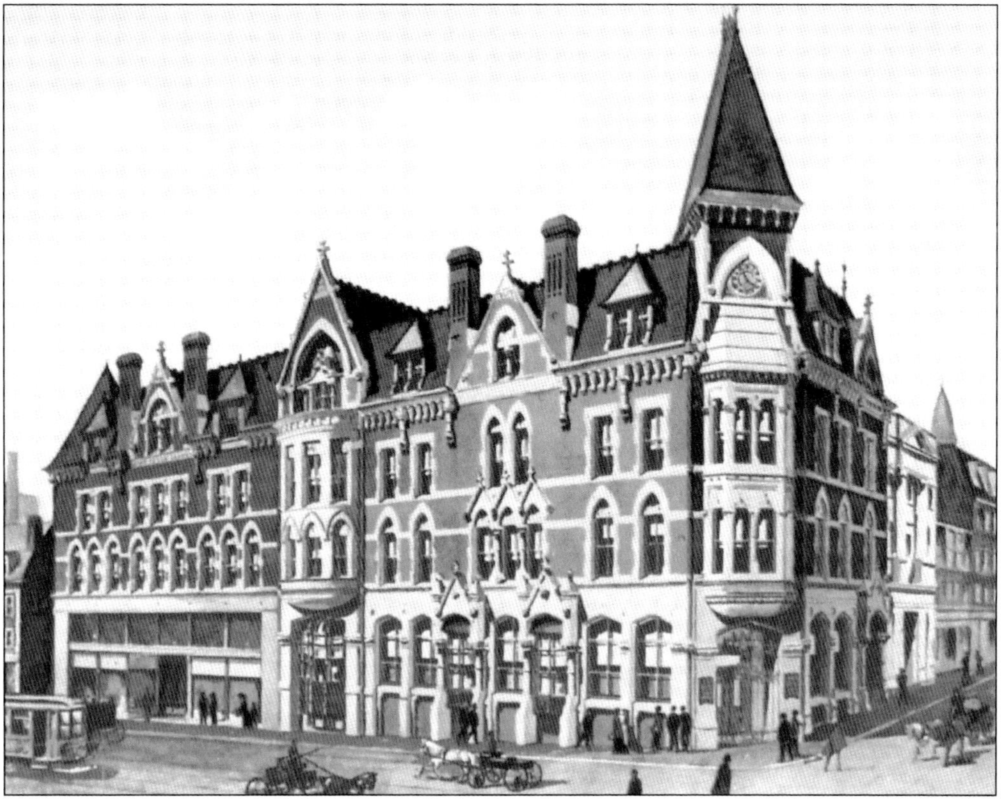
The 1874 Slater Trust Company Building, seen here in 1904, soon after it had been remodeled in commemoration of the 50th anniversary of the bank's founding. It stood at the southwest corner of Main Street and East Avenue. In 1922, it became the Slater Branch of the Industrial Trust Company. The building has since been replaced by the current Fleet Bank Building.

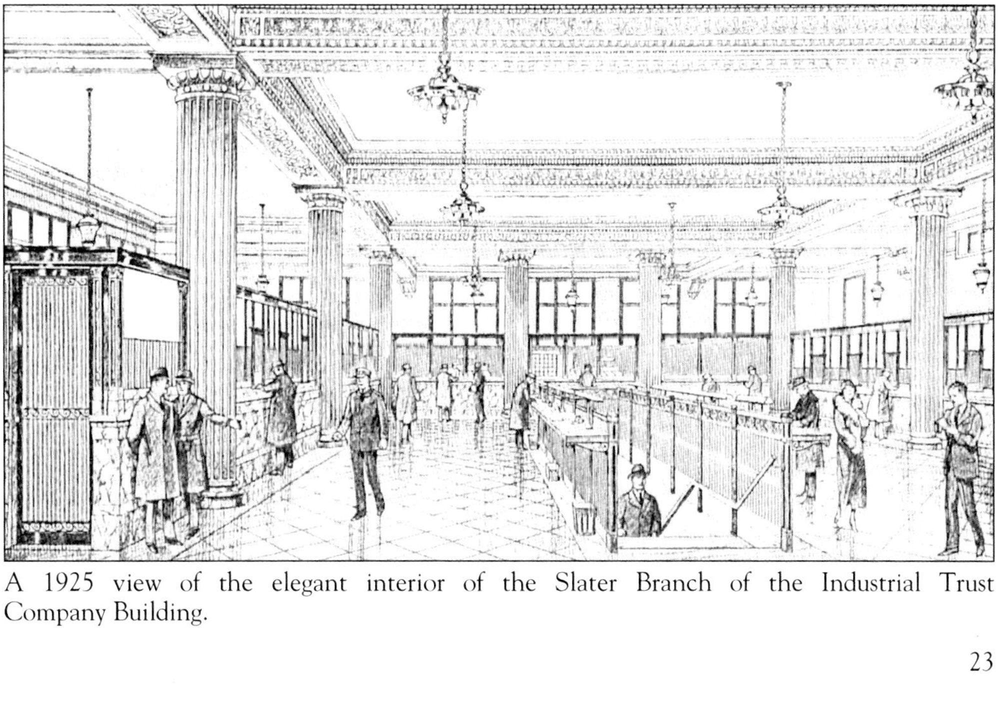
A 1925 view of the elegant interior of the Slater Branch of the Industrial Trust Company Building.

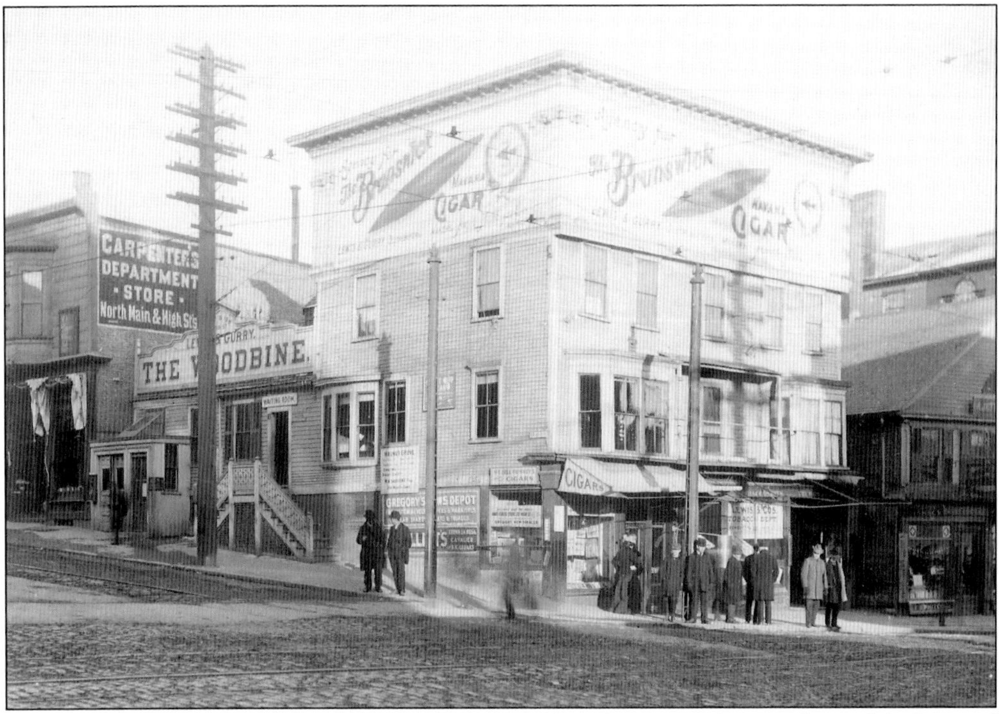

In this 1895 view of the northeast corner of Main and High Streets, the greatly-modified second home of Samuel Slater can be seen, which he purchased from David Toler (the original owner). Much enlarged and with new upper floors, it was primarily taken over by the flourishing tobacco and restaurant business of Enoch Lewis and Frank Gurry, called the "Woodbine." The Adams Drug Store was the last tenant before the building was razed to allow the construction of the current Peerless Building.

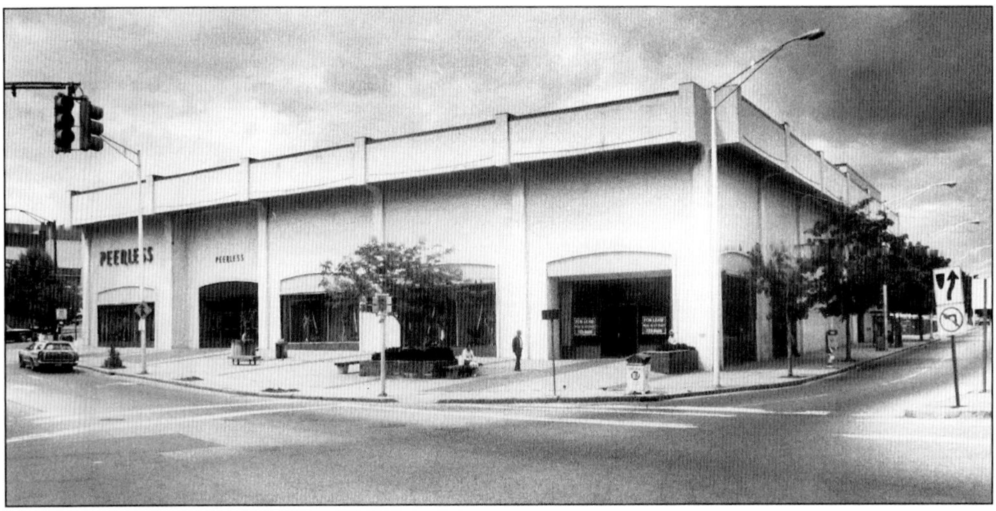

The April 1, 1970, opening of the Peerless Company's $1.2 million specialty store marked the culmination of a development which civic and business leaders defined as the "turning point" in the success of the Slater Urban Renewal Project. The building, bounded by High and Main Streets and Roosevelt Avenue, is currently being remodeled as a visitors' center and as the home for the city's Planning Department and Redevelopment Agency. (*Times*)

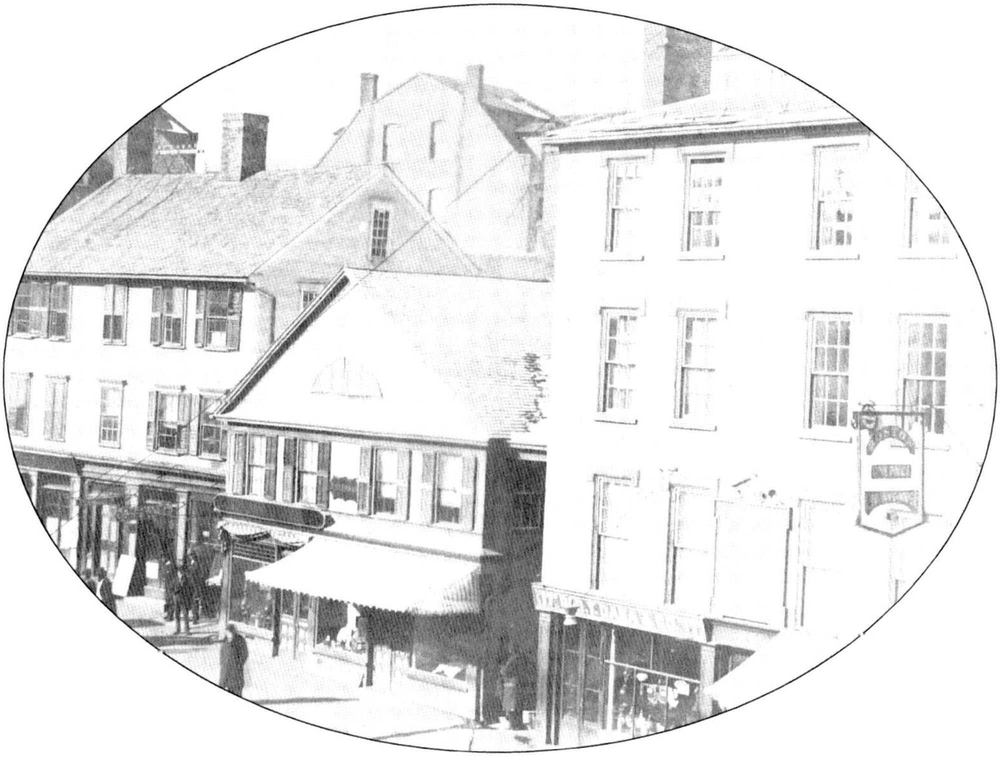

David Wilkinson built the Pawtucket Hotel in 1813, at the northwest corner of today's Roosevelt Avenue and Main Street. This picture shows the hotel in 1871.

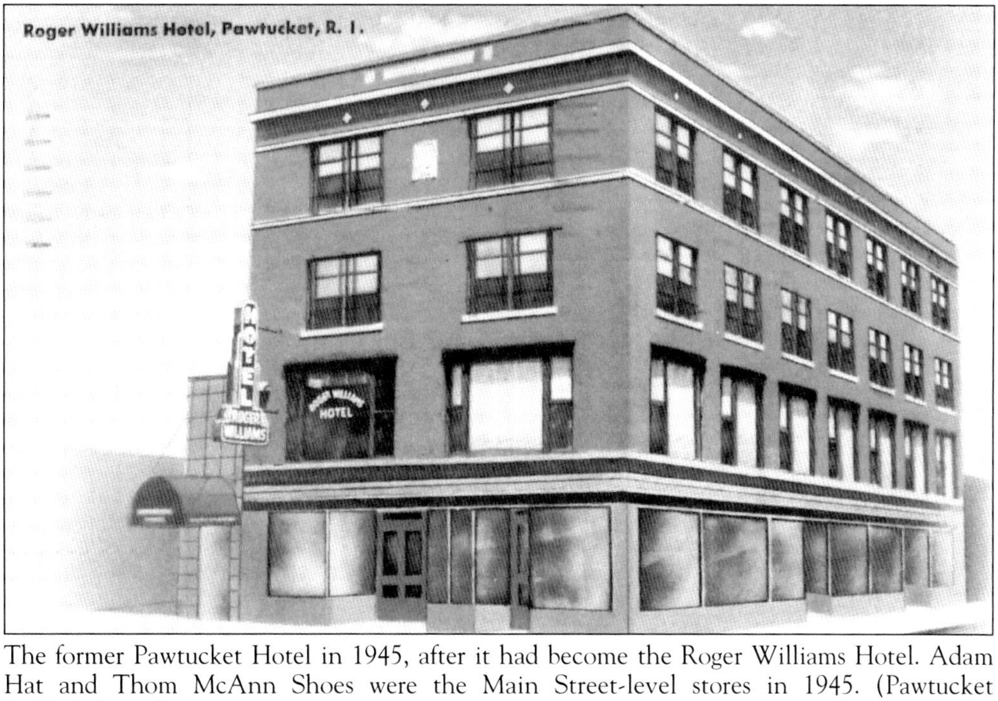

The former Pawtucket Hotel in 1945, after it had become the Roger Williams Hotel. Adam Hat and Thom McAnn Shoes were the Main Street-level stores in 1945. (Pawtucket Public Library.)

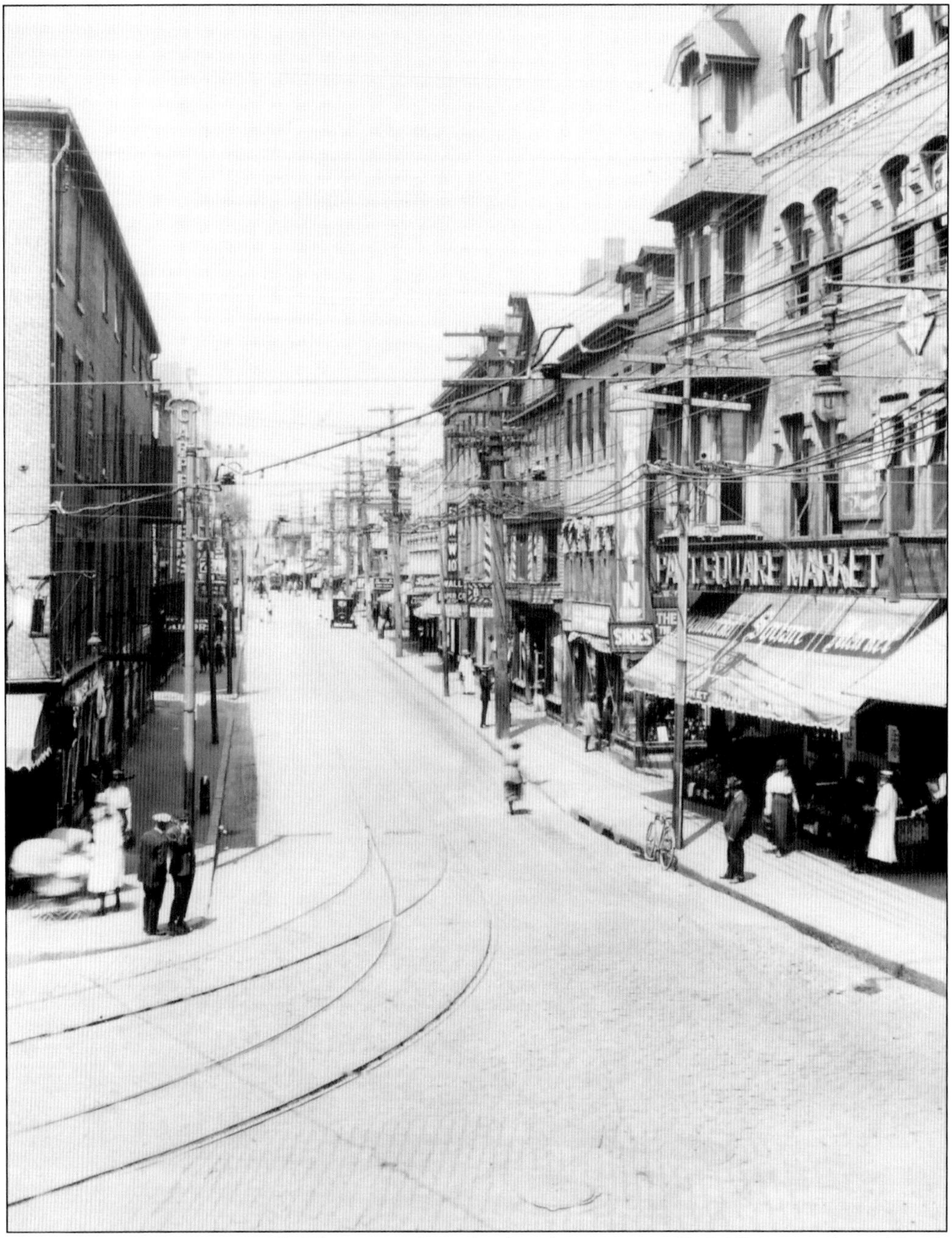

Main Street Square, *c*. 1925. The street directly ahead was originally Mill Street, later North Main Street, and, in 1933, the name was changed again: to Roosevelt Avenue, in honor of President Franklin D. Roosevelt.

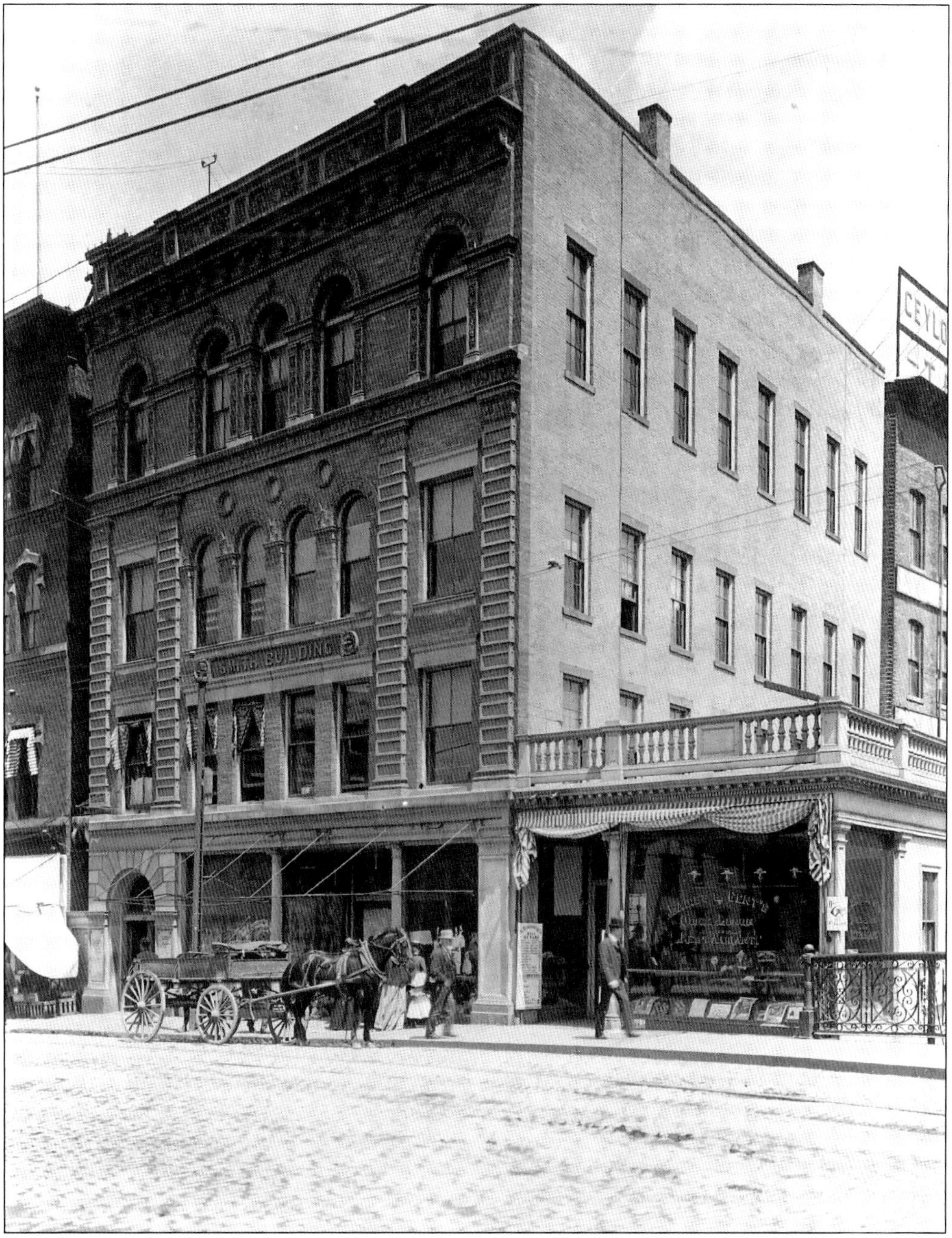

The Smith Building, on Main Street next to the Main Street Bridge, pictured in 1905. The photograph also shows, built over the river, Reuben Bloomberg's "Quick Lunch" restaurant, where the White Tower Restaurant would be in business in the 1930s, '40s, and '50s. These structures were lost to urban renewal in 1968. (Pawtucket Public Library.)

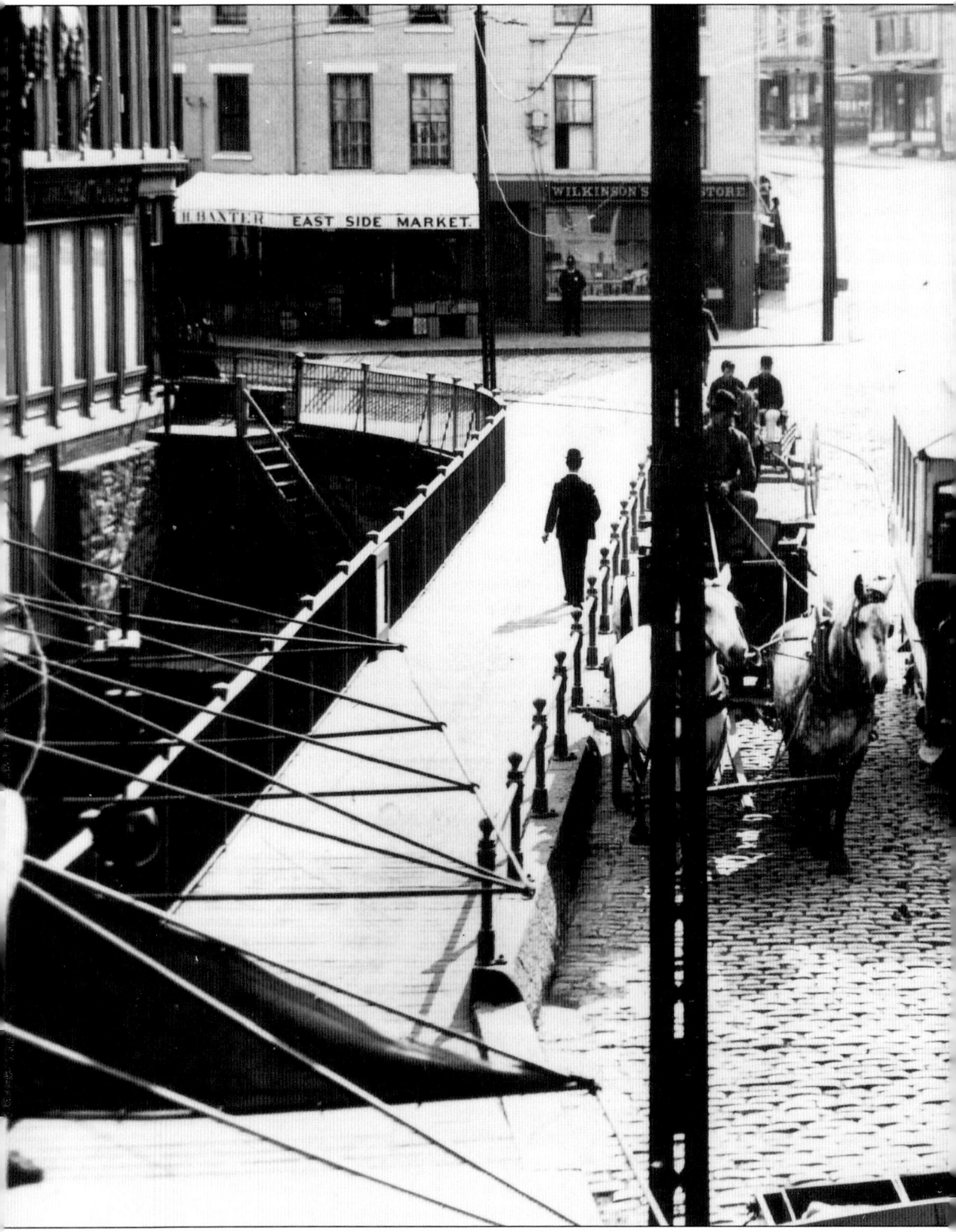

An 1894 view of the congested Main Street Bridge, looking east toward the junction of Broadway. This 1858 bridge was the fifth and last to span the falls. The first bridge was built

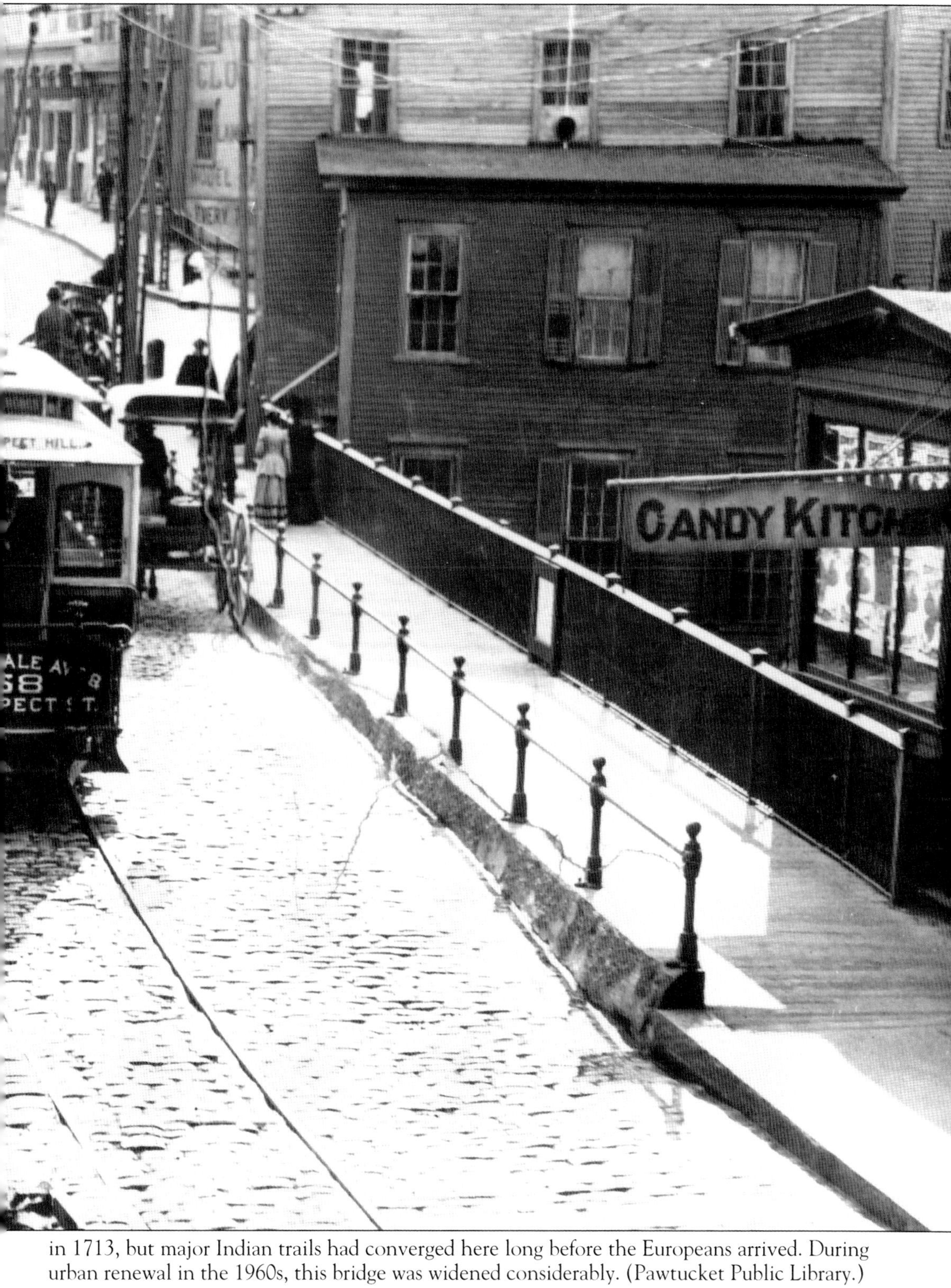

in 1713, but major Indian trails had converged here long before the Europeans arrived. During urban renewal in the 1960s, this bridge was widened considerably. (Pawtucket Public Library.)

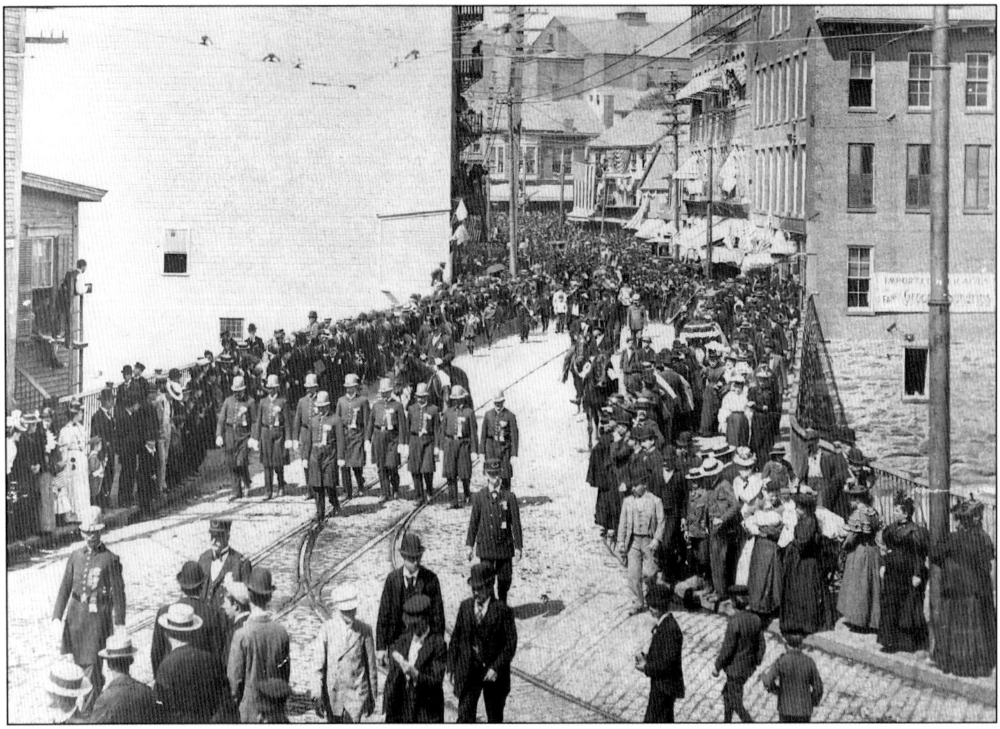

Policemen leading a Fourth of July parade over the Main Street Bridge, *c.* 1891. The building at the right of the bridge was the former Almy Block.

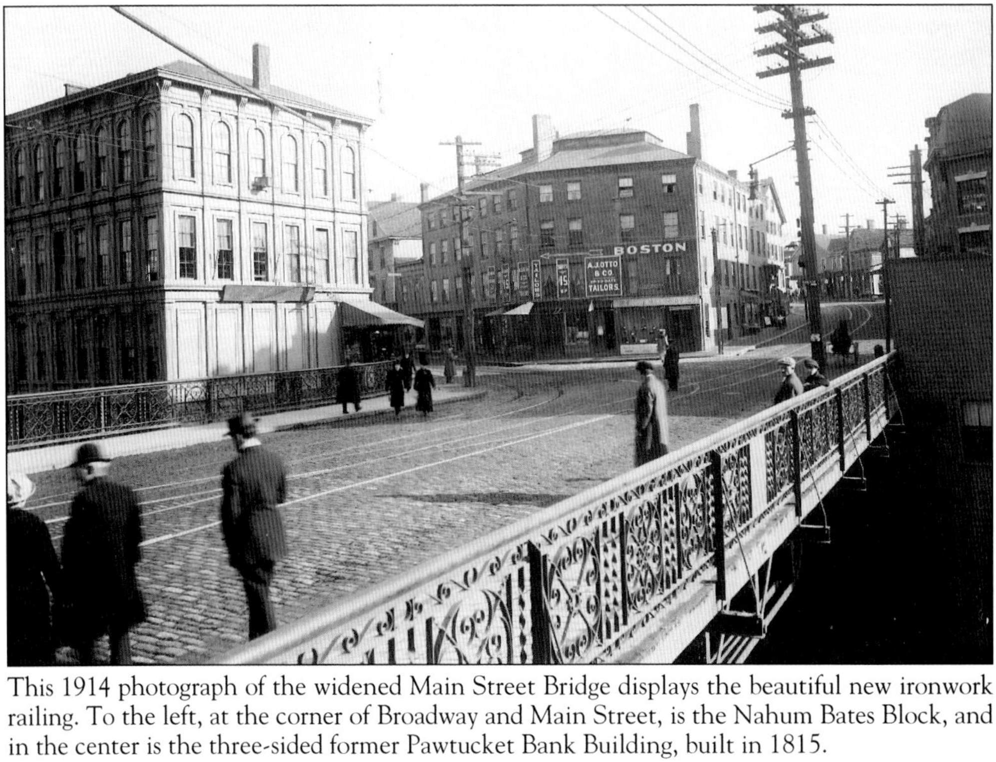

This 1914 photograph of the widened Main Street Bridge displays the beautiful new ironwork railing. To the left, at the corner of Broadway and Main Street, is the Nahum Bates Block, and in the center is the three-sided former Pawtucket Bank Building, built in 1815.

Two

Going to Work

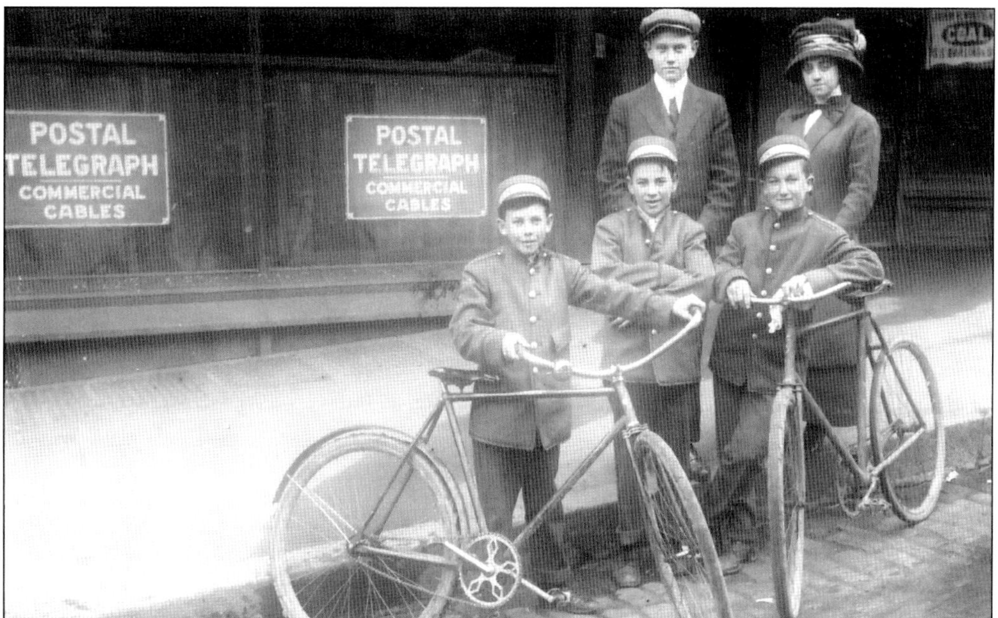

Telegraph messenger boys outside the telegraph station at 18 High Street, *c.* 1910. The boy on the left is George F. Redmond, brother of World War I hero Lawrence Redmond.

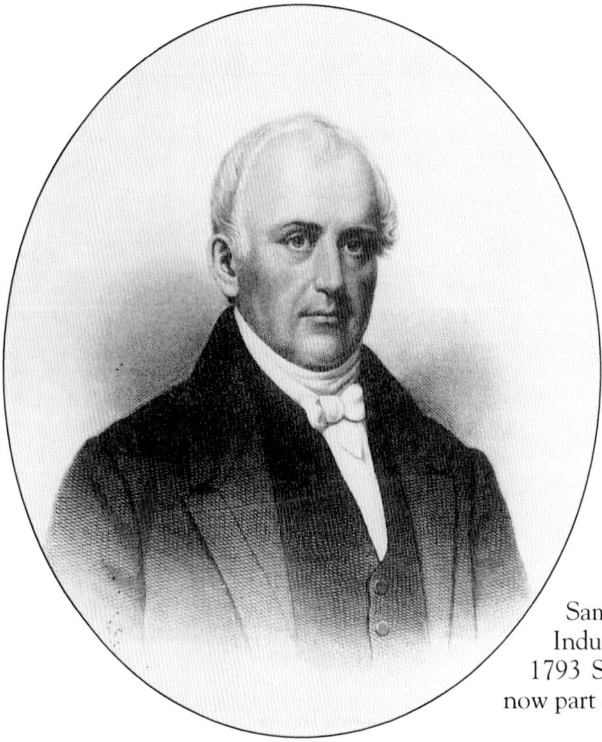

Samuel Slater, father of the American Industrial Revolution and builder of the 1793 Slater Mill at Pawtucket. The mill is now part of the Slater Mill Historic Site.

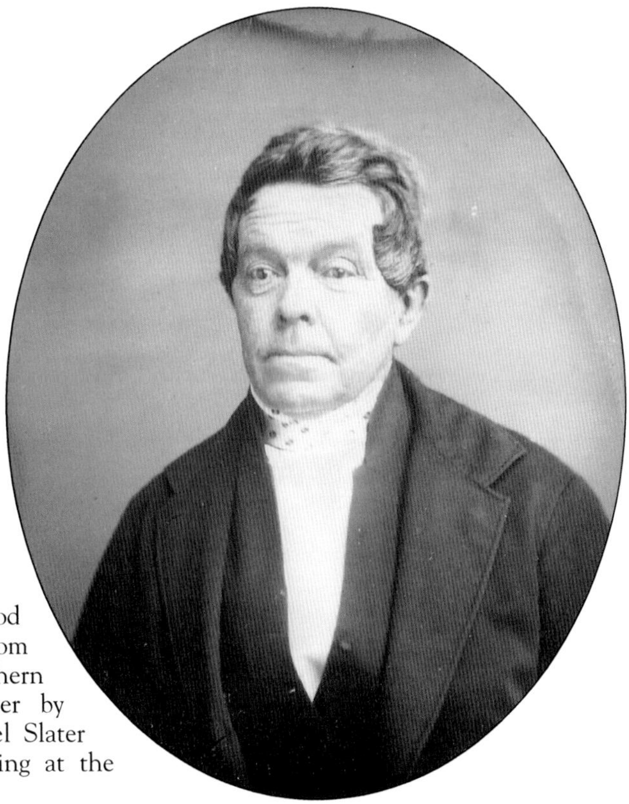

Joseph Hood (1790–1874). Hood came to America in 1810, from Rathfriland, Co. Down, Northern Ireland. He was a hand weaver by trade, and was invited by Samuel Slater to experiment with power weaving at the Slater Mill.

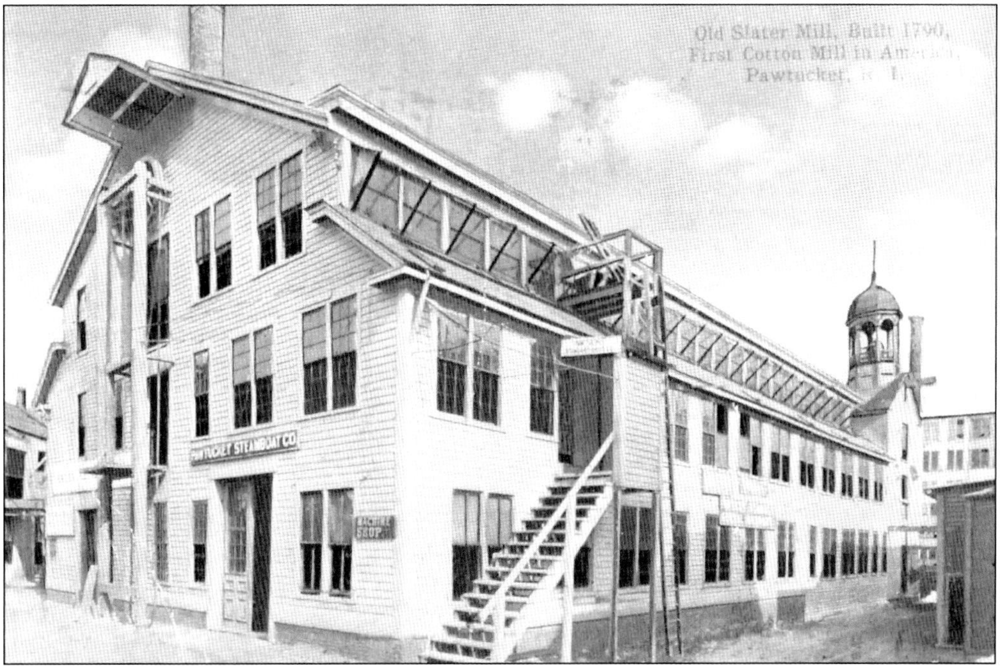

Old Slater Mill in 1872. The Pawtucket Steamboat Company, builders of early Pawtucket marine engines, occupied the first floor at this time.

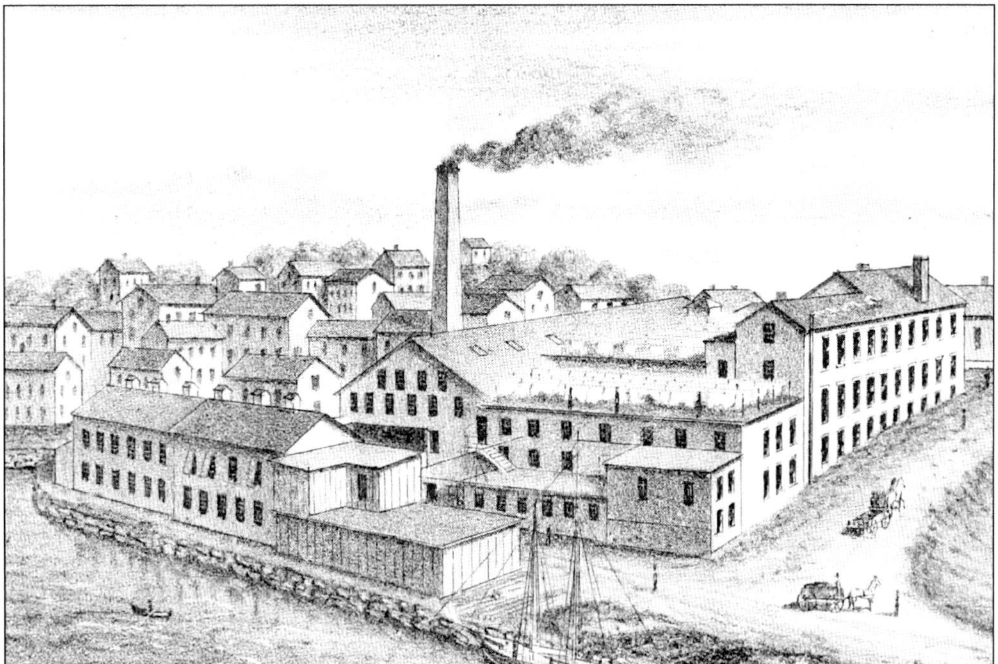

Hides drying on the roof of the James Davis Tannery in 1878. This tannery was located off Pleasant Street, by the old Town Landing on the Pawtucket River , opposite the location of today's Masonic Temple.

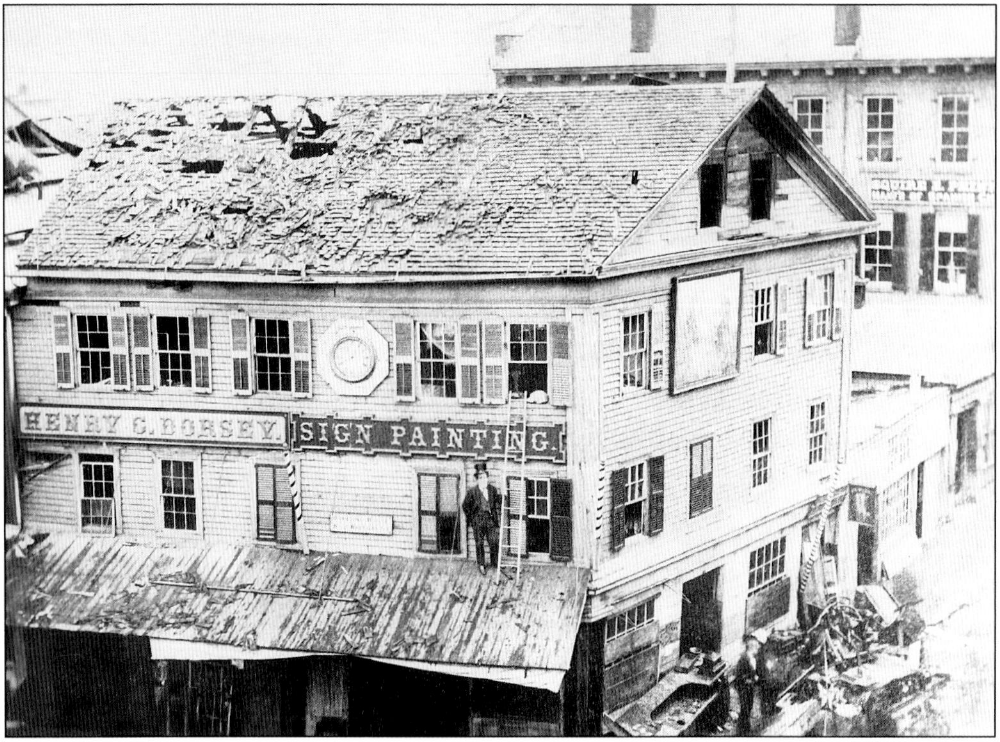

The Miller Building in Pawtucket Square (today the junction of Roosevelt Avenue and Main Street), after fire had destroyed it in January 1863. Henry C. Dorcey, noted sign painter and friend of the homeless and prisoners, stands by the ladder on the awning along Mill Street (now Roosevelt Avenue), posing for the camera.

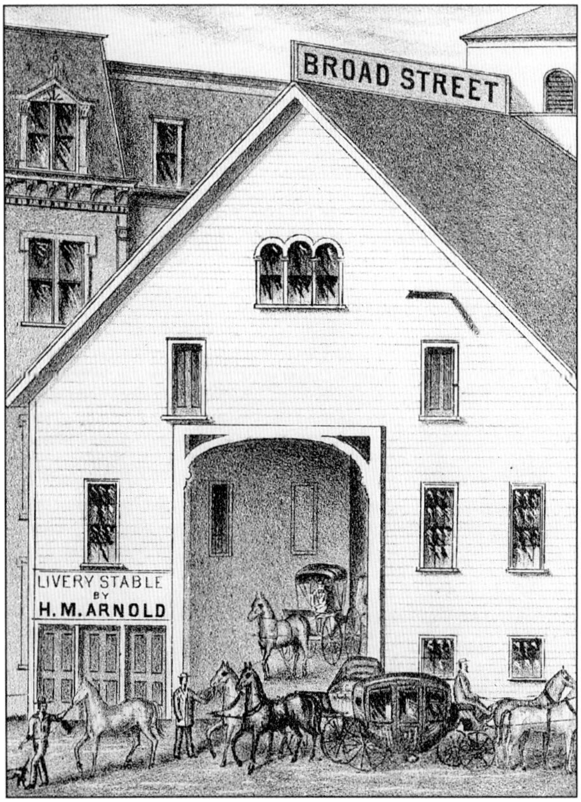

Arnold's Stable was located opposite the McDevitt Building and next to the Benedict House on Broad Street (across from its junction with North Union Street). This was a model operation, containing roomy apartments for horses and carriages, all removed from the main drive hall and with safety elevators and elegant waiting rooms for both ladies and gentlemen.

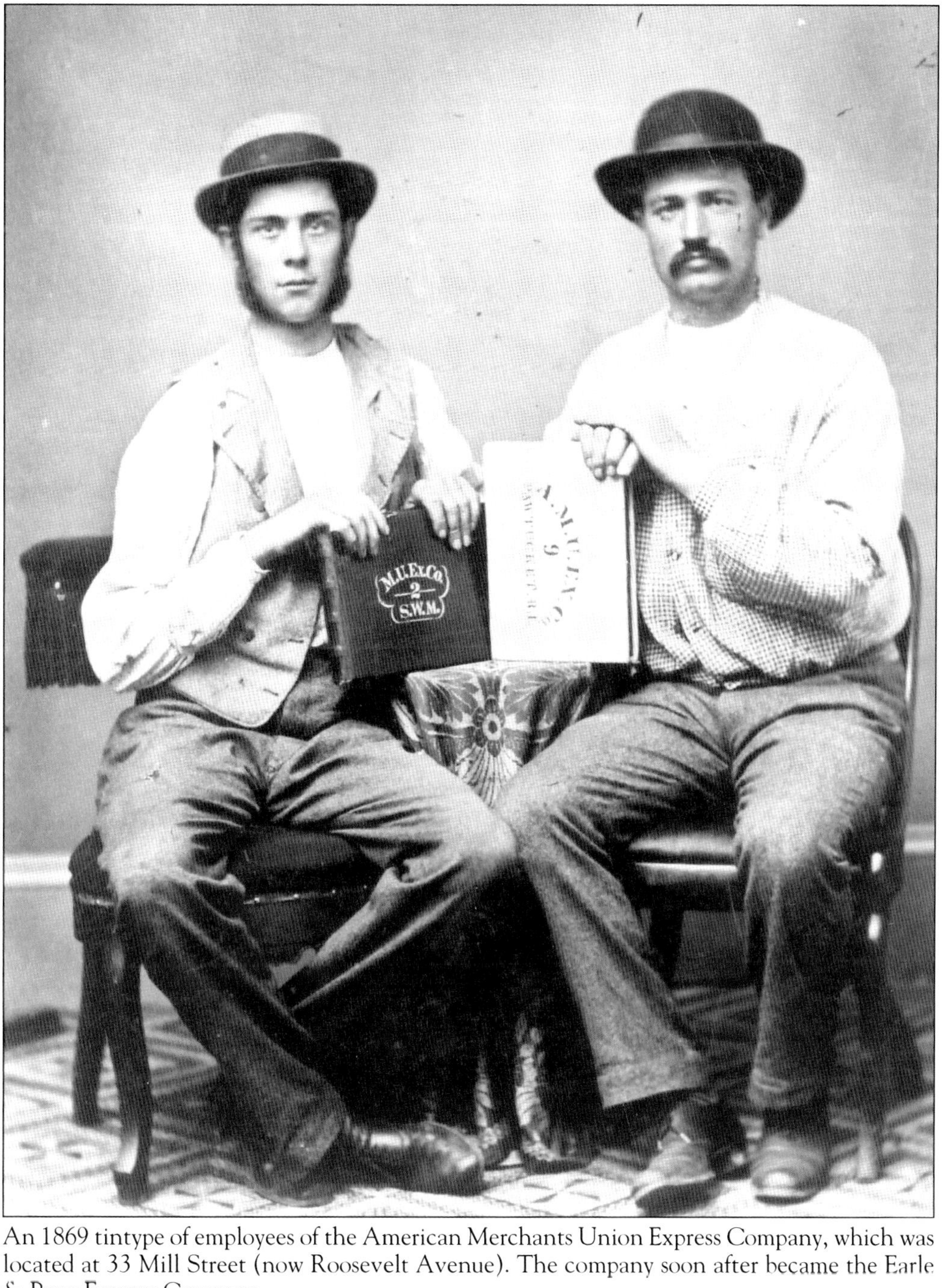

An 1869 tintype of employees of the American Merchants Union Express Company, which was located at 33 Mill Street (now Roosevelt Avenue). The company soon after became the Earle & Prew Express Company.

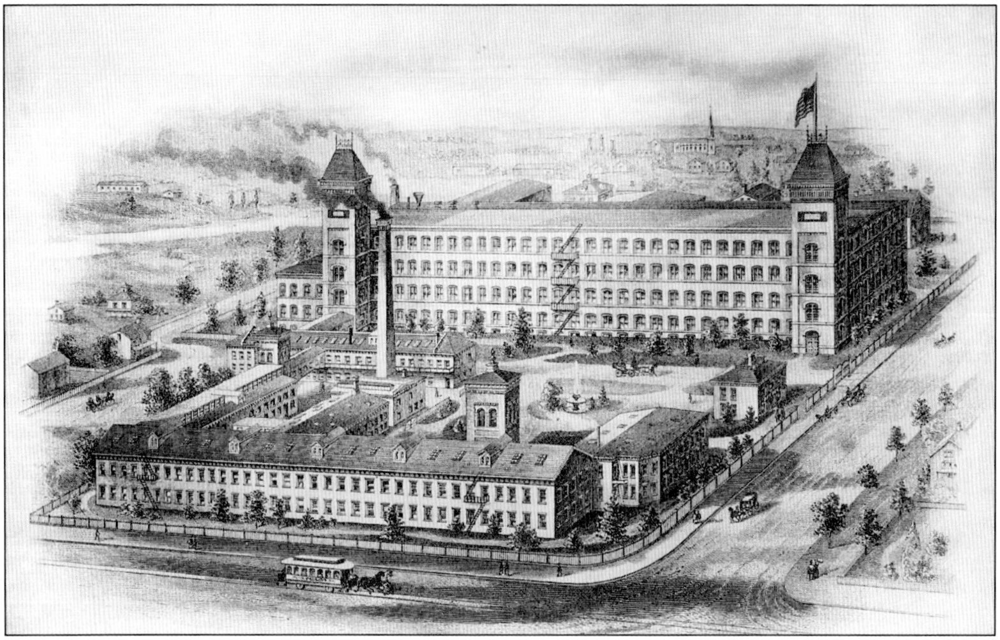

A view of the corner of Main and Pine Streets. The low buildings in the foreground were built for the American File Company in 1863. At that time the president was Stephen A. Jenks and the treasurer was Nahum Bates. The Slater Company purchased the buildings in 1868. Frank Crook Auto Sales was located here from 1935 to 1955, and today the buildings house Liberty International, Inc., Hill Office Supply, and the Rhode Island Supreme Court Judicial Records Center.

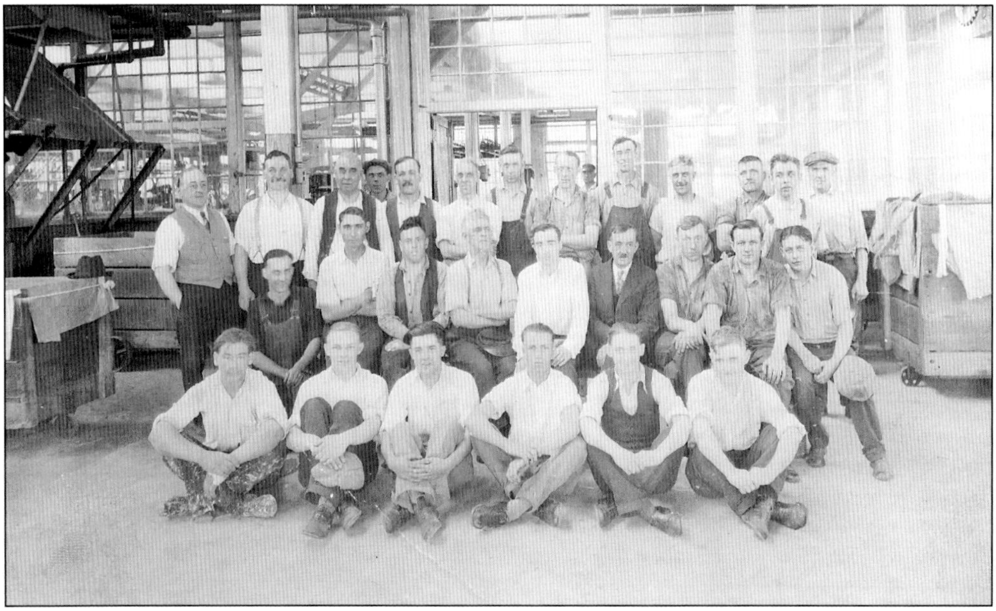

Employees of the Woodlawn Finishing Company in 1935. Founded in 1916, the company was located at 1 Moshassuck Street. The president was Maxwell C. Huntoon. Those pictured here include Charles W. Fleming and Louis J. Fleming (second row, fifth and sixth from left, respectively). The buildings are now occupied by Microfibres, Inc.

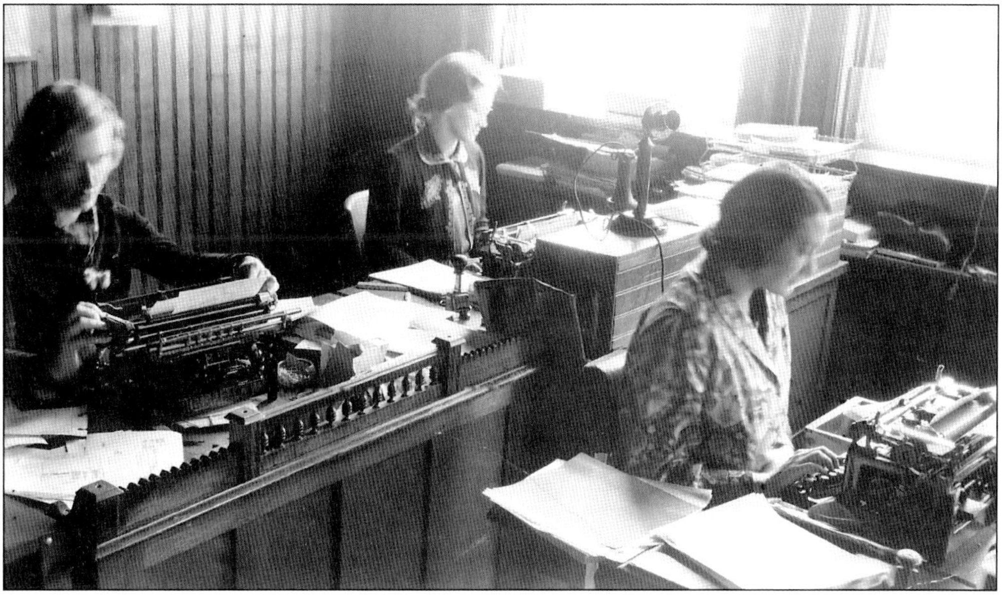

The clerical staff of the Narragansett Machine Company on Esten Avenue, *c.* 1928.

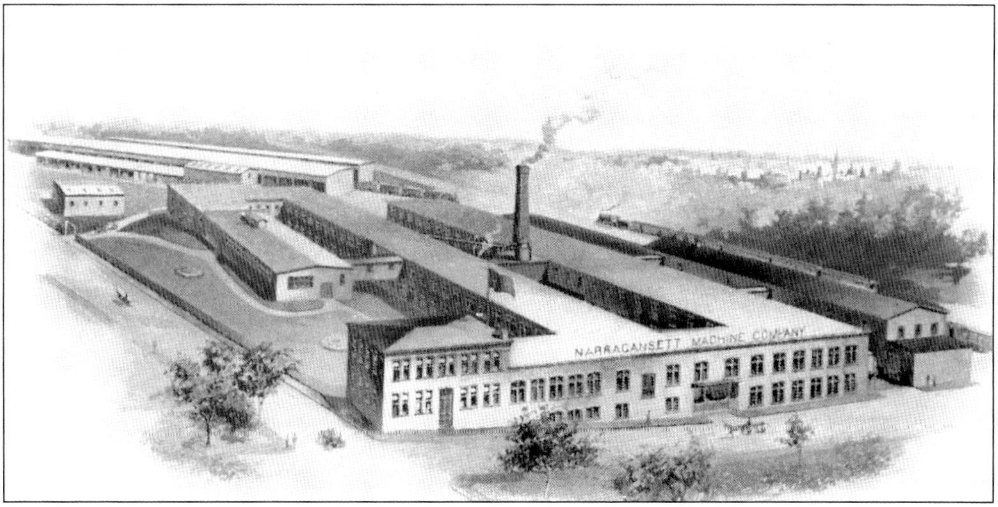

The Narragansett Machine Company was a manufacturer of light machinery, gymnastic apparatus, lockers, and bowling alley equipment. Its president was Albert J. Thornley. These buildings were located on Esten Street, at the foot of Vale Street. This photograph was taken in 1905.

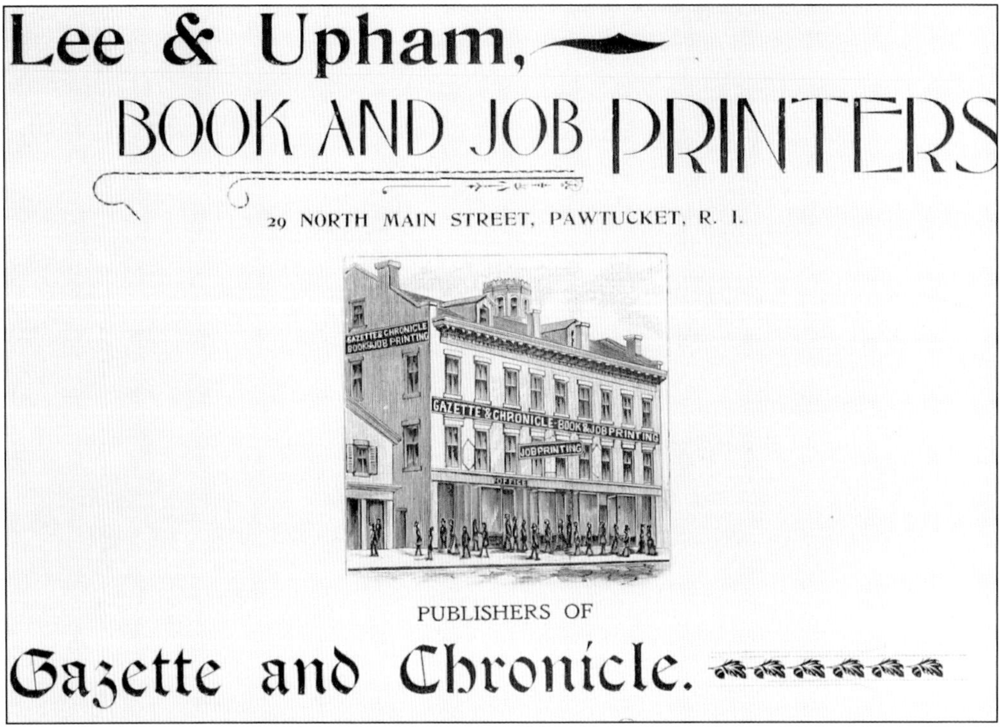

The *Pawtucket Gazette and Chronicle* newspaper offices were located at 29 North Main Street (now Roosevelt Avenue), in the Manchester Block. On the top floor of this building was an auditorium where, in 1850, the famous Jenny Lind sang. This illustration dates from 1897.

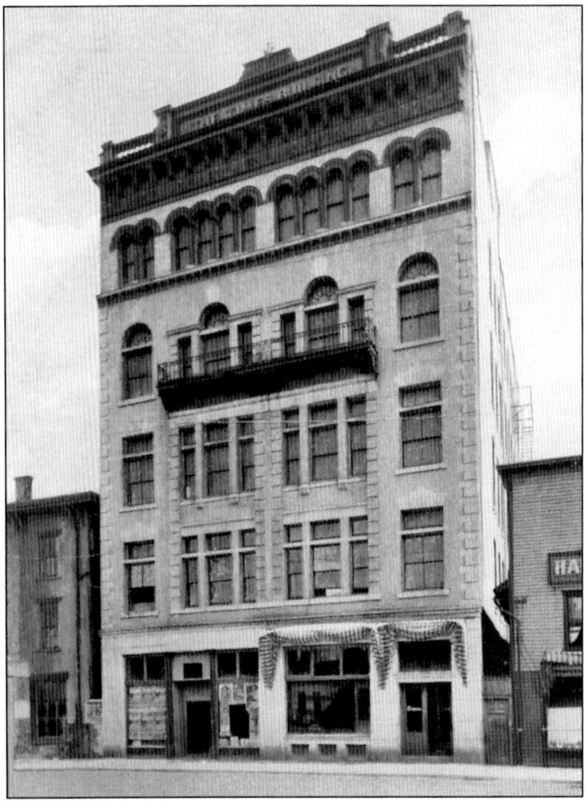

An 1895 photograph of the *Times* Building, in Times Square at 33 Exchange Street. Established in 1885, the paper has been in continuous circulation since. It was first known as the *Evening Times*, then as the *Pawtucket Times*, and today as the *Times*.

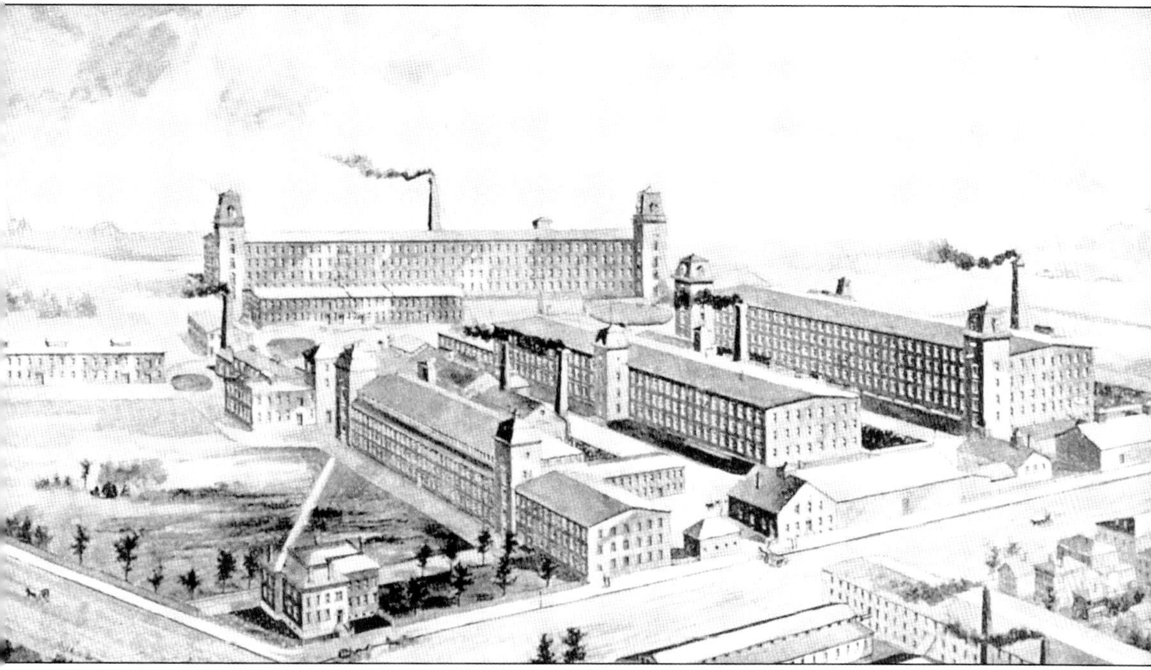

The eight mills, bleacheries, shops, and offices of the mill complex of J & P Coats, Ltd., at 366 Pine Street. J & P Coats was once the largest thread manufacturer in the world. Construction of the complex was completed between 1869 and 1919 and as early as 1876 it employed 1,400 people. Eventually, this figure rose to 4,000 people working in buildings which spread over 50 acres. J & P Coats merged with North Georgia Processing in 1951 and in 1952 merged again to become Coats & Clark, Inc. In 1964, the final shutdown was announced. The buildings now contain many small industries. This illustration dates from 1905.

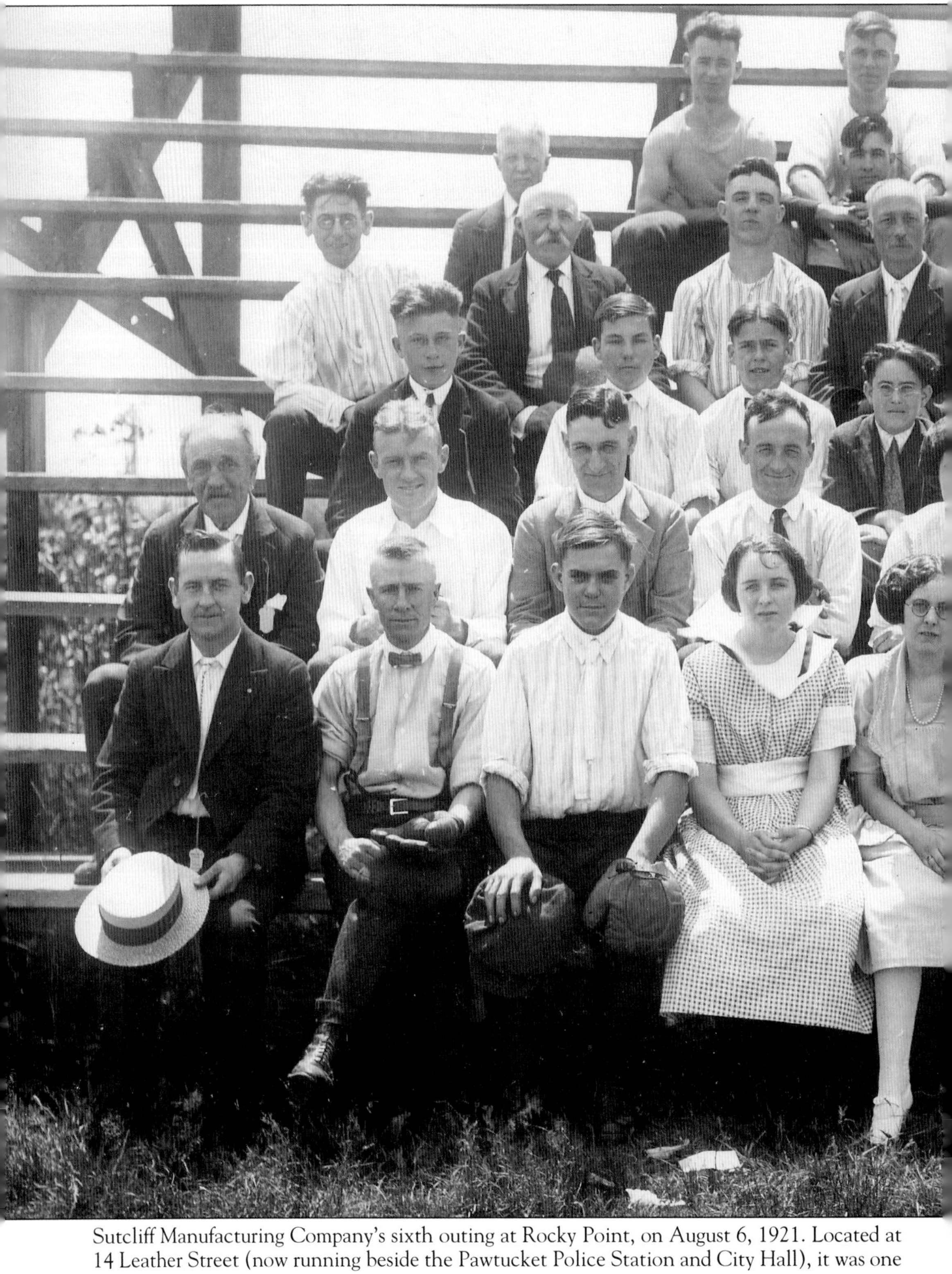

Sutcliff Manufacturing Company's sixth outing at Rocky Point, on August 6, 1921. Located at 14 Leather Street (now running beside the Pawtucket Police Station and City Hall), it was one

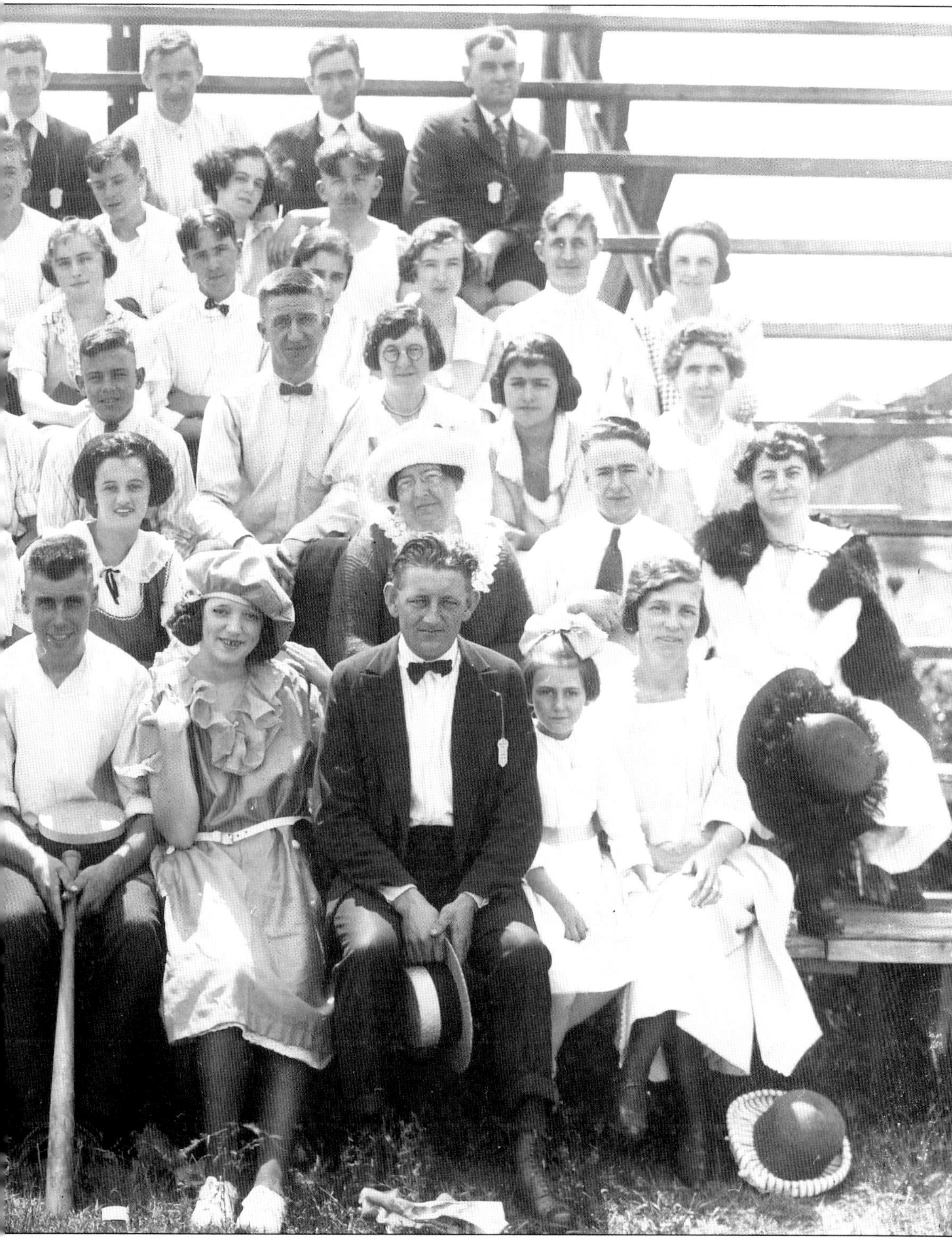

of the largest commercial printing establishments in the state. In 1924 Sutcliff moved to Cross Street, in Central Falls, Rhode Island.

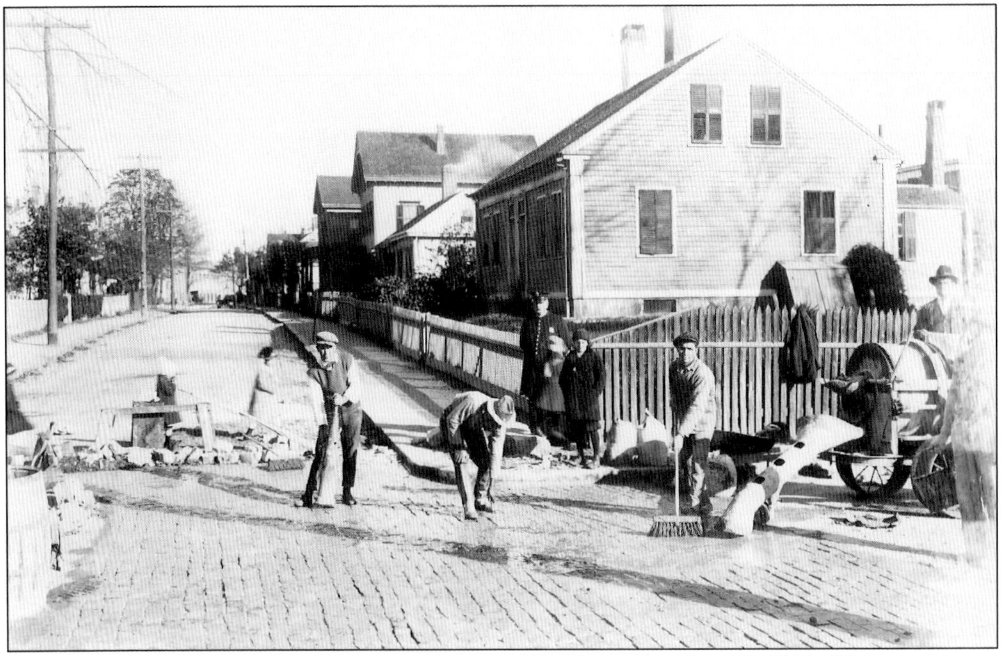

Workmen resurfacing Division Street with paving blocks on October 29, 1919. This view shows Division Street at its intersection with Elm Street, looking toward Main Street. Elm Street no longer exists as it is covered over by the Apex Store complex.

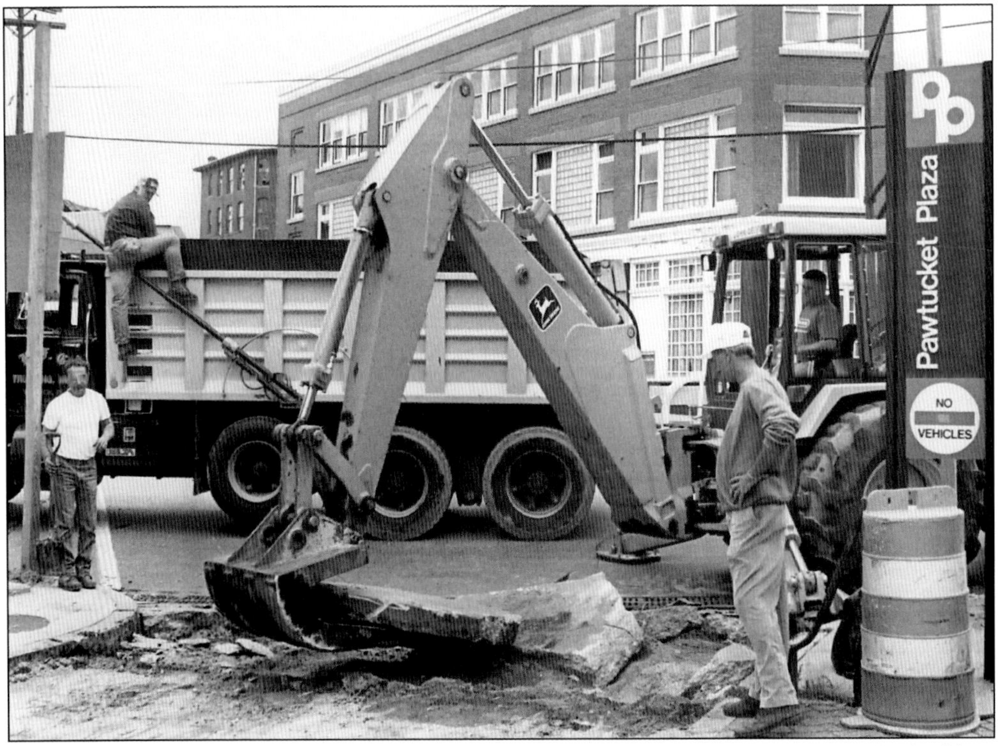

Construction at Pawtucket Plaza, at the corner of Broad and Main Streets, 1961. The building in the background was the Old Colony Bank Building (see p. 11). (*Times*.)

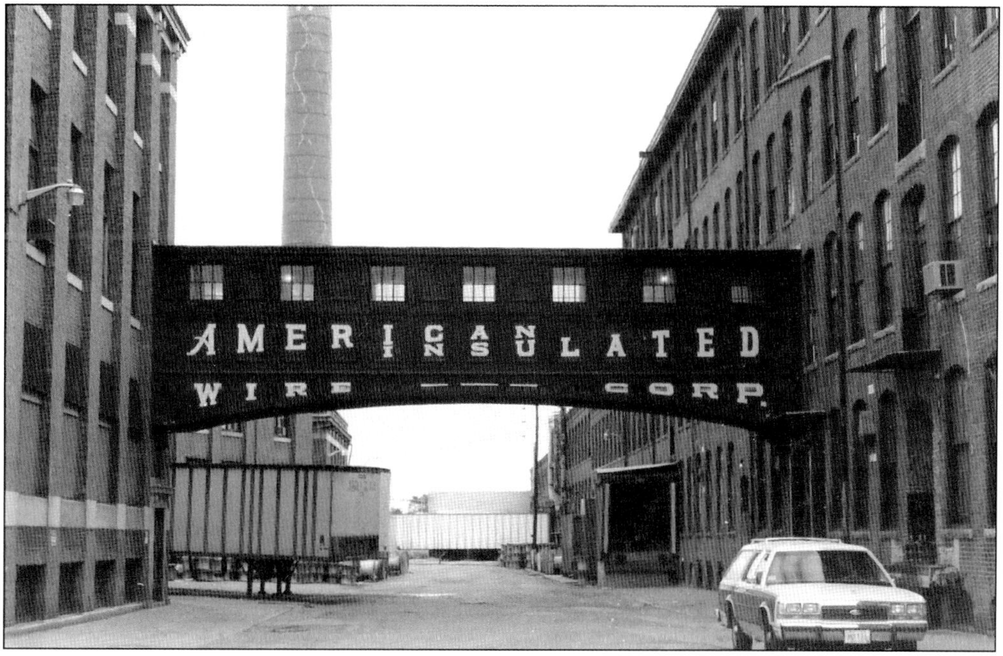

A complex of mill blocks in two groups, flanking Freeman Street off Central Avenue, near the Industrial Highway. Founded by H.O. Phillips as Phillips Insulated Wire Company in 1884, the first mill was constructed in 1883. There was subsequent construction in 1907 and 1915. In 1929, it became a division of the General Cable Corporation, and in 1947, it was renamed the American Insulated Wire Corporation.

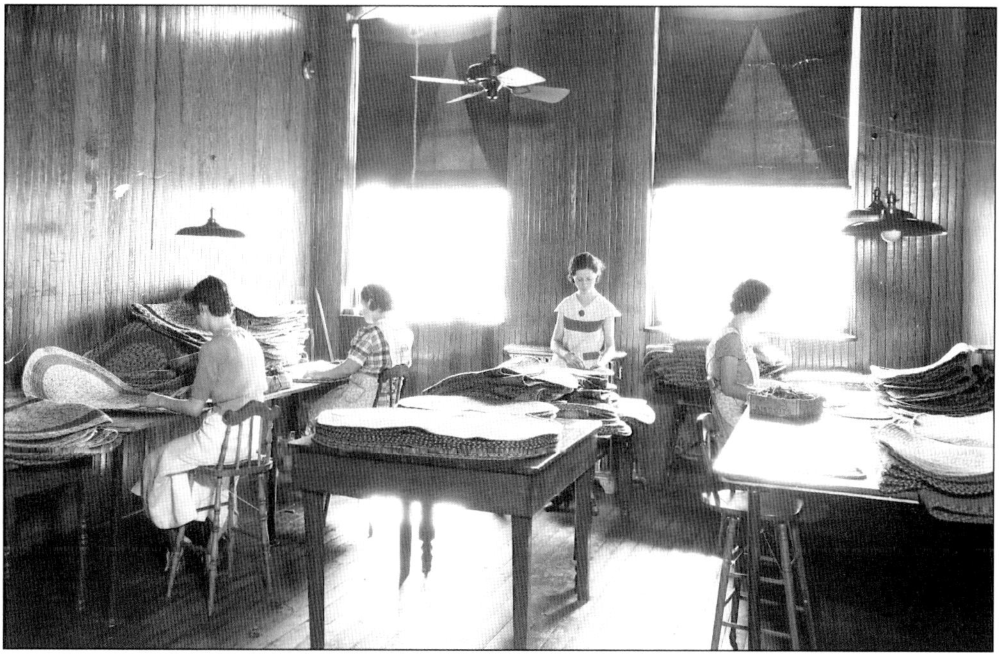

The inspection room at the former Braided Rug and Specialties Company, owned by Wesley Yando, at 28 Bayley Street in the Parkin Yarn Building. Those pictured here, in 1935, include Margaret Dacey (upper left) and Janet Speihardt (far right).

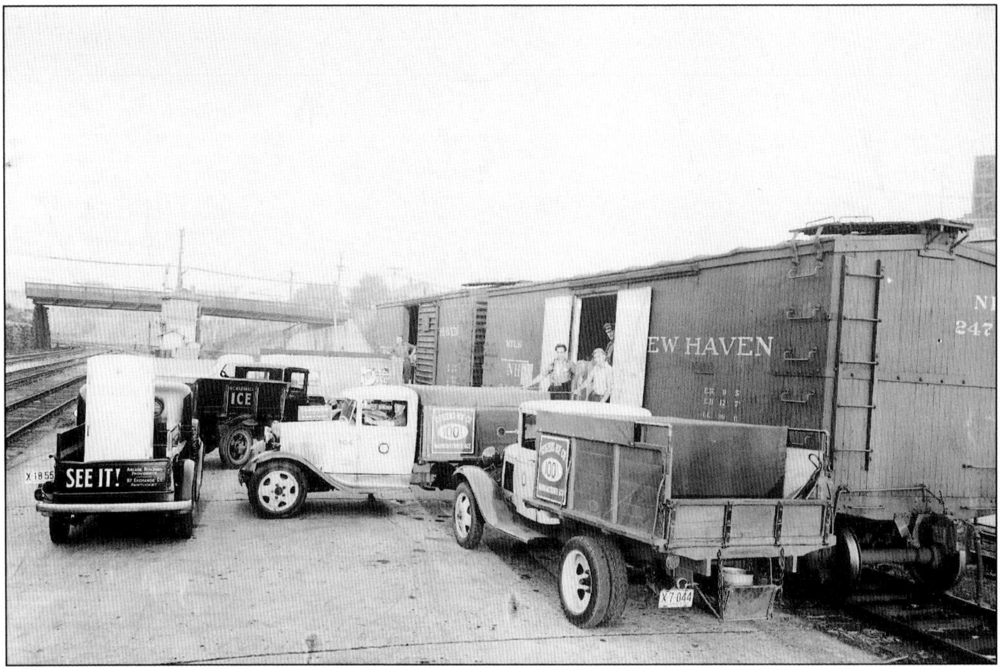

Trucks of the Citizens Ice Company in the 1930s, taking on ice refrigerators from railroad cars, at the Pawtucket freight yard off Goff Avenue. These refrigerators were then sold at their East Avenue headquarters.

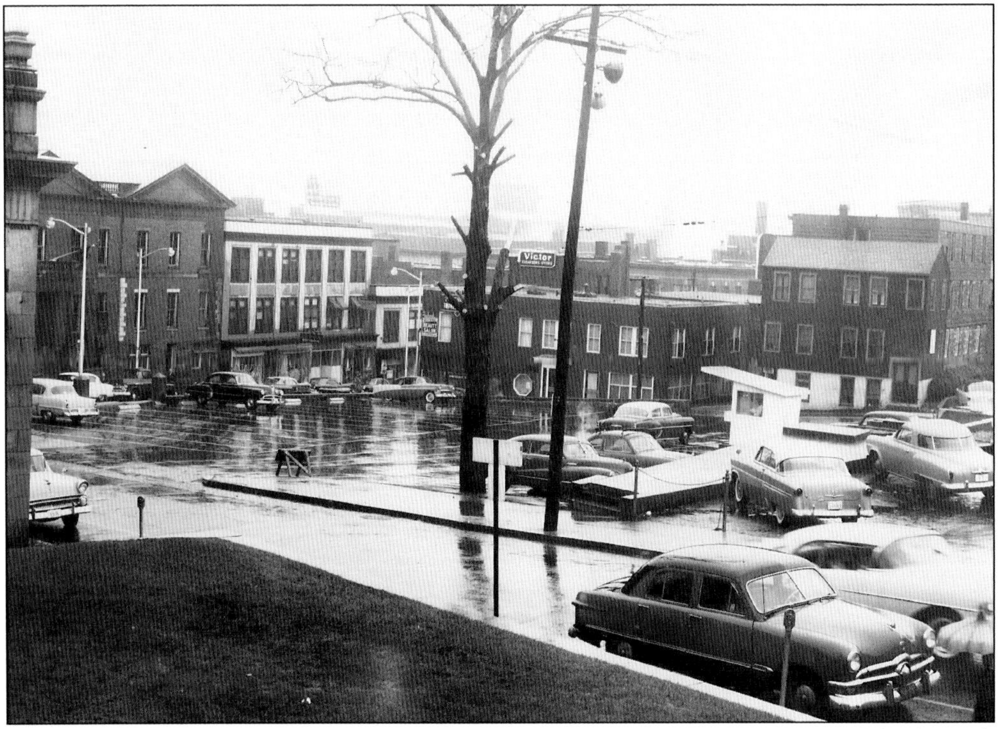

The first parking lot of Park & Shop, Inc., seen here *c.* 1960, on the former site of the burned-out First Baptist Church at the corner of High and Summer Streets.

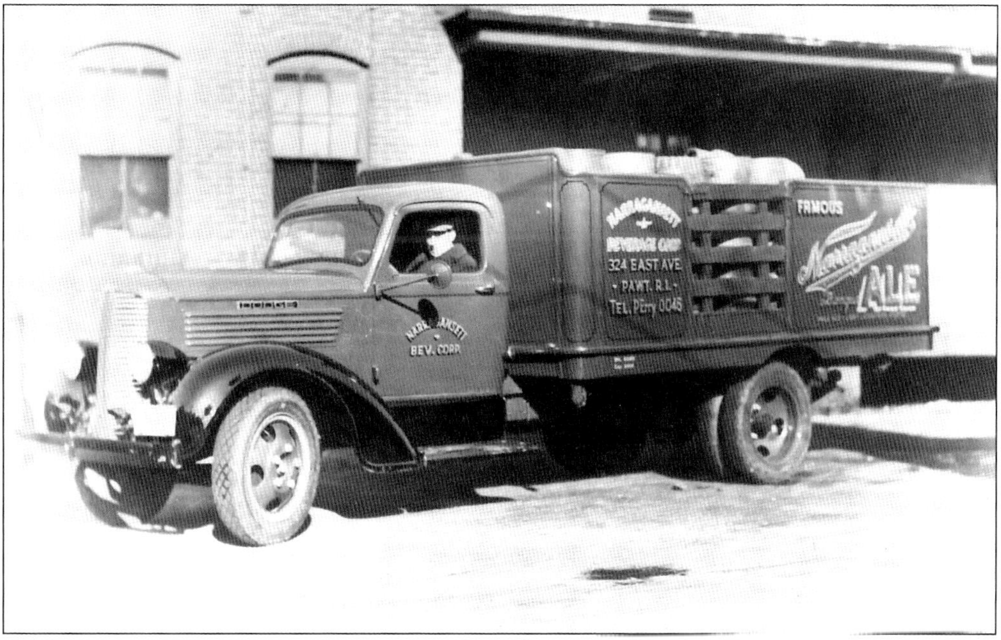

A Narragansett Beverage Corporation truck at the Pawtucket depot at 324 East Avenue, in 1944. The driver was John Precourt (1889–1952). The building has since been demolished.

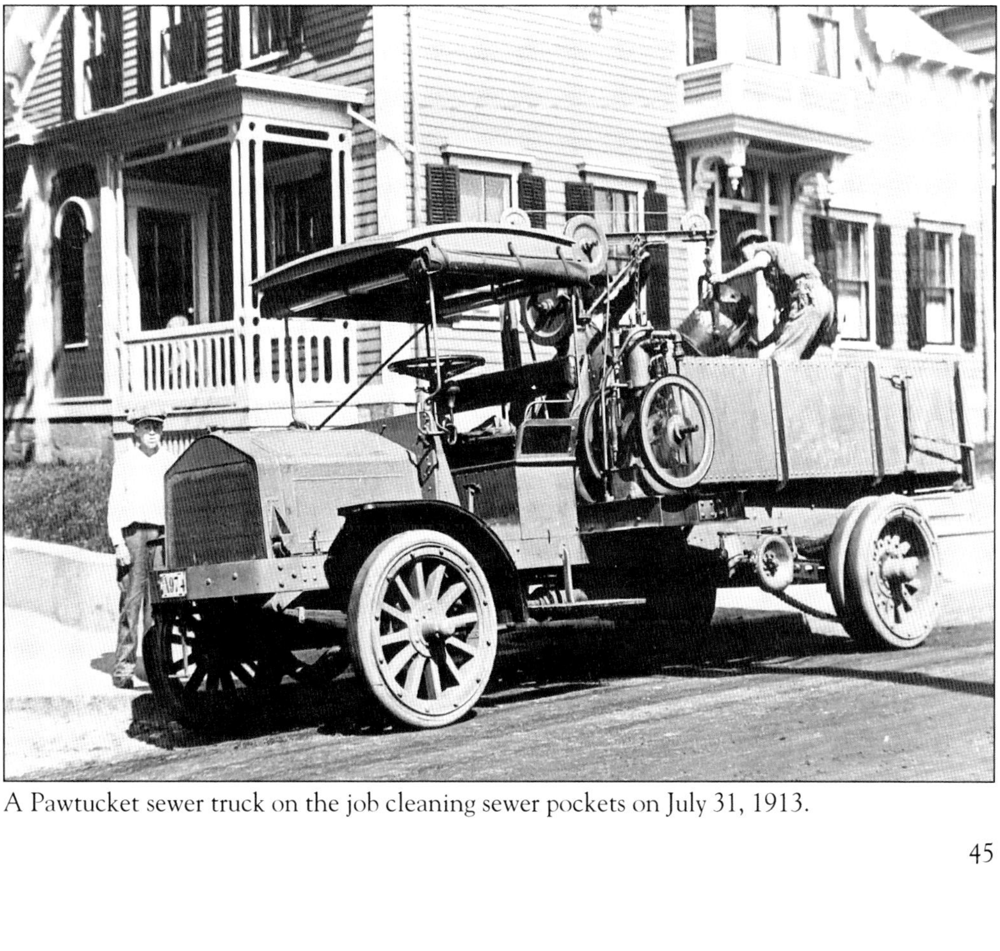
A Pawtucket sewer truck on the job cleaning sewer pockets on July 31, 1913.

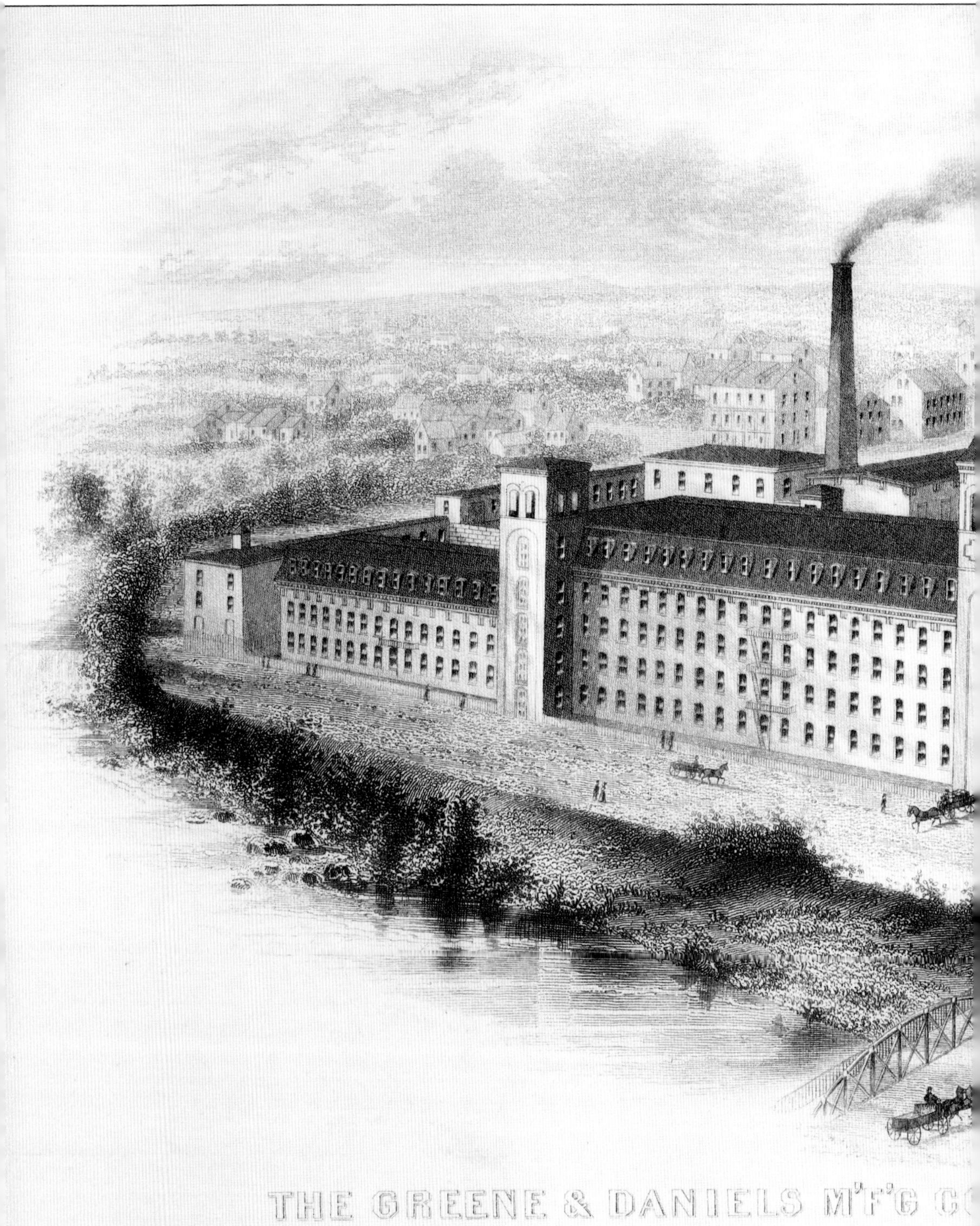

Benjamin F. Greene and Horace Daniels built these mills by the river at the foot of Central Avenue in the Pleasant View section of Pawtucket in 1860. They enlarged them in 1865. The mills cost $100,000, a great sum at that time, and ran 25,000 spindles, producing combed,

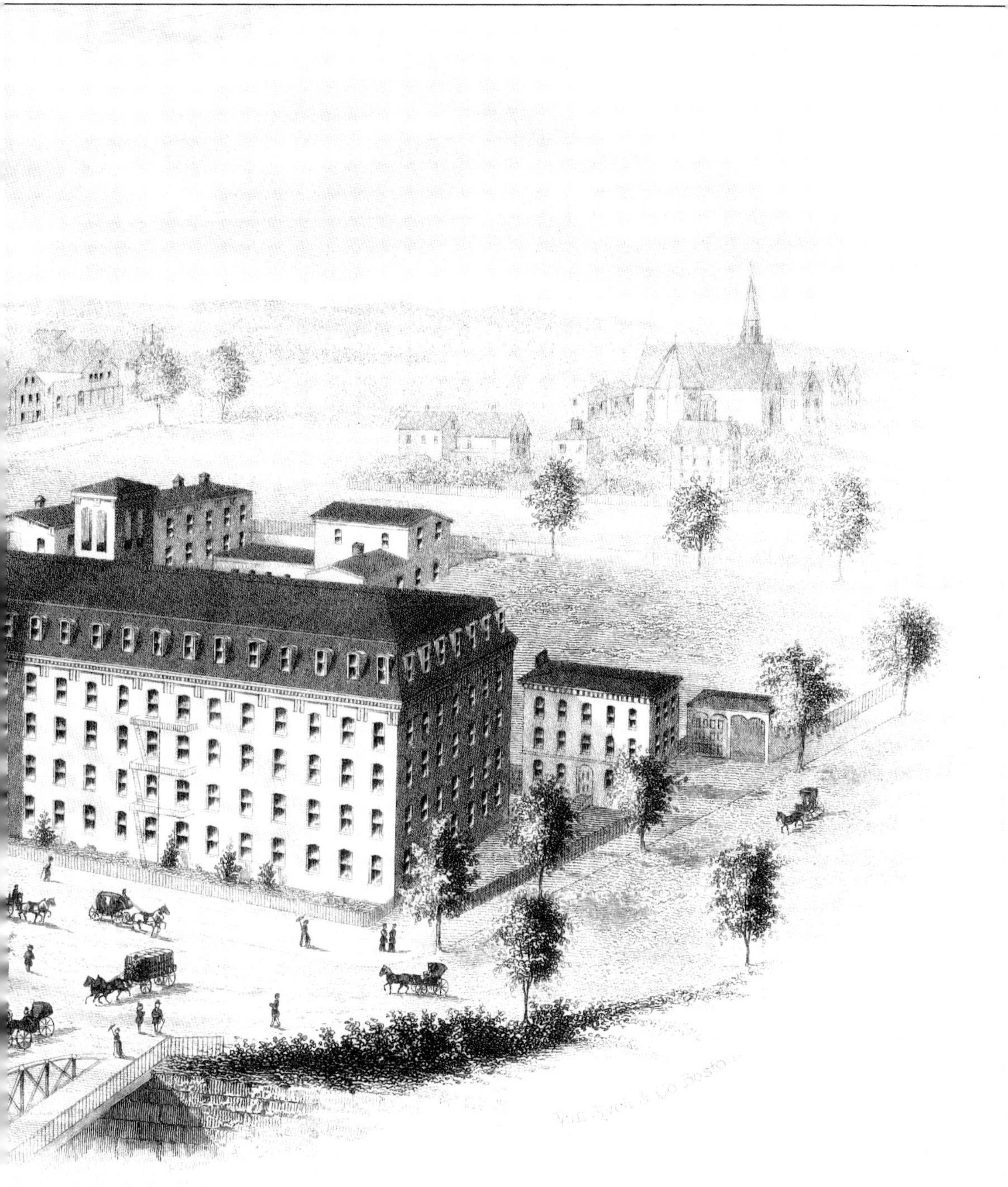

carded, and gassed yarns as well as threads, twine, and chain warps. In 1987, these mills were converted to condominiums, called the Blackstone Landing.

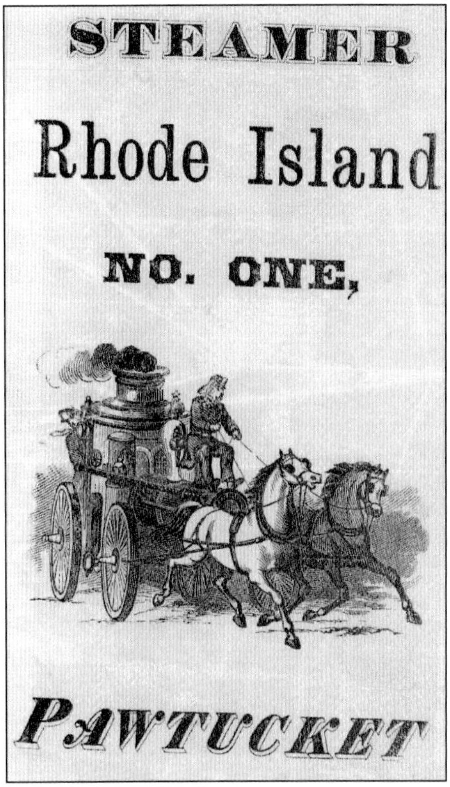

This silk badge shows a fire team from Rhode Island Company No. 1, *c.* 1880. It was located at the corner of Washington and Brown Streets in Woodlawn. The foreman was George W. Chaplin, the engineer was William J. Daggett, and the driver was John Oldham.

The Rhode Island Company's "Hay Cart" was built in 1844 by the Bates Company in Philadelphia, but perfected in 1848 by Pawtucket's famous builder of fire engines, William Jeffers. The old "Hay Cart" gained its reputation at a 1852 New Bedford exhibition, with a perpendicular play of water of 200 or more feet. This old pumper is now displayed in the Hall of Fame in Phoenix, Arizona. (Pawtucket Public Library.)

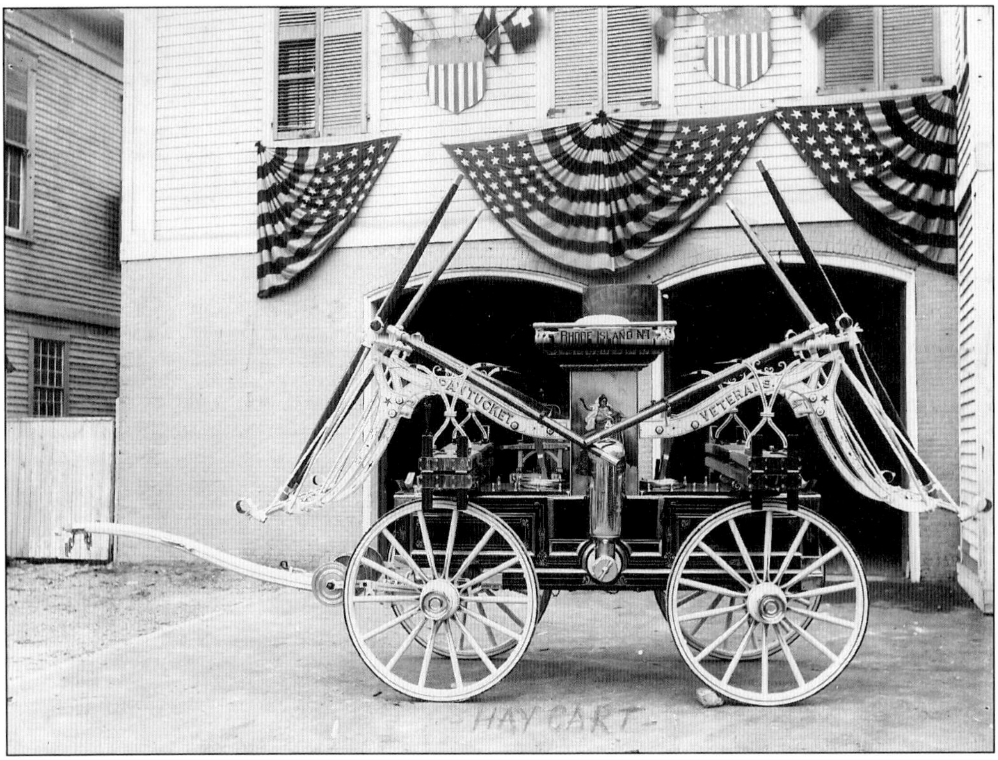

The seal of the Pawtucket Police Association, incorporated in 1889.

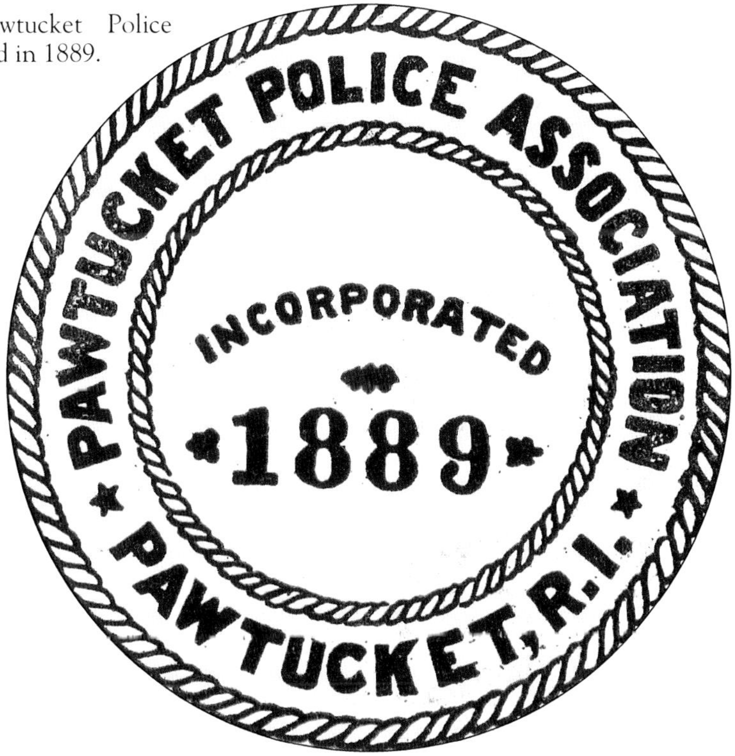

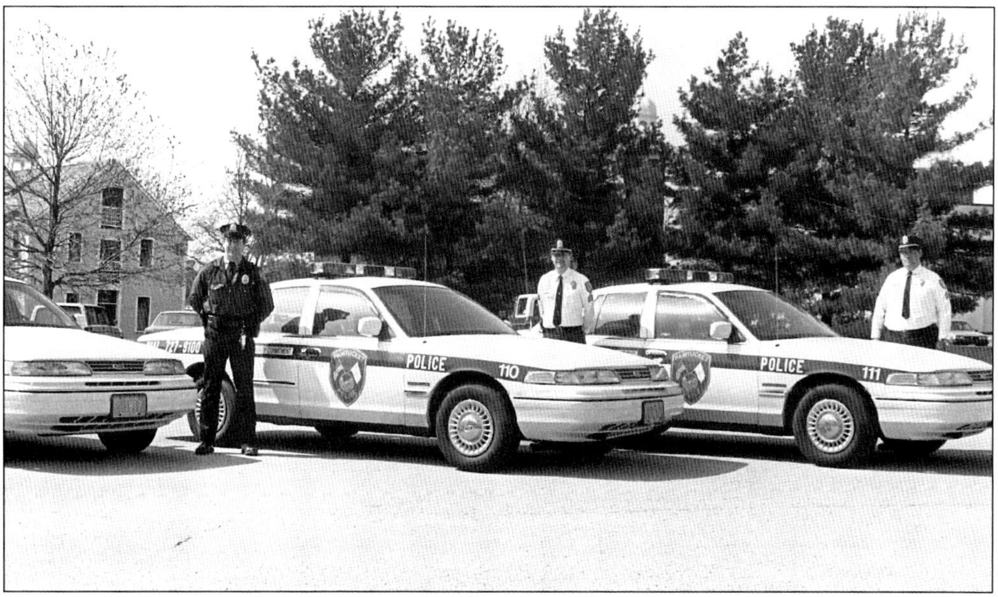

In this April 21, 1993 photograph are, from left to right, Officer Stephan Allcock, Sergeant Joseph Monteiro, and Sergeant John Monteiro, showing off new Pawtucket police cruisers. (*Times*.)

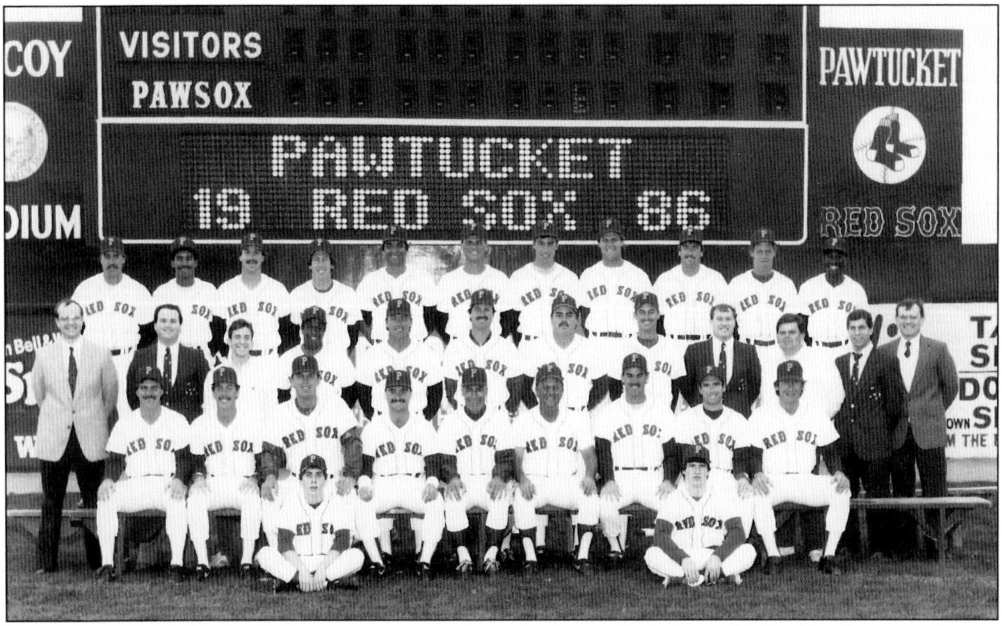

The 1986 Pawtucket Red Sox. From 1987 to 1994, the "Pawsox" established eight consecutive single season attendance records. On June 21, 1994, they celebrated their four millionth fan during owner Ben Mondor's eighteen-year regime.

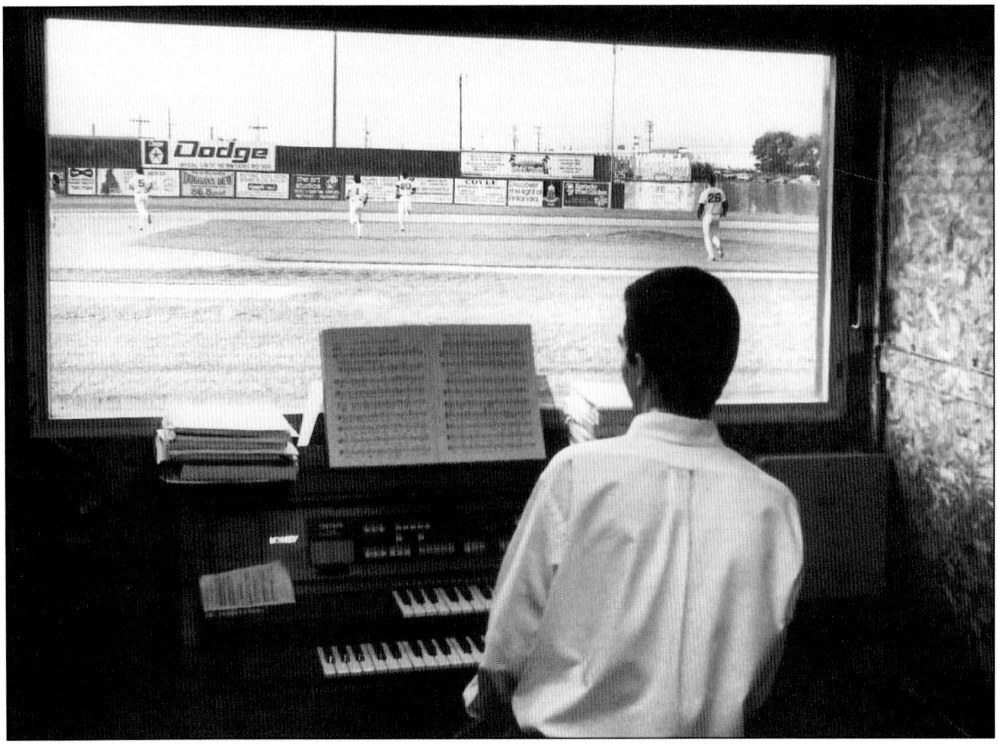

A new organ aroused the spirits of Pawtucket Red Sox fans at McCoy Stadium in June 1986. Joe Carvalho is shown at the console. This is a rare image, because taped music replaced the organ soon afterward. (*Times*.)

Three

GOING SHOPPING

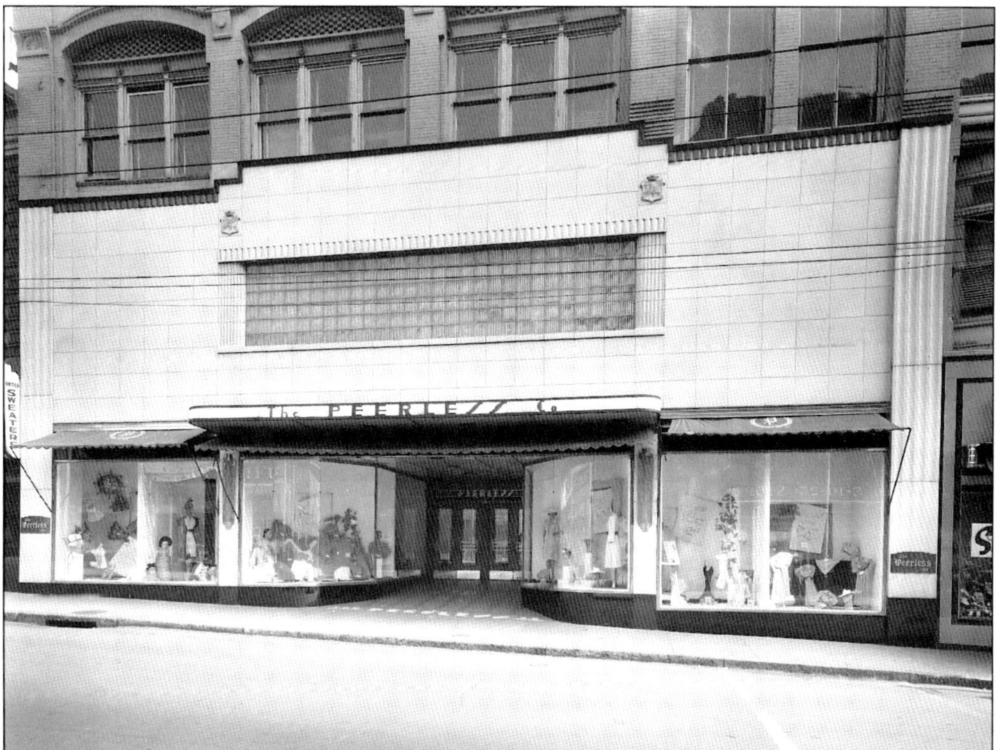

This Art Deco facade identifies the first location of the Peerless Company in Pawtucket, the Music Hall Building on Main Street in downtown Pawtucket, seen here in 1937. The building was torn down in 1970.

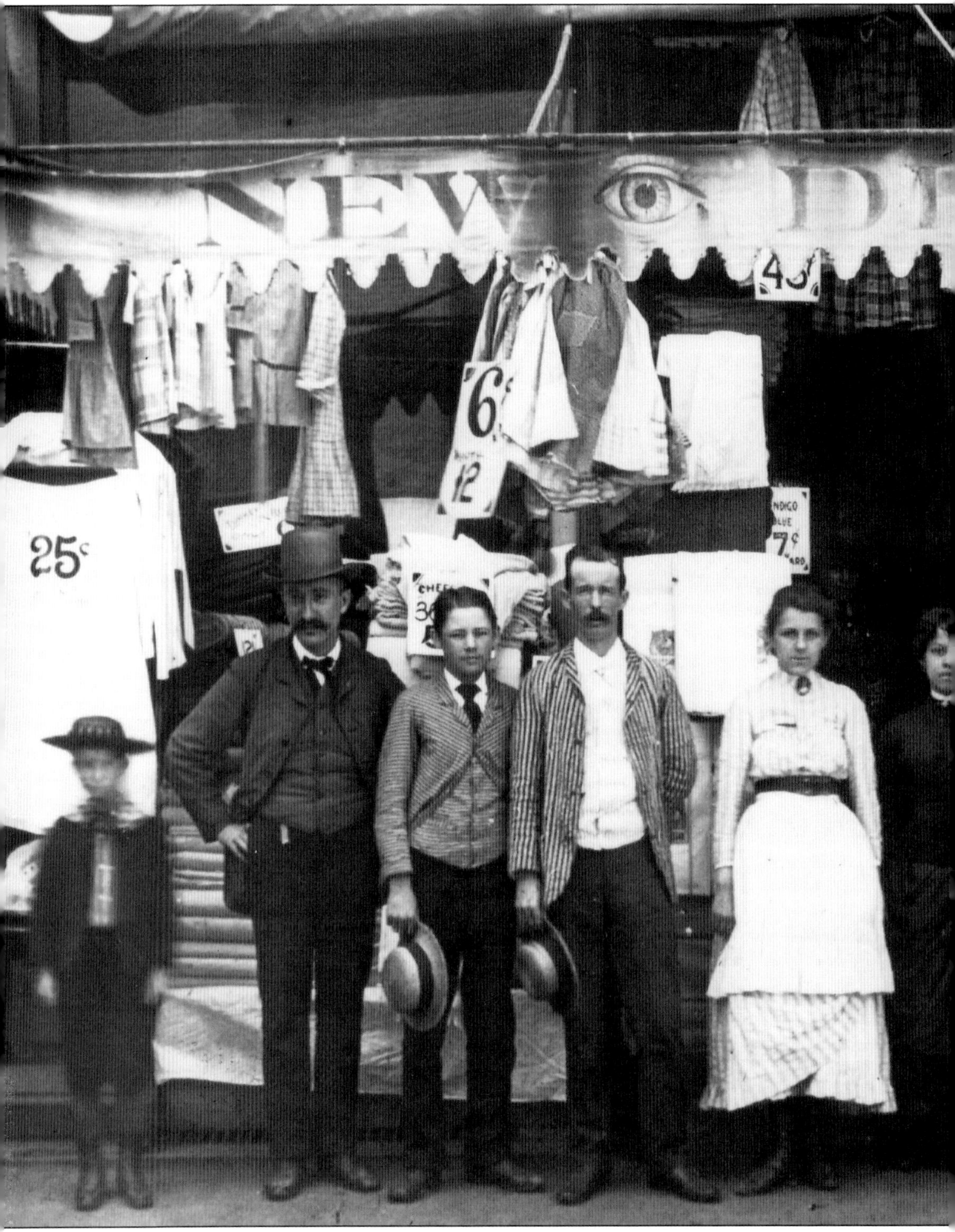

This photograph, taken in 1886, shows the New Idea Store, founded by Jacob Shartenberg and situated in the John Blake Read Block at 96 Main Street in Pawtucket Square. As business

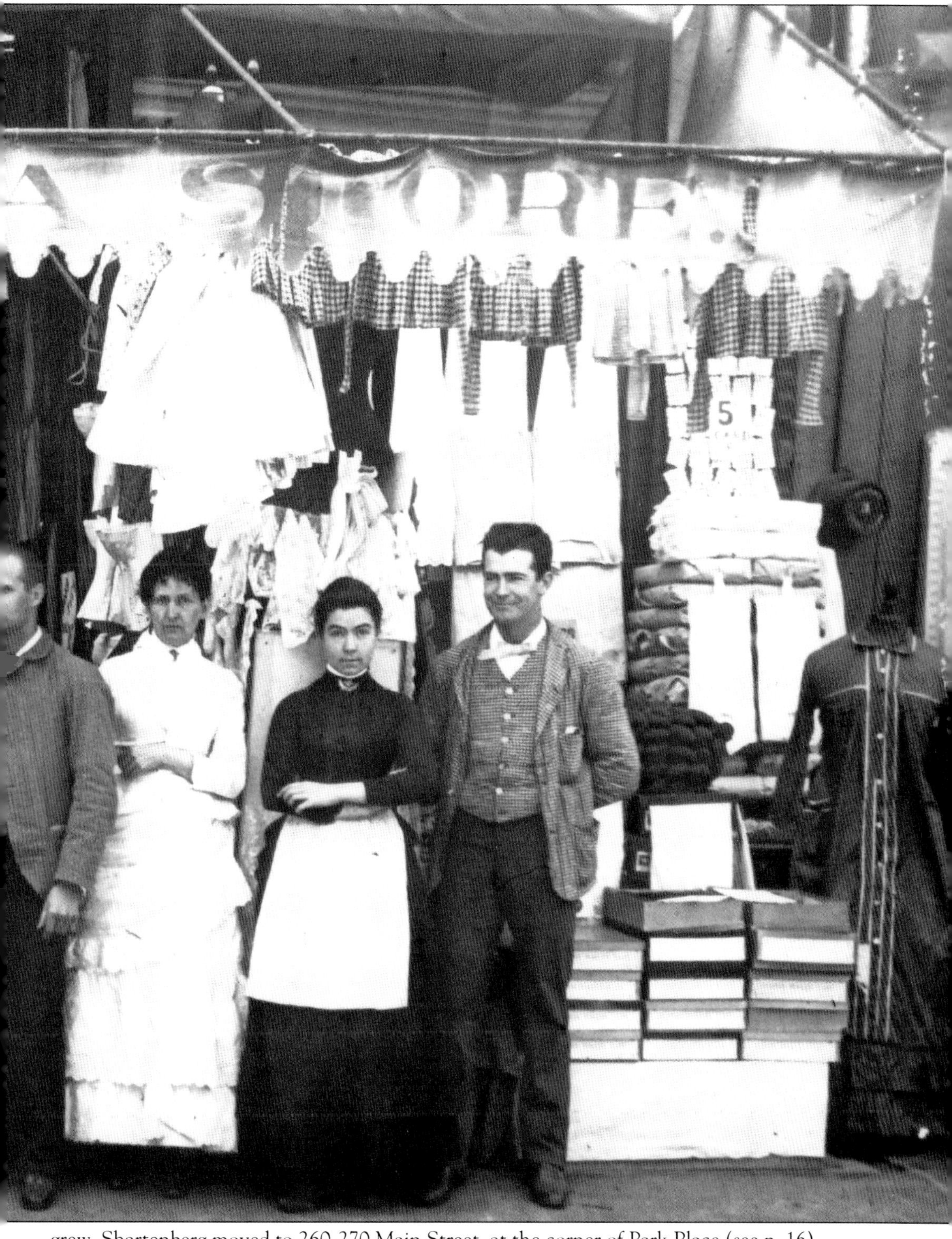

grew, Shartenberg moved to 260-270 Main Street, at the corner of Park Place (see p. 16).

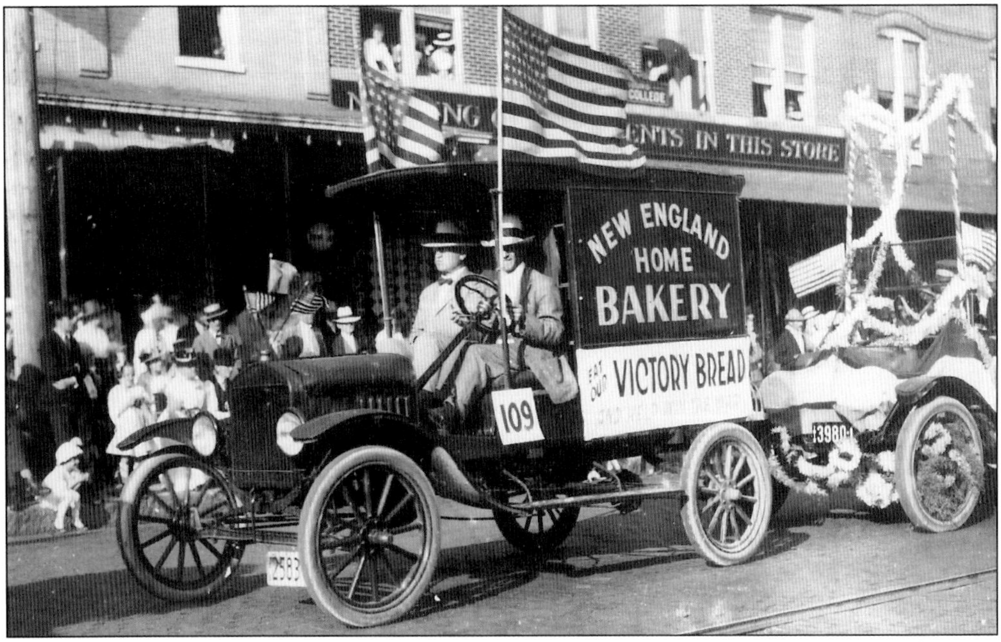

The Commercial Parade on the Fourth of July, 1917, aroused patriotism during World War I. F.W. Woolworth's Five & Ten Cent Store, at 242-244 Main Street, is in the background. The New England Bakery, founded by Henry J. Blais and the bakers of Bamby Bread, became the Ward Bakery.

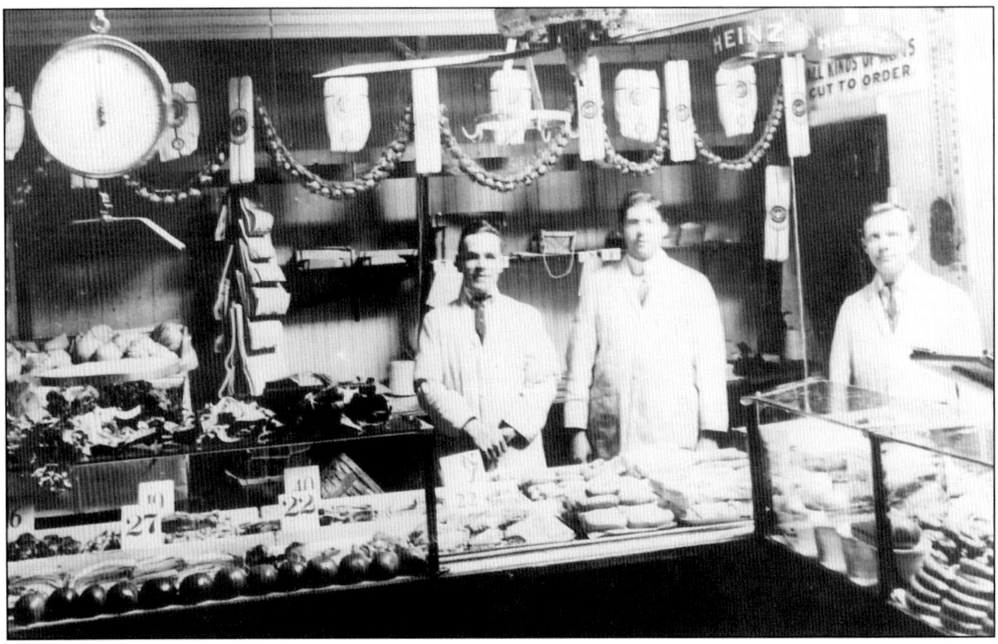

Lemuel Whitney, Inc., a meat market, was in the Odd Fellow Building at 319 Main Street. This photograph was taken between 1913 and 1918.

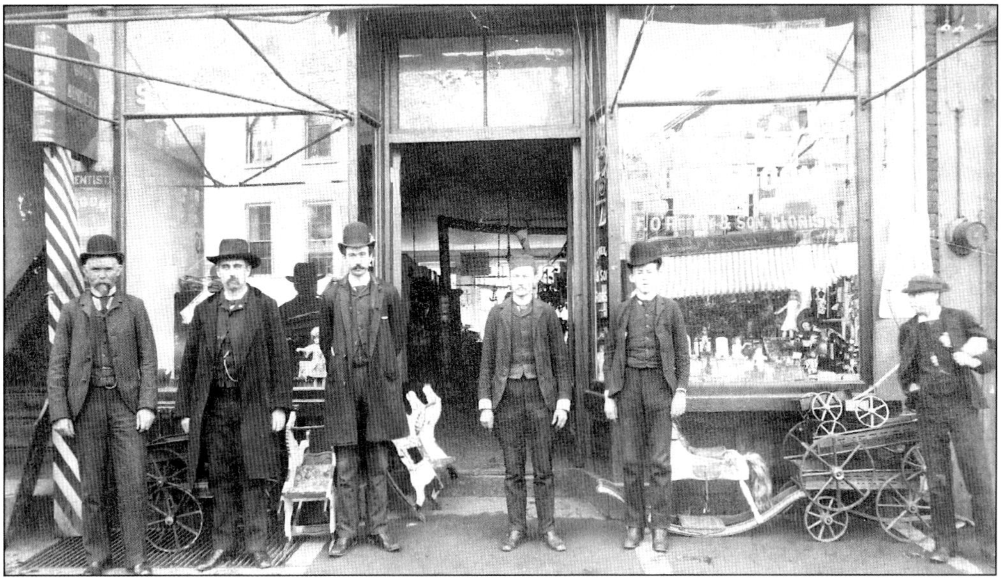

An 1888 view of 96 Main Street, in the John Blake Read Block at Main Street Square in downtown Pawtucket. Pictured are, from left to right: Frank O'Reilly, florist; Edward P. Tobie, agent and reporter for the *Providence Daily Journal and Bulletin*; Peter R. O'Reilly, florist; Crossely Crossely, purveyor of periodicals, stationery, etc.; Crossley's son; and unknown. This was the first office of the *Providence Journal/Bulletin* in Pawtucket.

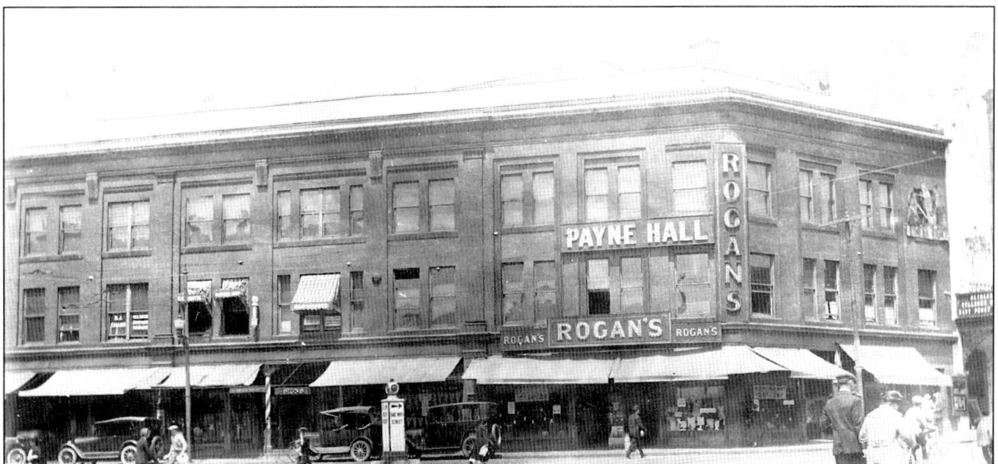

This c. 1925 picture shows Edward J. Rogan's Men's Clothing Store at 1-3 Railroad Avenue (later Goff Avenue) at the corner of Broad Street, and the Payne Building at 7 Railroad Avenue. Upstairs in the Payne Building was duck pin bowling, a favorite of Pawtucket's bowlers. The Leroy Theater can be seen at the far right on Broad Street. The Payne Building was torn down to make way for the Circulator Road.

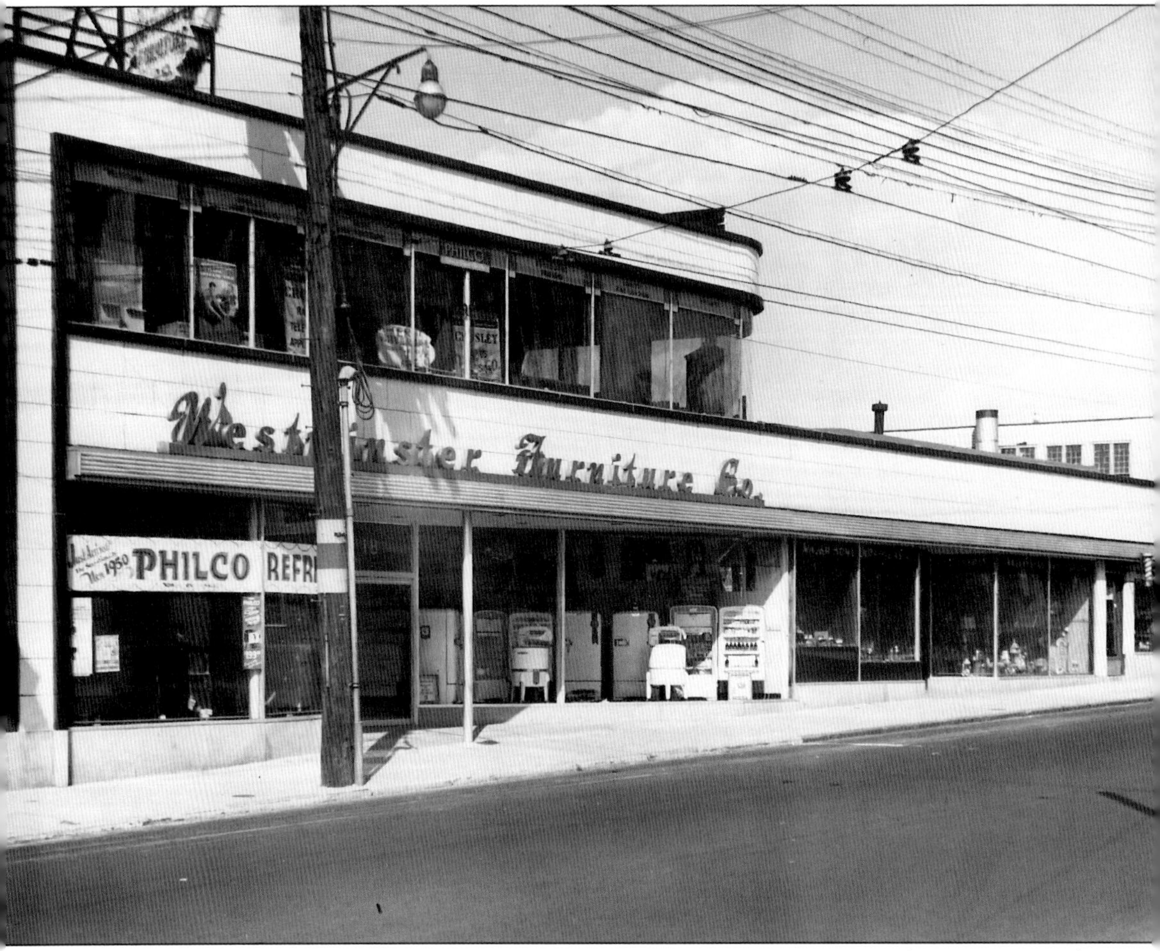

The Westminster Furniture Company started business in 1938 at 18 Broadway. In 1948, the architectural firm of Monahan and Meikle designed the Art Deco facade and made interior alterations. The company was owned by Barney Buckler. This photograph was taken in 1950.

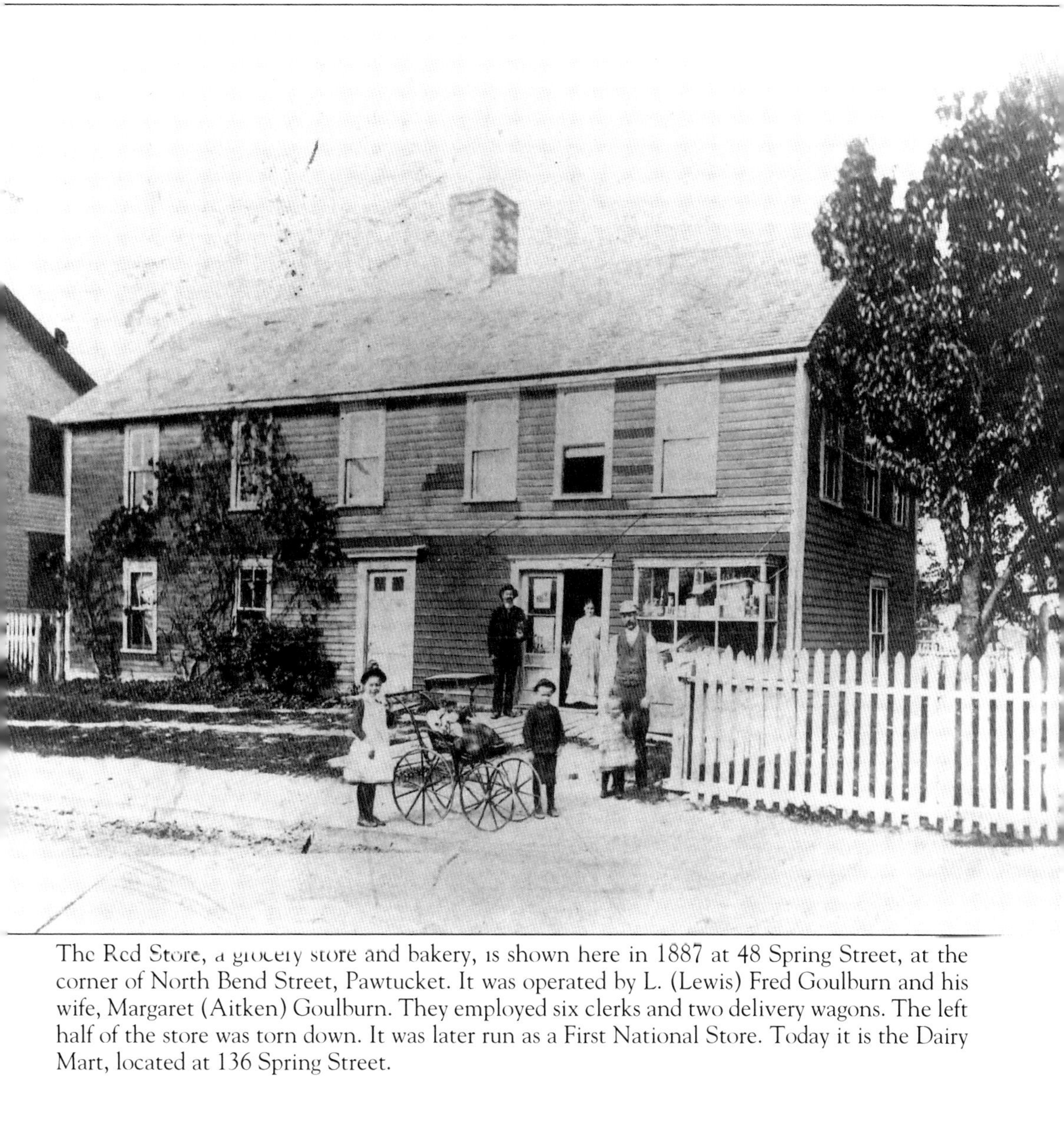

The Red Store, a grocery store and bakery, is shown here in 1887 at 48 Spring Street, at the corner of North Bend Street, Pawtucket. It was operated by L. (Lewis) Fred Goulburn and his wife, Margaret (Aitken) Goulburn. They employed six clerks and two delivery wagons. The left half of the store was torn down. It was later run as a First National Store. Today it is the Dairy Mart, located at 136 Spring Street.

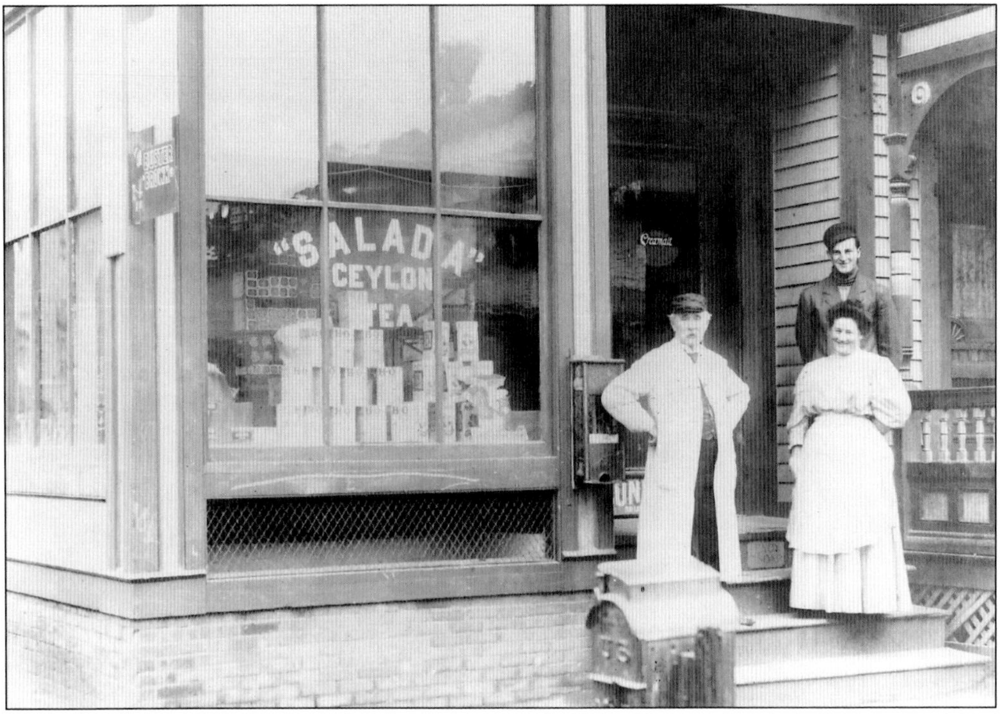

Roberts' Market, at the corner of Cole Street and Clark Avenue in Pleasant View, c. 1905. On the steps of the market are Richard Roberts (left), his daughter Isabel Hilton Roberts (right), and George M. Marsh of 70 Appleton Avenue (standing at the rear).

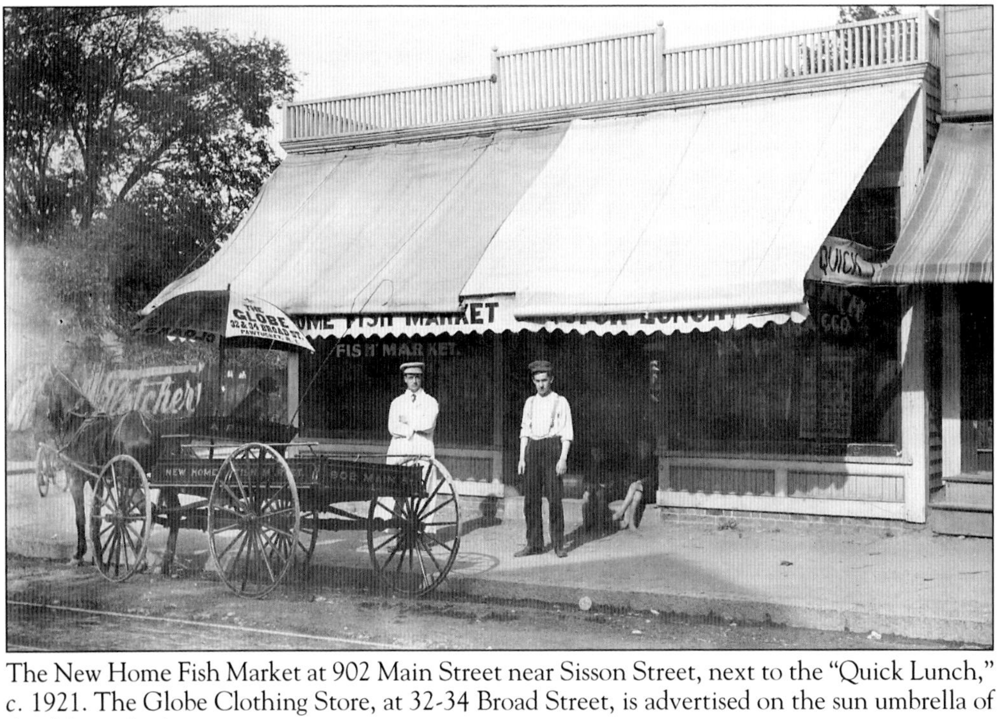

The New Home Fish Market at 902 Main Street near Sisson Street, next to the "Quick Lunch," c. 1921. The Globe Clothing Store, at 32-34 Broad Street, is advertised on the sun umbrella of the fish market's wagon.

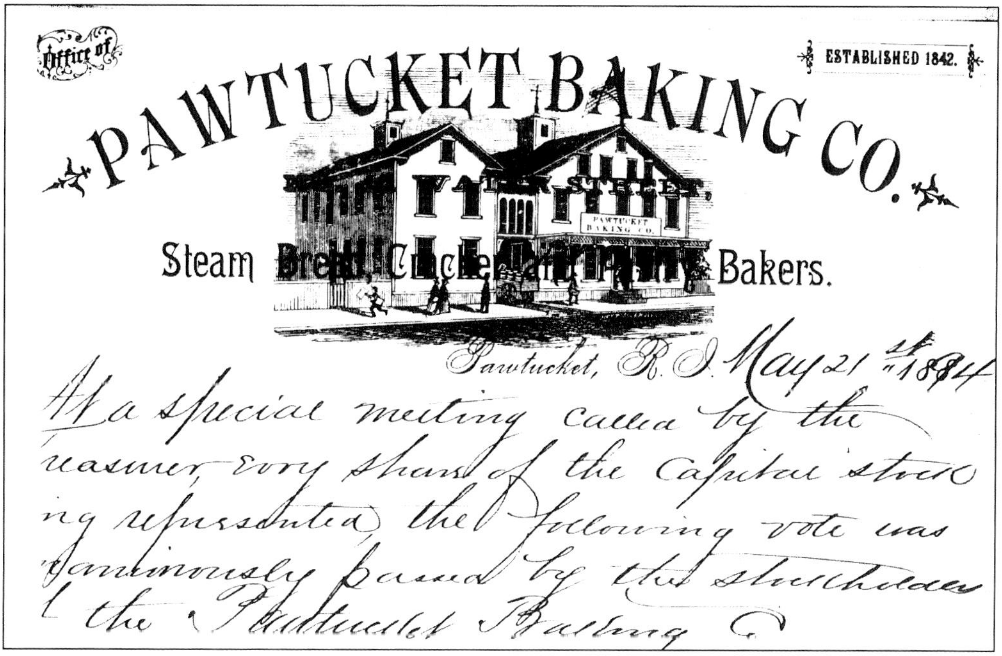
Office of
ESTABLISHED 1842.
PAWTUCKET BAKING CO.
Steam Bread, Cracker and Pastry Bakers.
Pawtucket, R. I. May 21st 1884
At a special meeting called by the
reasurer, every share of the capital stock
ng represented, the following vote was
nanimously passed by the stockholders
the Pawtucket Baking Co

A letterhead from the Pawtucket Baking Company. Marcus L. Dean, the founder, expanded his thriving business in 1860 by constructing the buildings shown above on Water Street. The new buildings had 100 feet of frontage, beginning at Main Street. The property is now covered by the Apex Company complex.

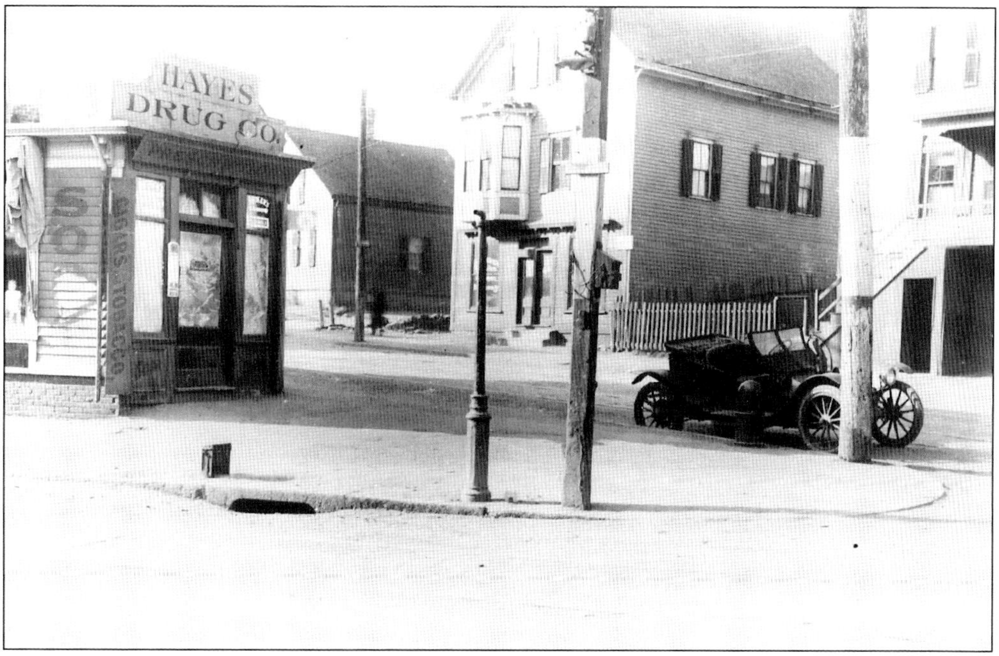

Hayes Drug Company, at the junction of East and Pawtucket Avenues, in 1914. The company was founded by Frank J. Hayes in 1910. Pharmacists Henry L. Bessette and Bernard F. Keenan continued from 1956 until 1968. The building was torn down about 1973. The auto belonged to photographer Albert Vandall.

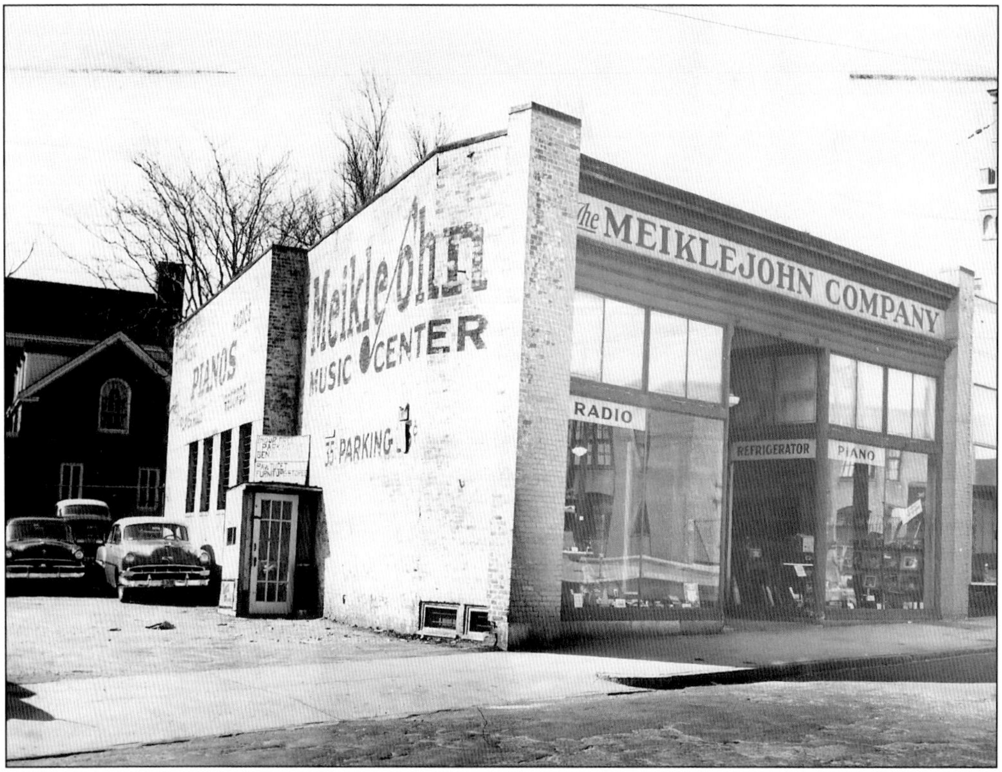

A March 1954 view of Meiklejohn Music Center (owned by James H. Meiklejohn) at 45 Park Place, just off Main Street. The firm was established in 1884. For many years, the Meiklejohn Auditorium stood adjacent to this store, where the parking lot is to the left. Big name concerts were staged here and championship roller polo was played. The auditorium, subsequently used for storage, was finally destroyed by fire in 1933. (*Times.*)

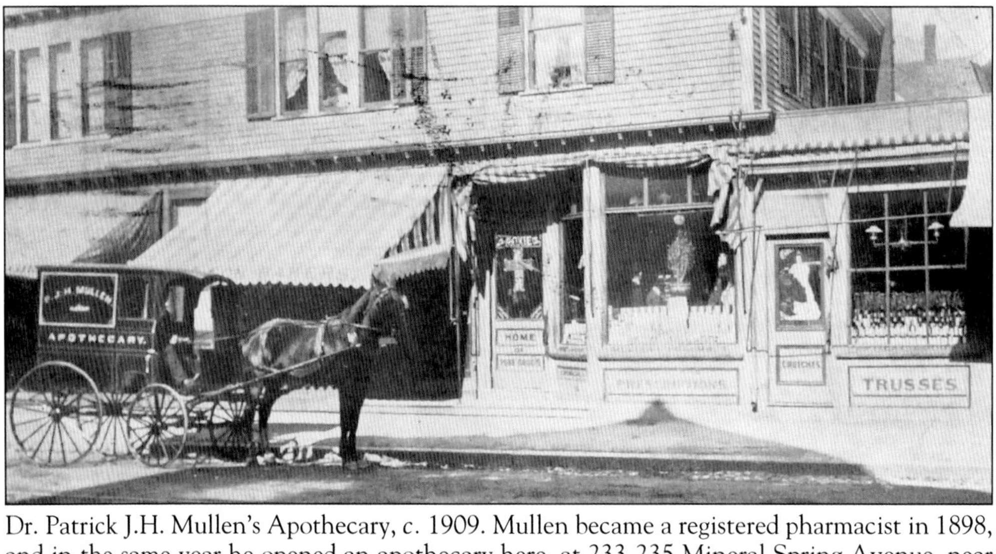

Dr. Patrick J.H. Mullen's Apothecary, *c.* 1909. Mullen became a registered pharmacist in 1898, and in the same year he opened an apothecary here, at 233-235 Mineral Spring Avenue, near the "Four Corners" at Lonsdale Avenue. Mullen played an active role in the development of Woodlawn. For years, he practiced optometry and devoted considerable time to real estate.

Four

Going to School

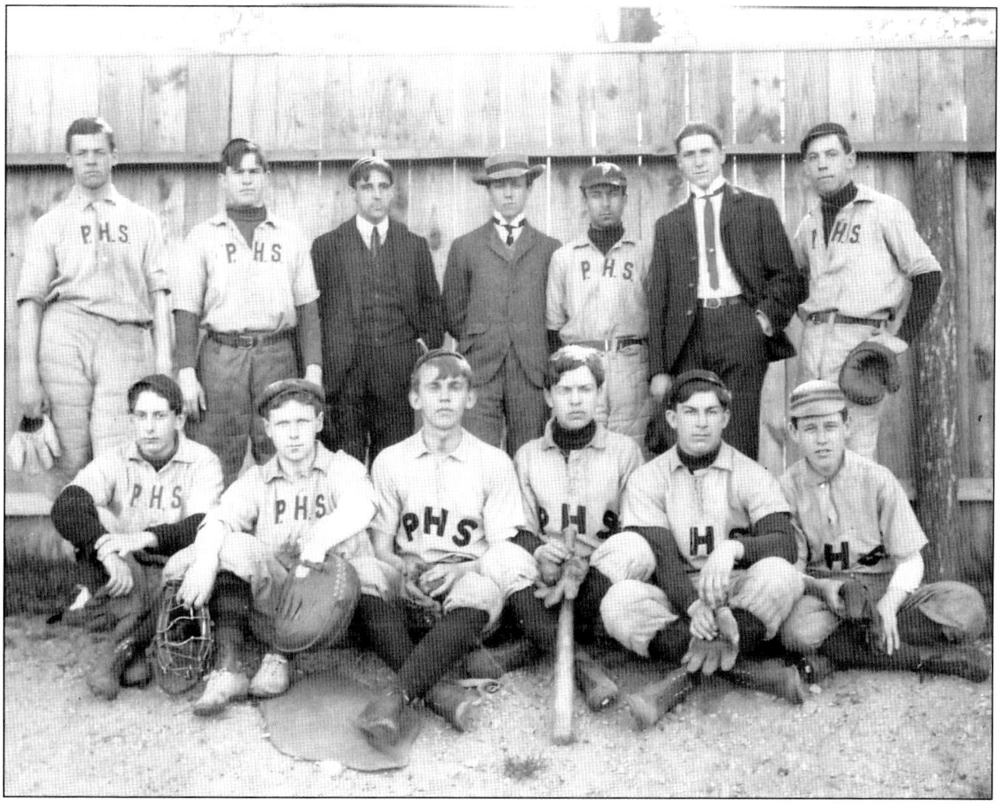

The Pawtucket High School baseball team, *c.* 1903. Pictured here are, from left to right: (front row) Ernest Fuller, Elmer Davis, George Stone Emerson, Edwin C. Colwell, Leppy Hammond, and Howard Payne; (back row) Fulton Redmond, Morton French, Charles W. Perry, Gene Jackson, Frank Vanada, the coach (name unknown), and William R. Walker.

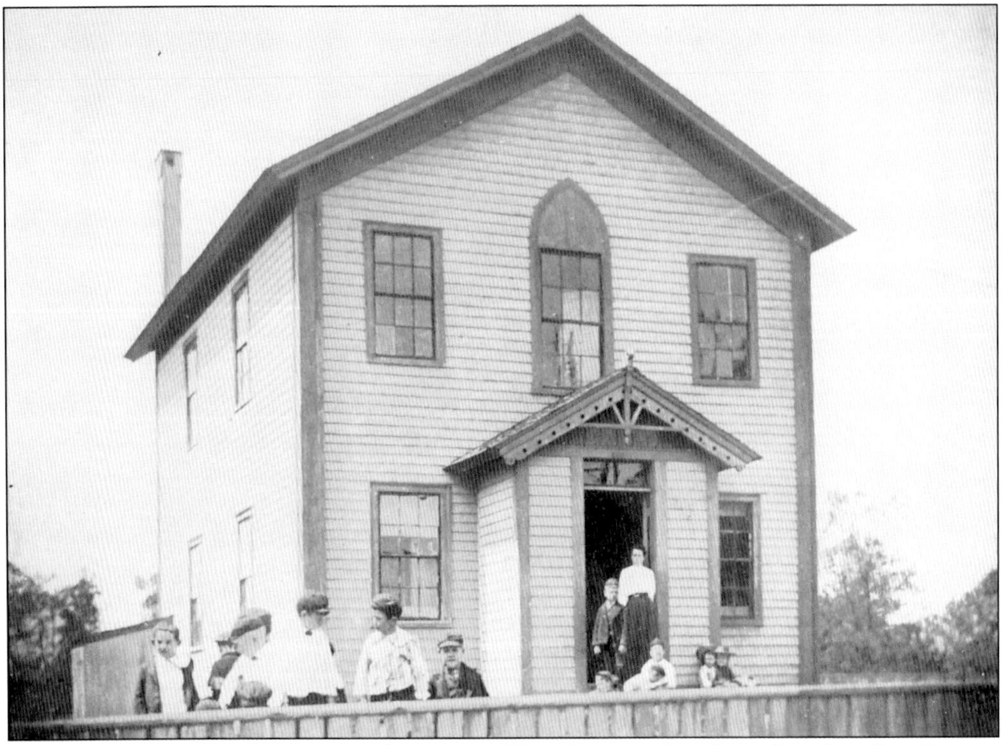

The old Prospect Street School, built *c.* 1870. This photograph is from the 1910 City Report. Originally known as the Dunnell's Print Works School, it was replaced in 1908 by a new brick Prospect Street School. The old schoolhouse was modified into a four-apartment structure, and was finally torn down by the city in the 1970s.

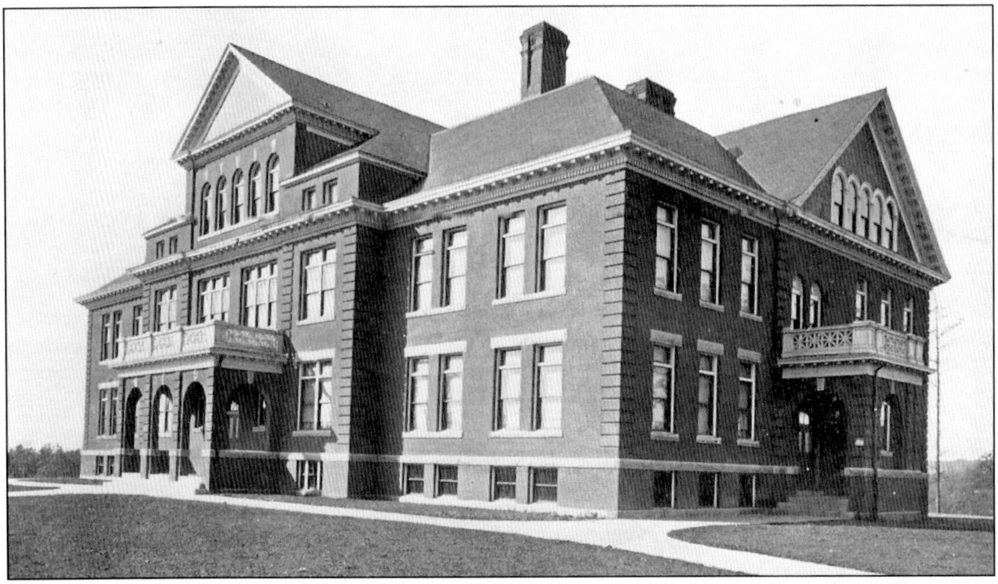

The new Prospect Street School, at 325 Prospect Street, was built in 1908 and razed in 1971. This photograph is from the 1910 City Report.

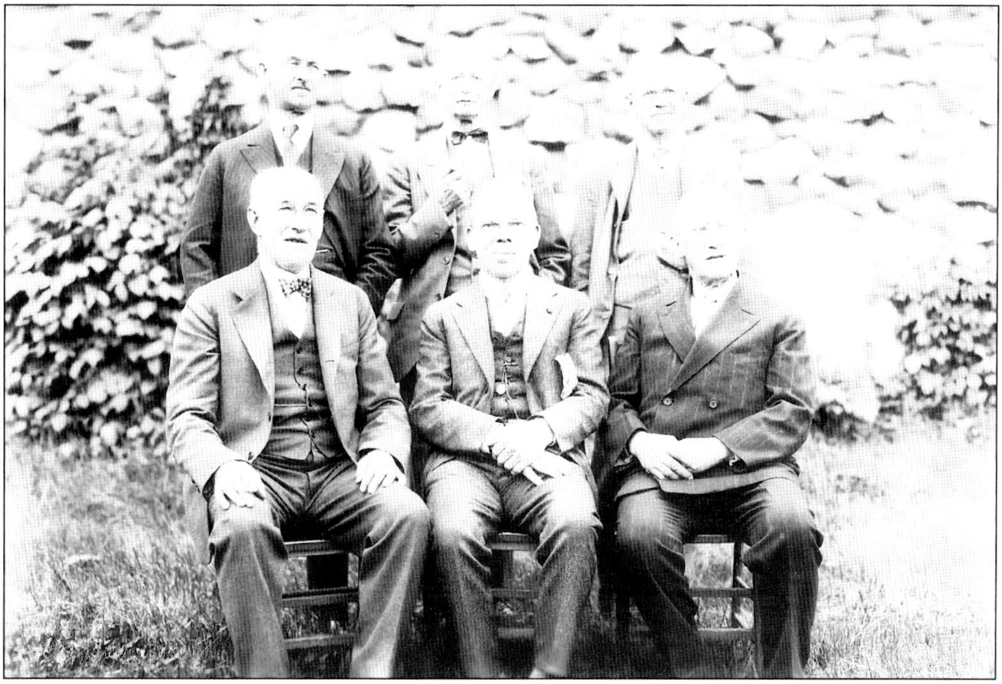

The 1930 reunion of the Pawtucket High School Class of 1886. Seen here are, from left to right: (front row) Charles S. Foster, William L. Perkins, and George M. Rex; (back row) Sam H. Roberts, Shirley Green, and Roger Clapp.

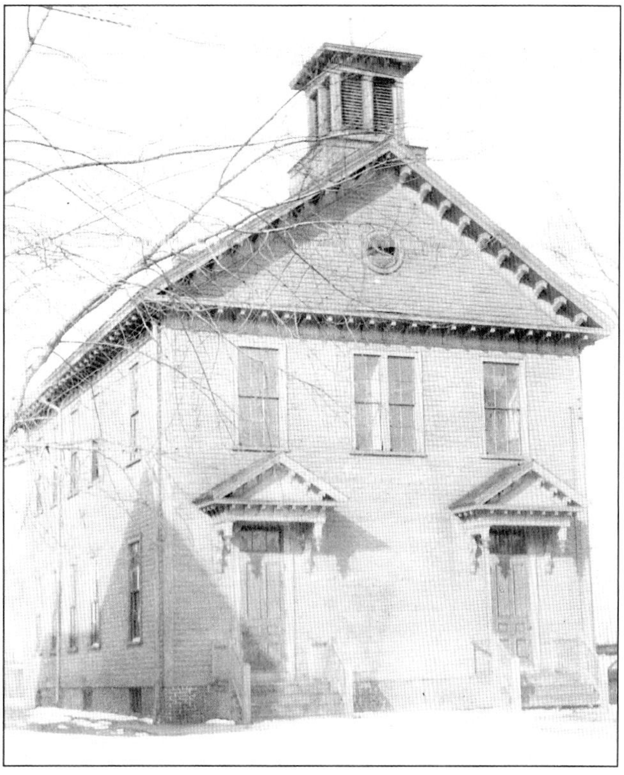

The Brook Street Grammar School was built in 1876 and closed out as a school about 1922. It was sold by the City to Patrick J. McGartlen in 1930 and converted into a private residence. It is still standing, at 130 Armistice Boulevard. This photograph was taken in 1887. (*Times*.)

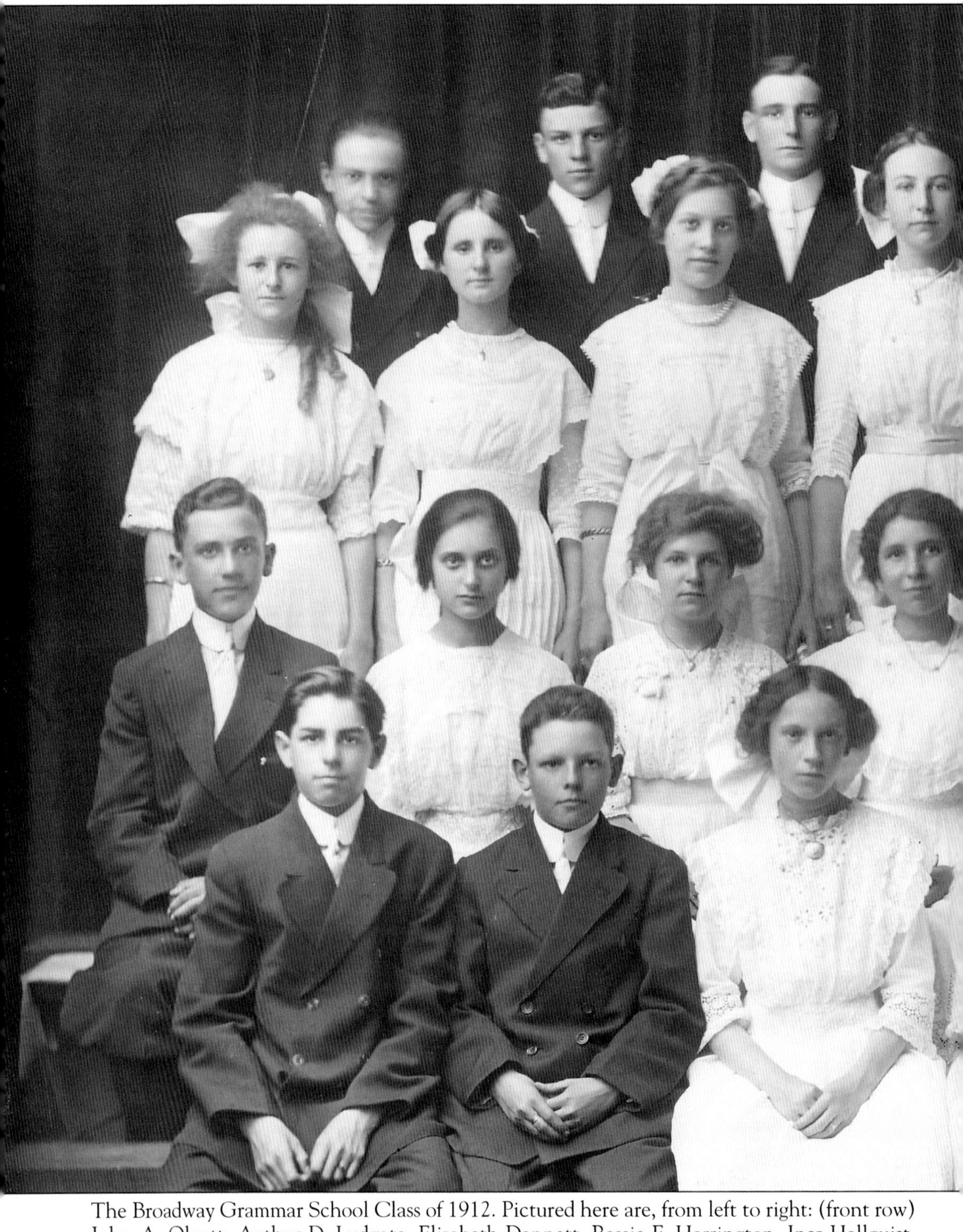

The Broadway Grammar School Class of 1912. Pictured here are, from left to right: (front row) John A. Olyott, Authur D. Ludgate, Elizabeth Dennett, Bessie F. Harrington, Inez Hallquist, T. Francis Vance, and Ralph Hallquist; (second row) Agnew McRae, Esther Kanowski, Marion Heimer, Myra Wassmer, Ruth Armour, Harriet Wightman, Miriam Crawford, and

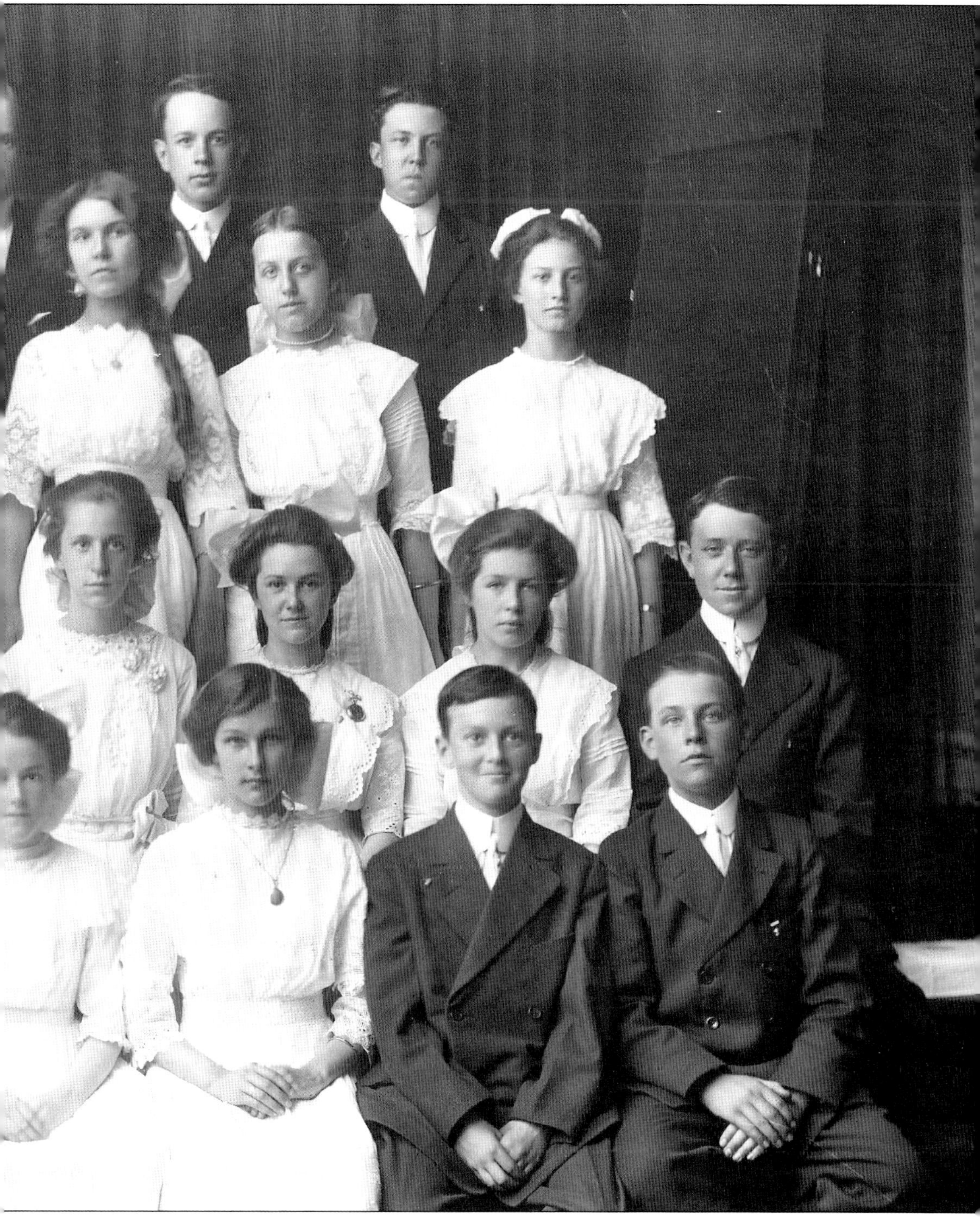

Lester Wightman; (third row) Mildred Wadsworth, H. Seaver Gorman, Leah Seaver, Helen Lewis, Gladys Foot, Ethel Wilson, and Ethel Hines; (back row) Richard Haslam, Lester Stauff, William Lynch, David Valentine, Samuel W. Chantler, and Herbert Ellis. (Pawtucket Public Library.)

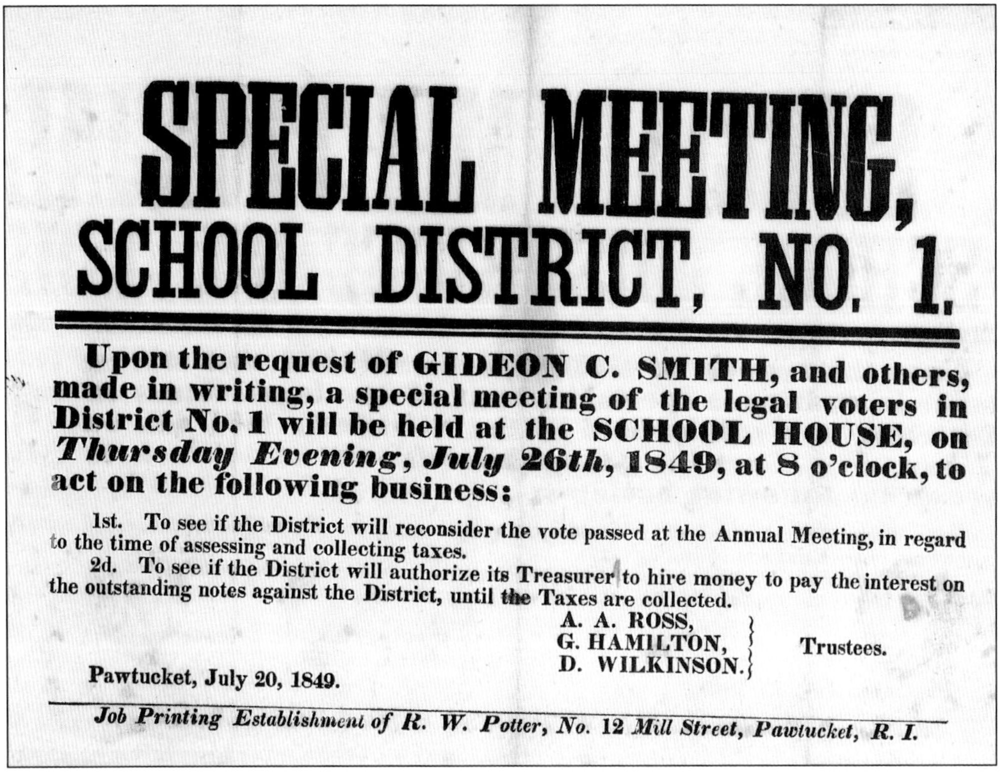

SPECIAL MEETING, SCHOOL DISTRICT, NO. 1.

Upon the request of GIDEON C. SMITH, and others, made in writing, a special meeting of the legal voters in District No. 1 will be held at the SCHOOL HOUSE, on *Thursday Evening, July 26th*, 1849, at 8 o'clock, to act on the following business:

1st. To see if the District will reconsider the vote passed at the Annual Meeting, in regard to the time of assessing and collecting taxes.

2d. To see if the District will authorize its Treasurer to hire money to pay the interest on the outstanding notes against the District, until the Taxes are collected.

A. A. ROSS,
G. HAMILTON,
D. WILKINSON. } Trustees.

Pawtucket, July 20, 1849.

Job Printing Establishment of R. W. Potter, No. 12 Mill Street, Pawtucket, R. I.

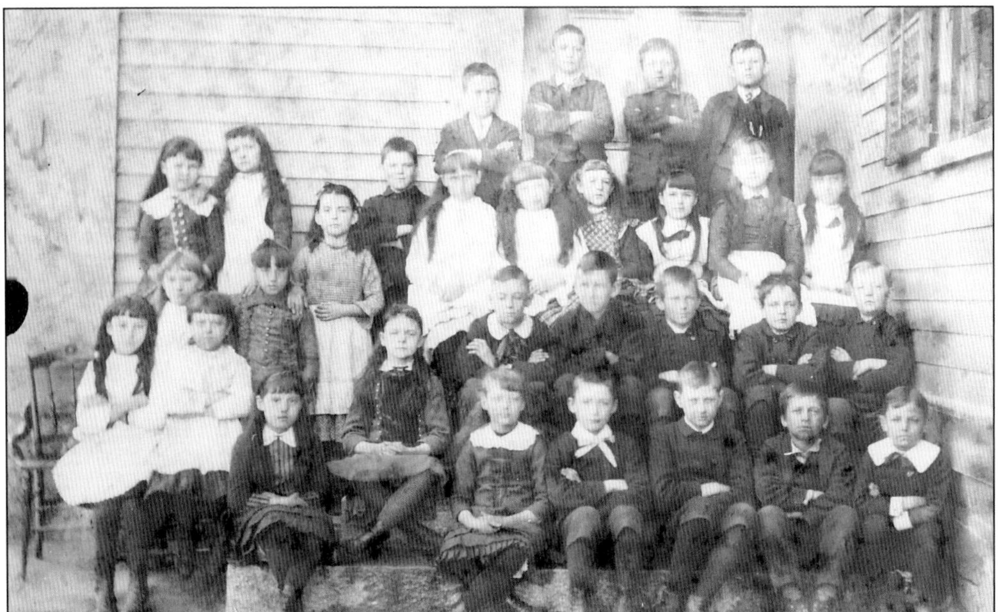

A class at the Church Hill School, *c.* 1885. Irving Perrin can be seen in the front row, third from the right.

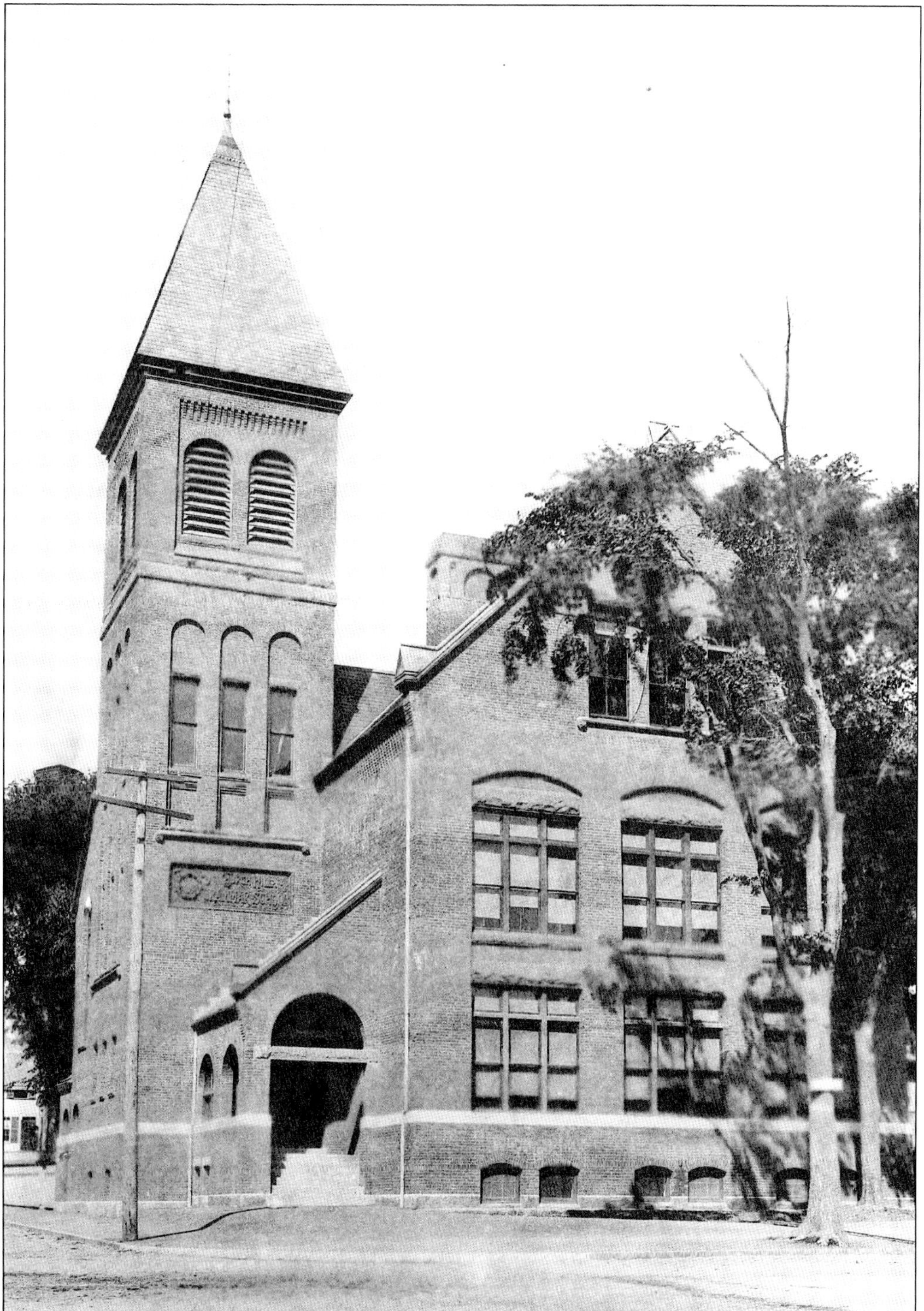

A view of the Church Hill School at Park Place and Church Street in 1890. This building replaced an earlier wooden structure. The fanciful Queen Anne-style building was rededicated in September 1987 as the Edward T. Creamer Pawtucket School Administration Building.

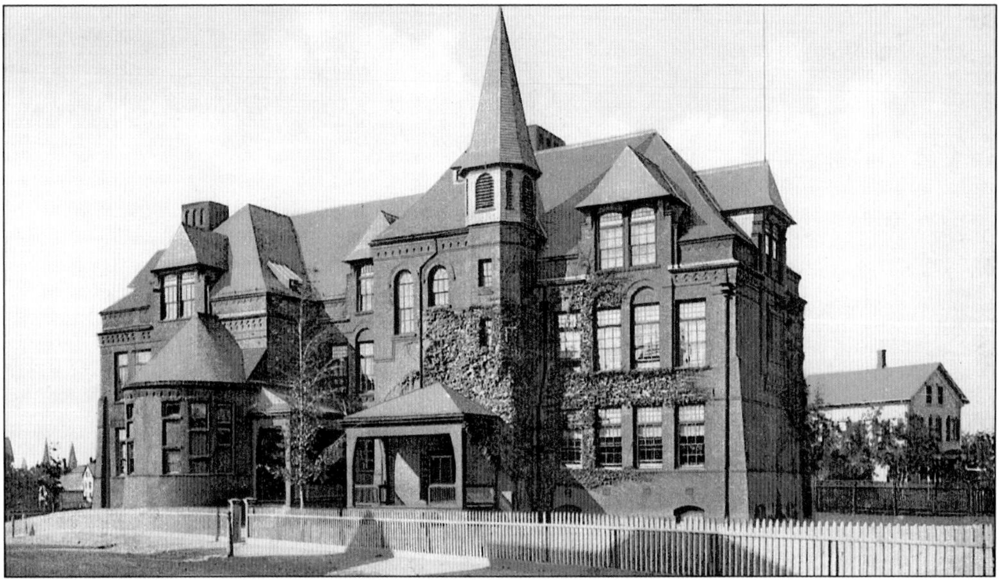

The Garden Street School around the turn of the century. The right half was built in 1888 and the addition to the left was built by Pawtucket architect William R. Walker in 1892–93. The school is no longer standing.

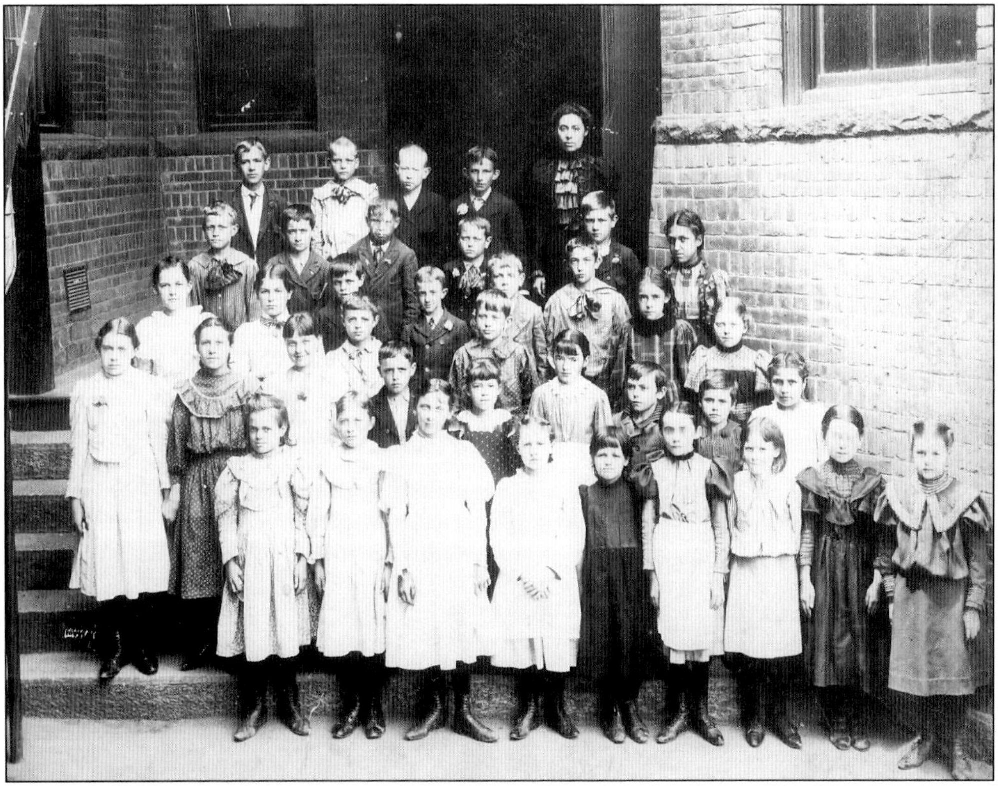

Garden Street School students, *c.* 1894. Roy Roberts can be seen in the third row, third from the left.

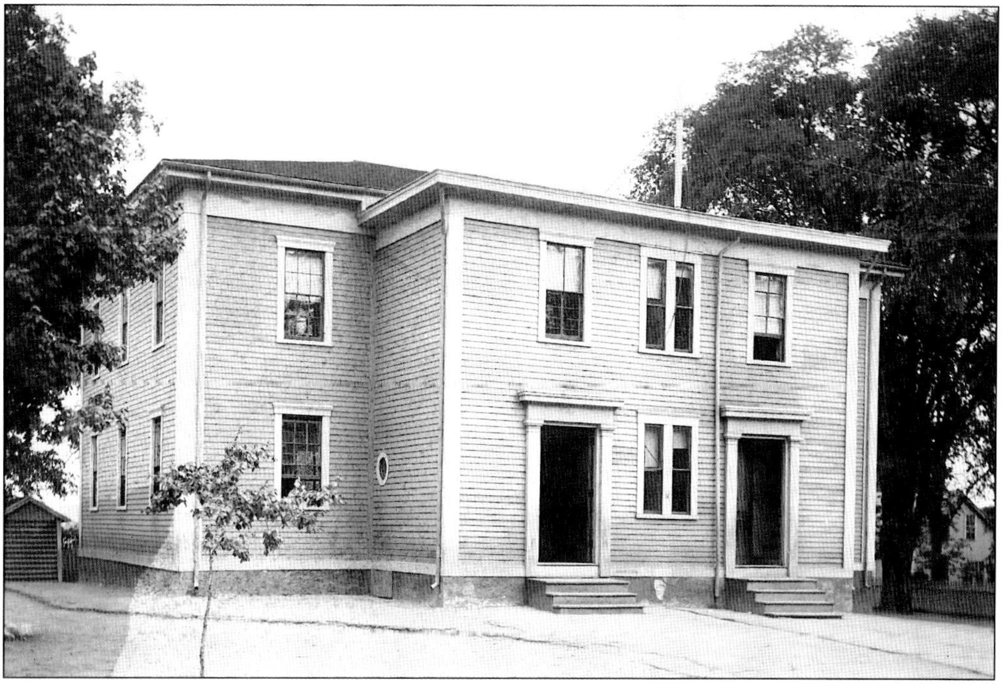

The Summit Street High School, at the corner of Summit and Johnson Streets, *c.* 1904. This was formerly the Pawtucket High School (established in 1885 under William E. Tolman), and was later a fresh (open) air school. It was torn down around 1932.

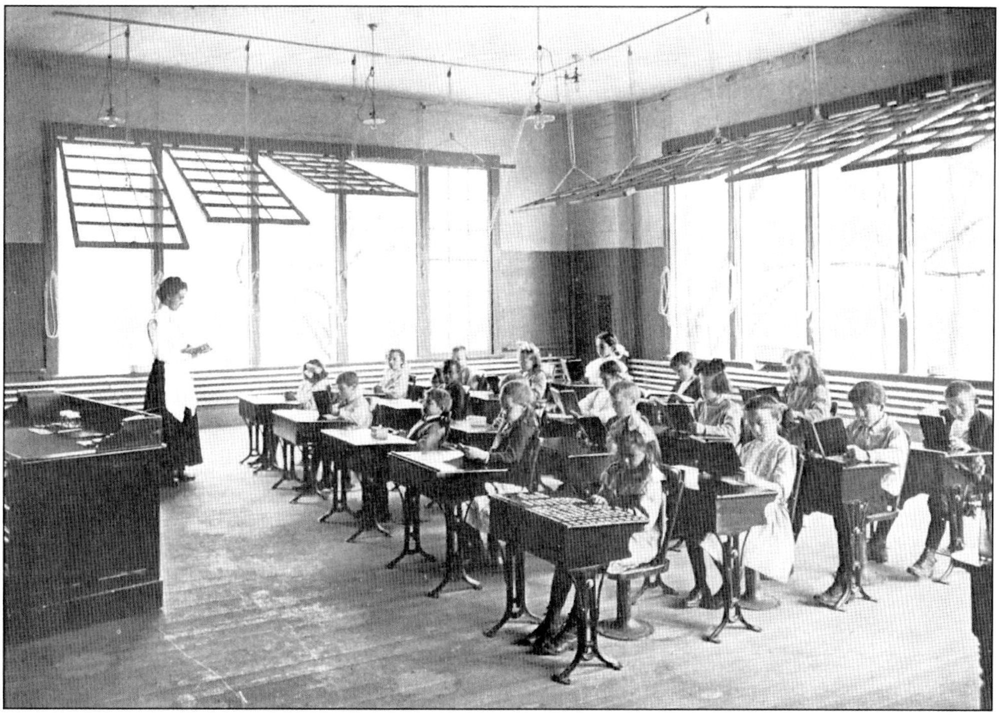

A classroom view of the Summit Street Fresh Air School. The photograph is from the 1910 City Report.

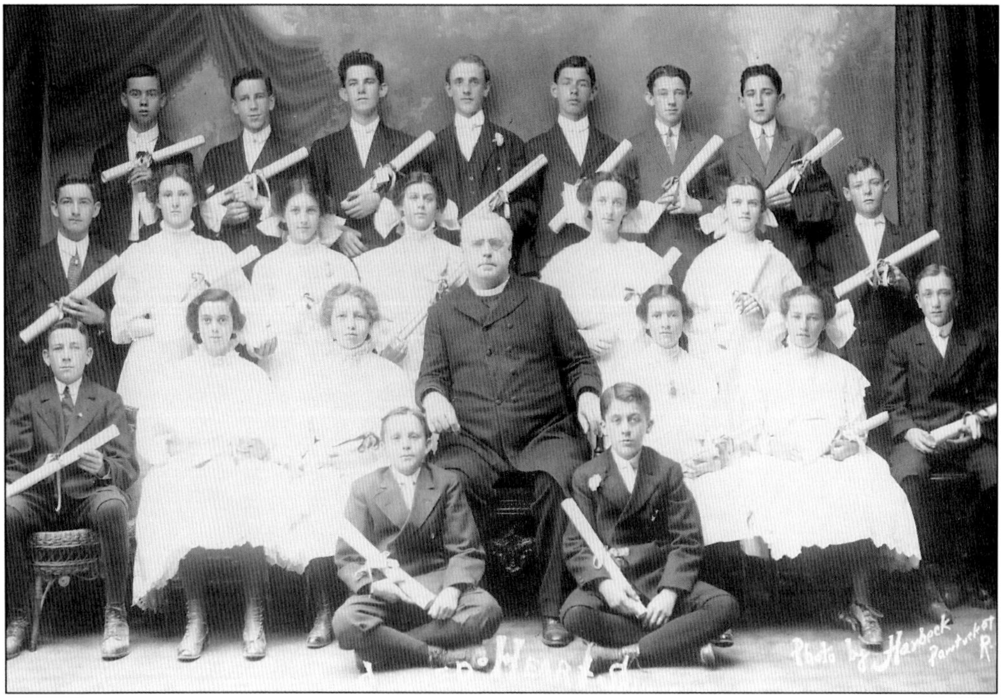

The Class of 1909 at the Sacred Heart School in Pleasant View.

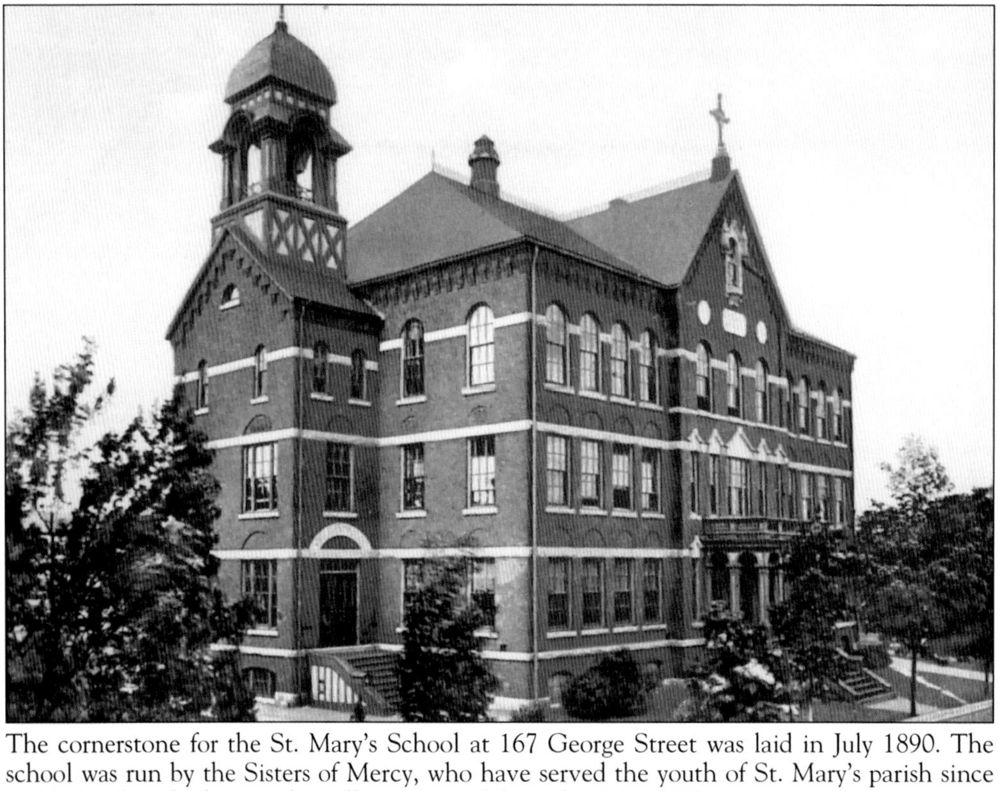

The cornerstone for the St. Mary's School at 167 George Street was laid in July 1890. The school was run by the Sisters of Mercy, who have served the youth of St. Mary's parish since 1854. One hundred years of excellence was celebrated in May 1992.

Five

Showing Respect

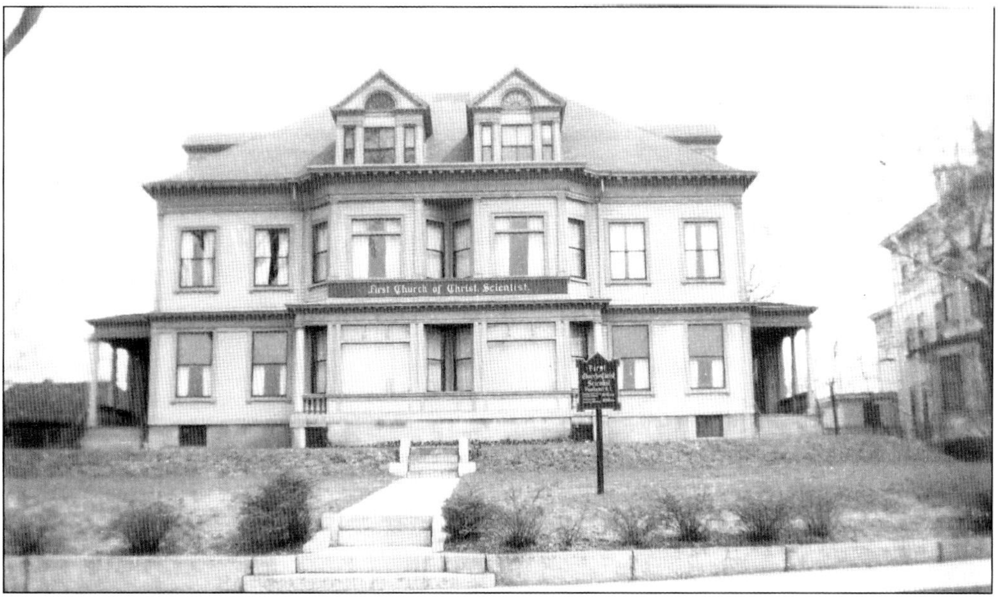

Inventor Henry Herbert Sheldon, who made his fortune from real estate and construction, built this home on Park Place in 1896. It was taken over by the Christian Science Church from 1933 to 1969. In 1980 it was torn down by the Pawtucket Savings and Trust Company to create a parking lot.

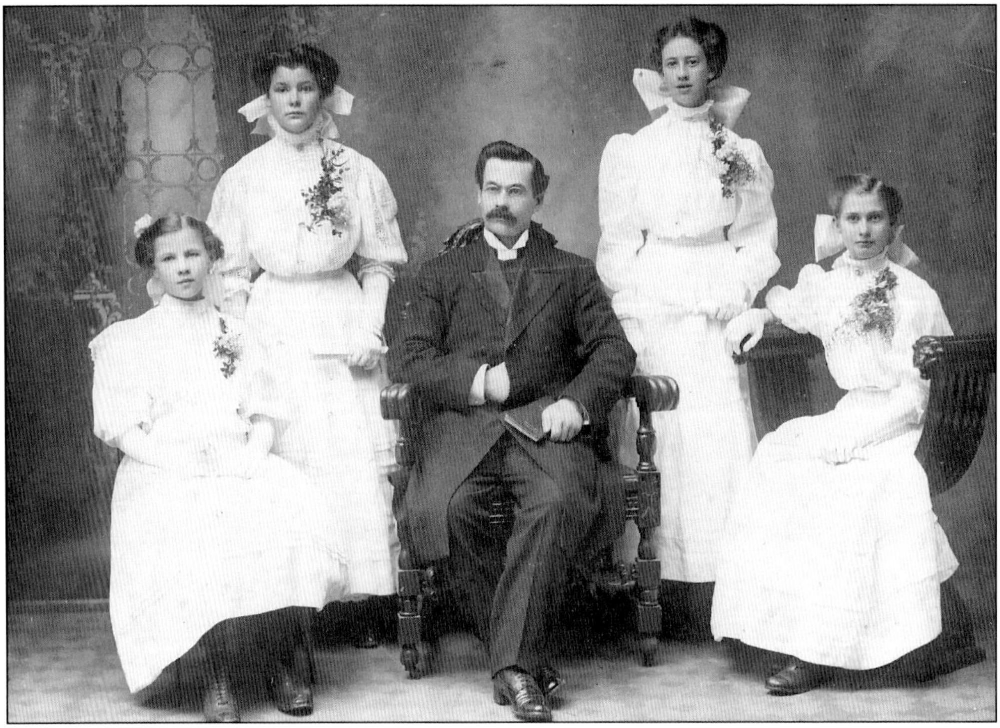

The 1908 Sunday School class of the Swedish Congregational Church on Elm Street. Founded in 1892, it is now the Covenant Congregational Church on Glenwood Avenue, Pawtucket. Seen here are, from left to right: Ellen (Nordquist) Harvey, Alice Enander, Reverend Olaf Ohlson (pastor), Anna Oden, and Segrid (Carlson) Lundquist.

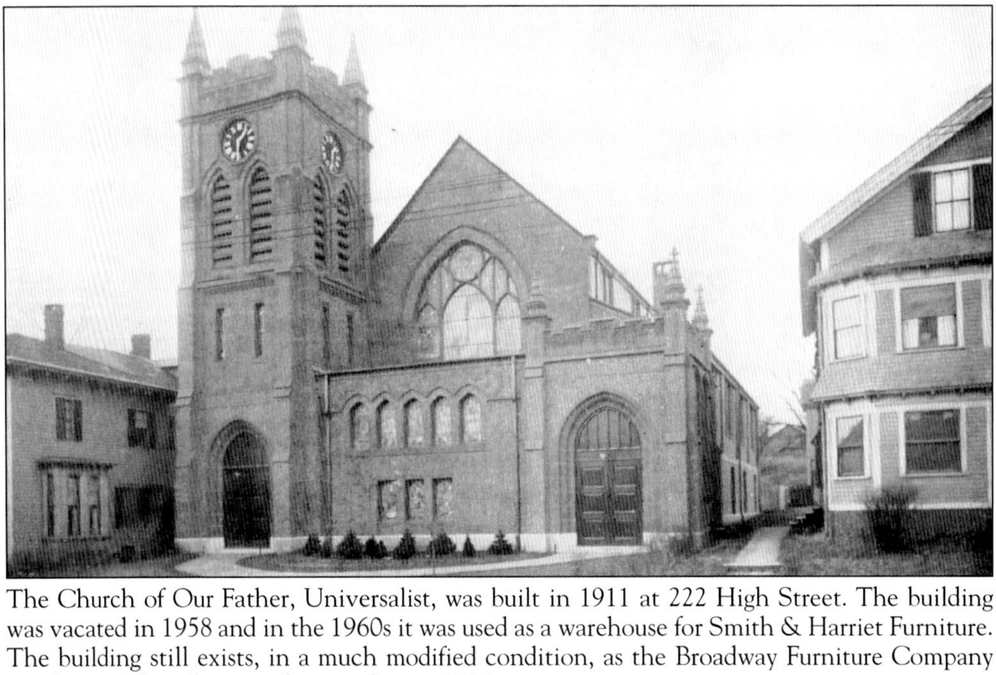

The Church of Our Father, Universalist, was built in 1911 at 222 High Street. The building was vacated in 1958 and in the 1960s it was used as a warehouse for Smith & Harriet Furniture. The building still exists, in a much modified condition, as the Broadway Furniture Company warehouse. This photograph was taken *c.* 1940.

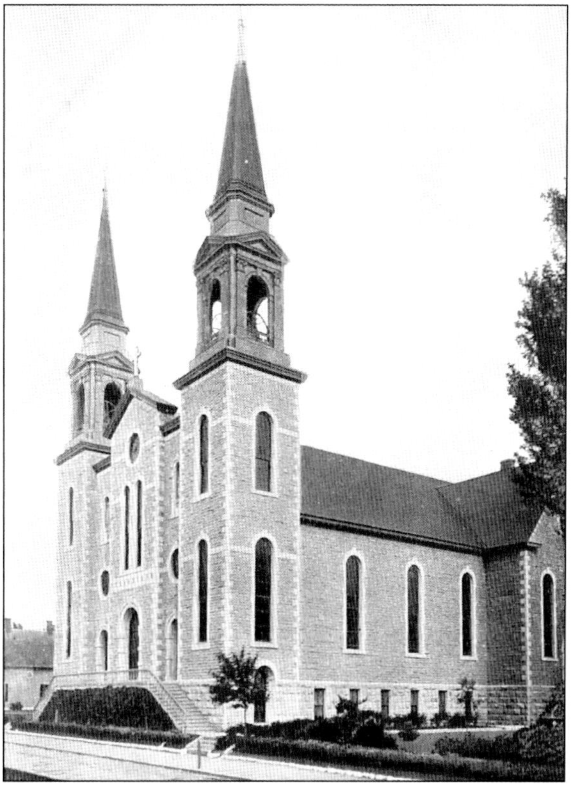

The St. Jean Baptiste Church on Quincy Avenue. Built in 1895 to serve a swelling French population, it was destroyed by fire in October 1918. It is seen here about 1900.

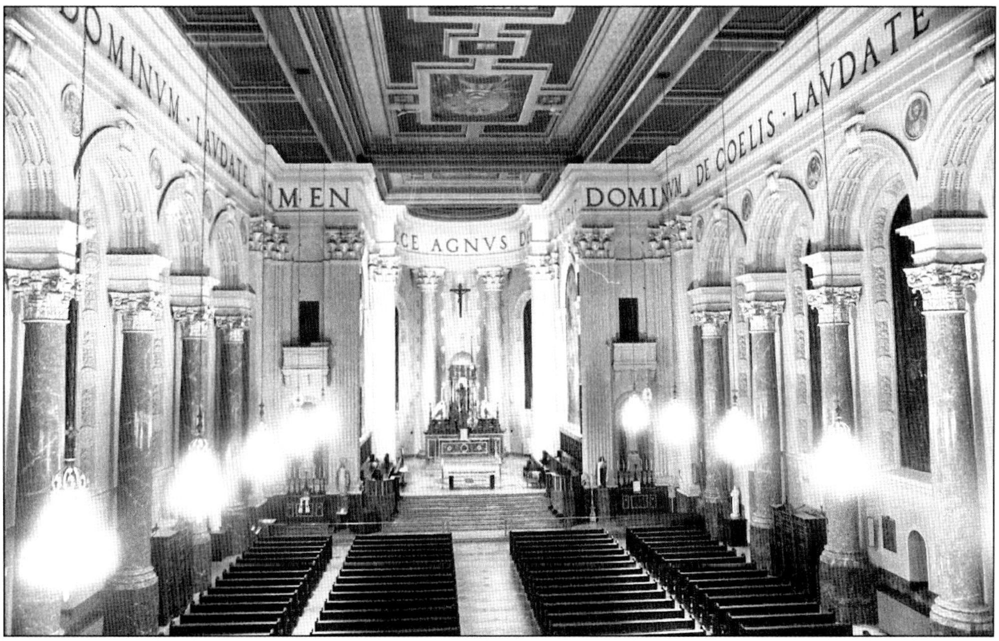

The construction of the St. John the Baptist Church (formerly the St. Jean Baptiste Church) was started in 1925 and completed in 1927, to replace the earlier church building (see above) which burned down in 1918. It is adorned with many art treasures. This interior view of the cathedral-like edifice was taken in 1986. (*Times.*)

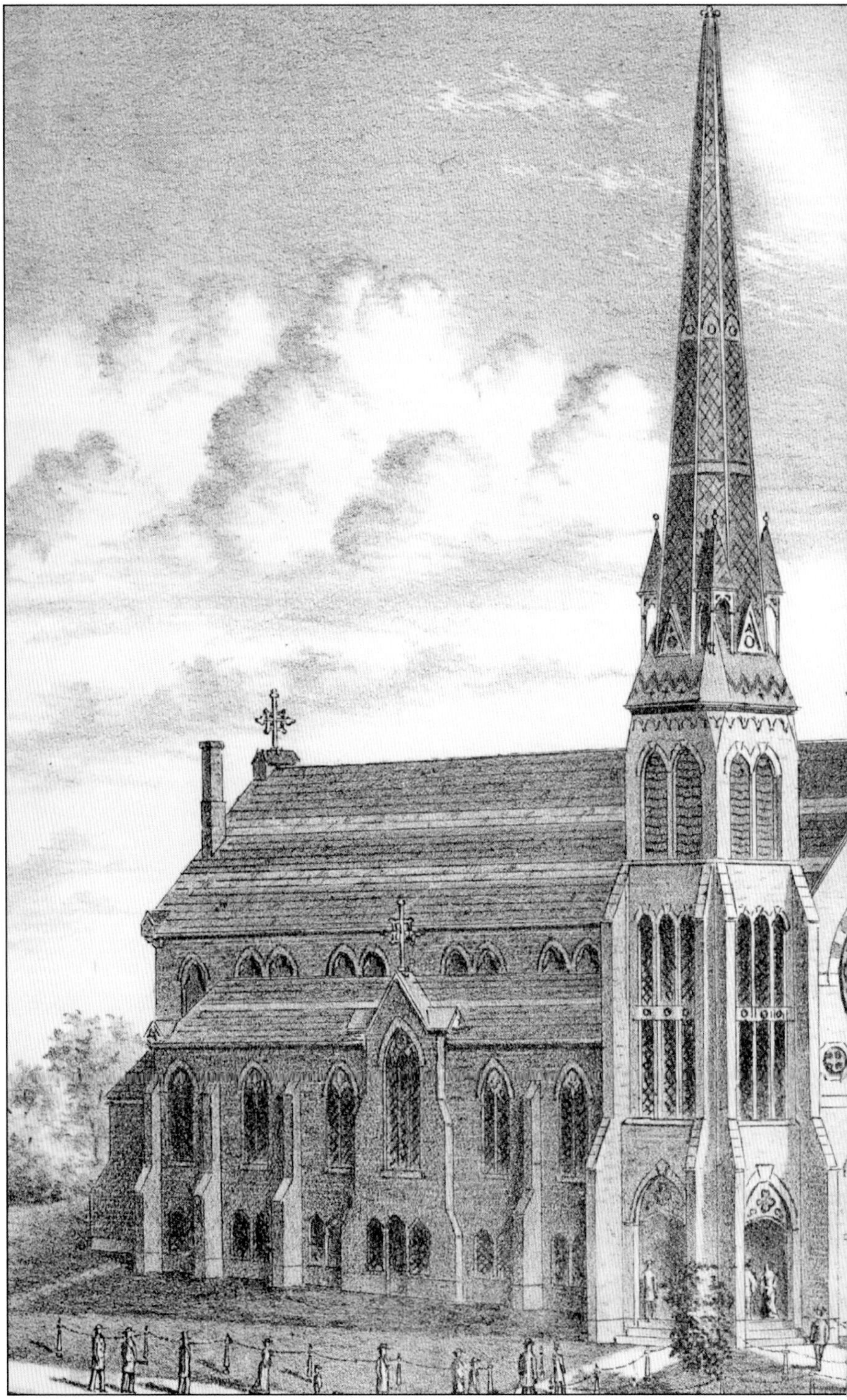

St. Joseph's Roman Catholic Church was formed on January 26, 1874. This church building, at the corner of Walcott and South Bend Streets, was completed on October 10, 1878. Reverend Henry F. Kinnerney was pastor from

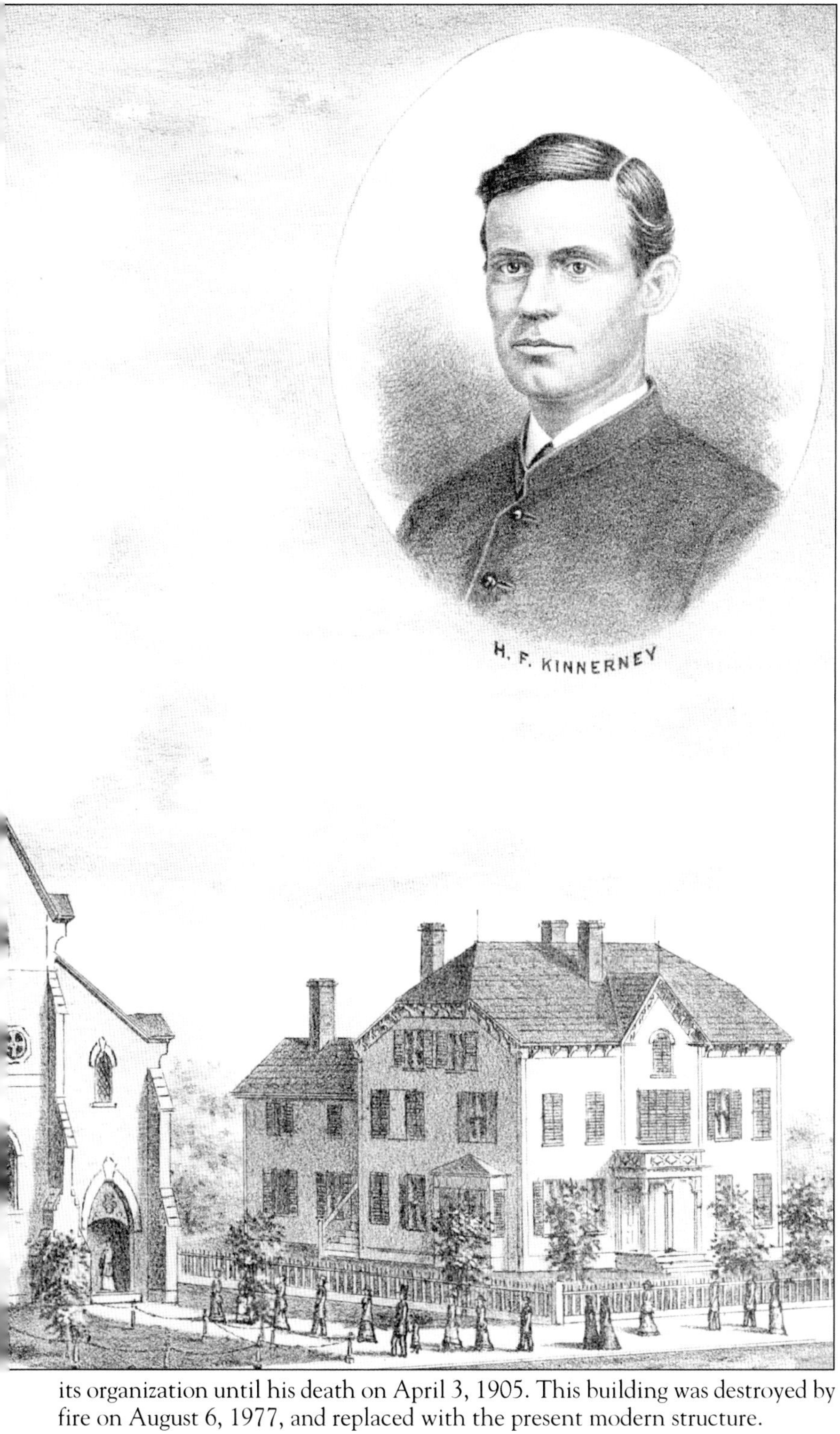

its organization until his death on April 3, 1905. This building was destroyed by fire on August 6, 1977, and replaced with the present modern structure.

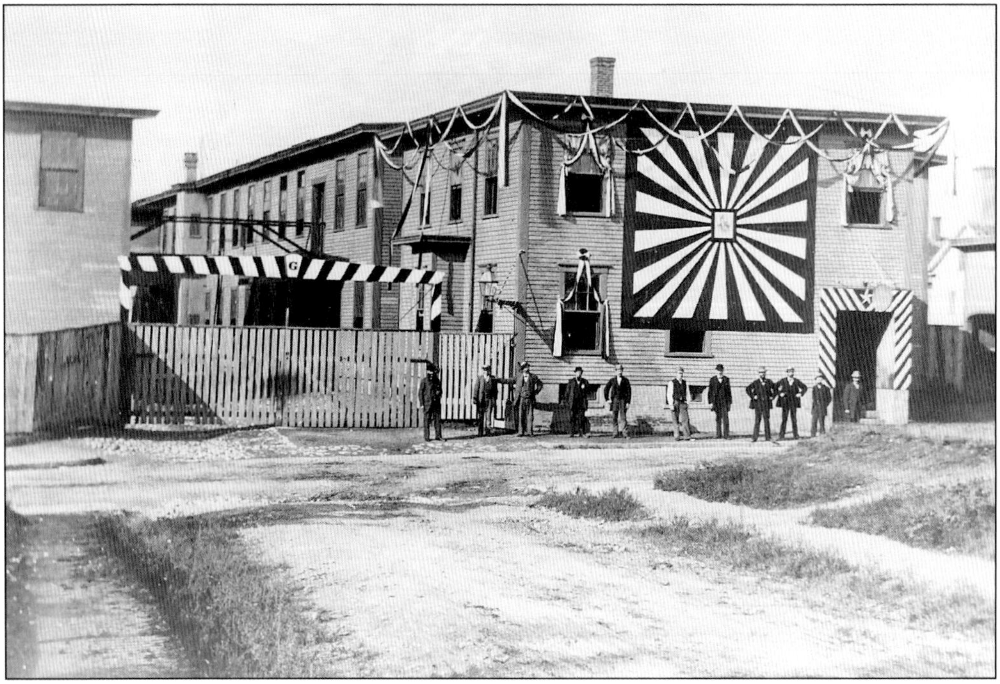

The Fales and Jenks Machine Company, located at 118 Dexter Street near Clay Street, is seen draped for the death of President Garfield in September 1881. (Pawtucket Public Library.)

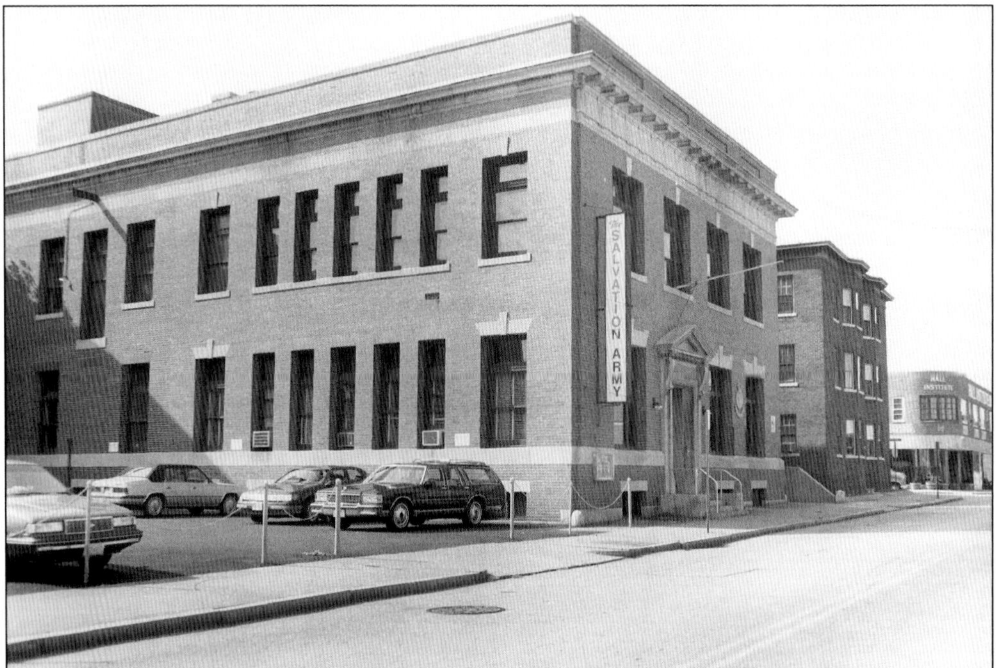

The Salvation Army came to Pawtucket in 1895. They were originally located on High Street, then moved to the "Rough and Ready" fire station on Main Street in 1921, and finally returned to 102 High Street, moving into the vacant telephone company building in October 1960. This photograph was taken on September 3, 1988. (*Times*.)

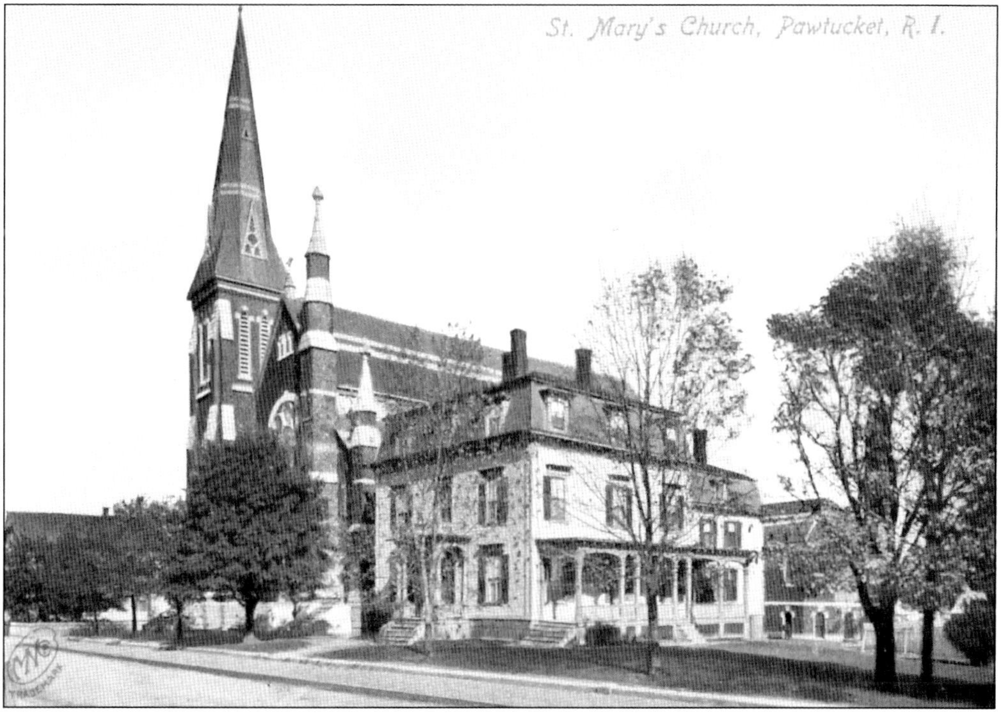

St. Mary's Church, designed by architect James Murphy and located at the corner of Pine and Grace Streets, replaced the old St. Mary's in 1887. The old rectory, built next to the church by Reverend Patrick Grace Delany, was moved to Randall Street (the rear of St. Mary's School/Convent) in 1911.

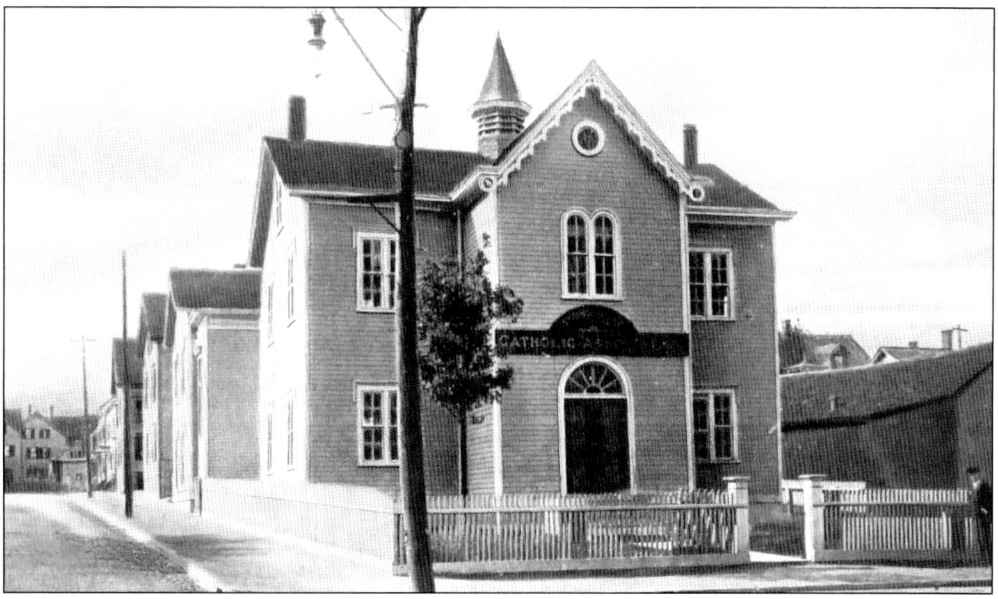

This building was constructed at the corner of Grace and George Streets by St. Mary's Church in 1854, and it is believed to be the state's oldest parochial school. It was used until the 1890s. Later, it was used as a gym, a men's club, and finally as a CYO center. It was purchased by the Pawtucket Redevelopment Agency in 1976, and then demolished.

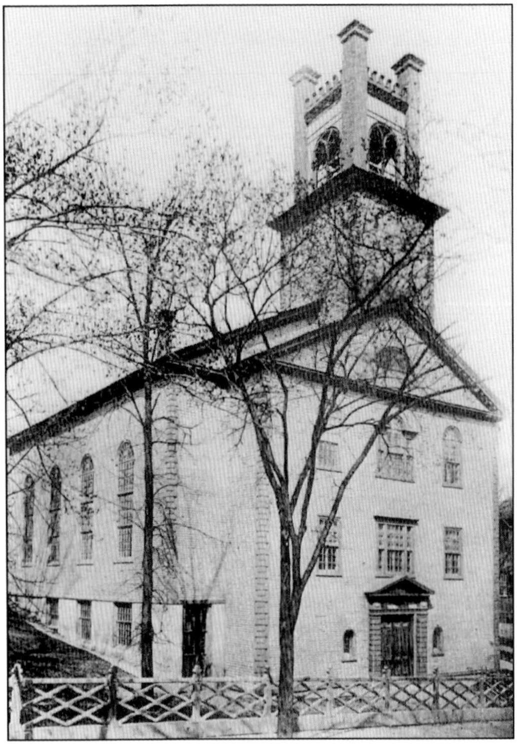

The old St. Paul's Episcopal Church, built part-way down Church Street Hill from the present church, was consecrated on October 17, 1817. The original steeple was replaced with this tower in 1843. The church bell was cast by Paul Revere and it still exists as part of the present church building, shown below.

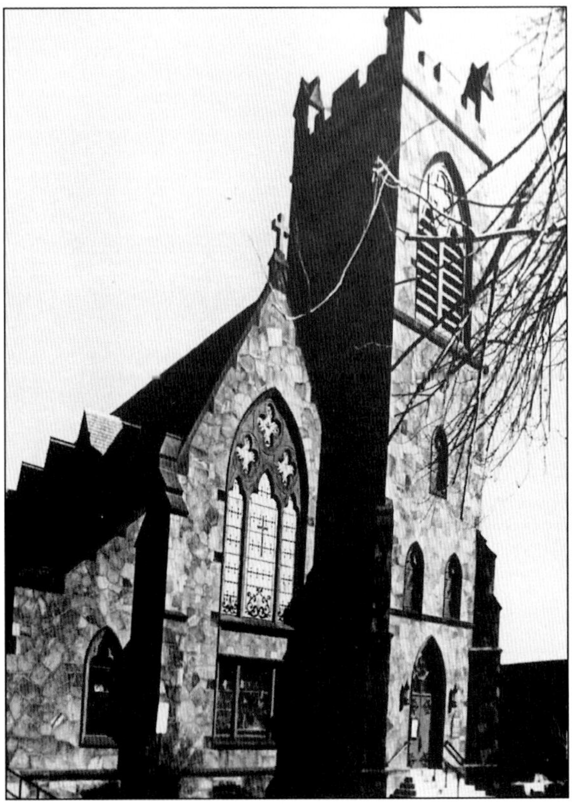

The present-day St. Paul's Episcopal Church on Park Place, with its massive tower and beautiful stained-glass windows, is designed in the fifteenth-century Gothic style. The first service in this building was held on Maundy Thursday in 1902. This photograph was taken in 1990.

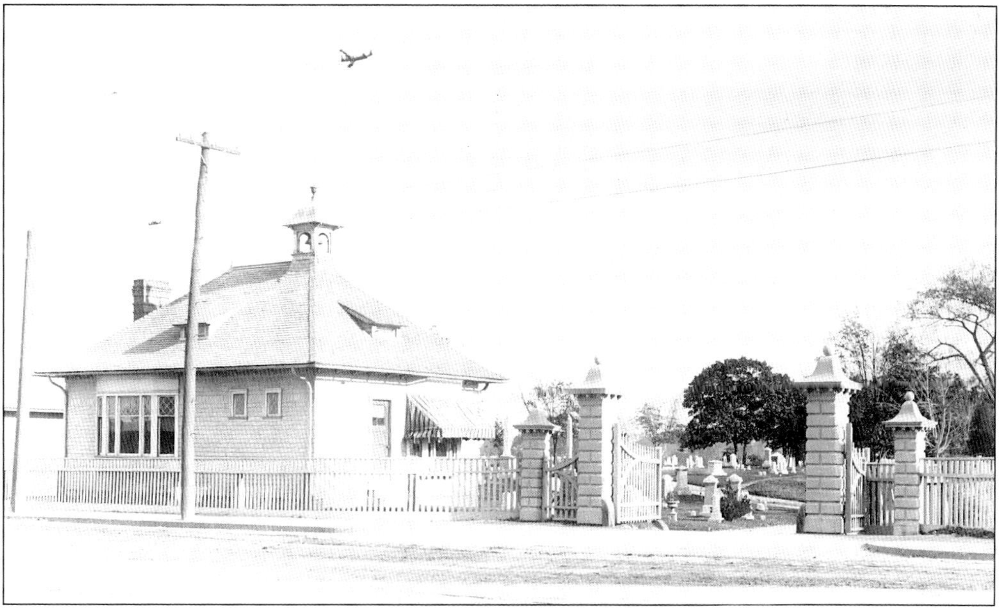

A view of the Royal Square gates to Oak Grove Cemetery, as seen in 1902.. New gates, by architect Robert C.N. Monahan, replaced these gates in 1912 and remain today.

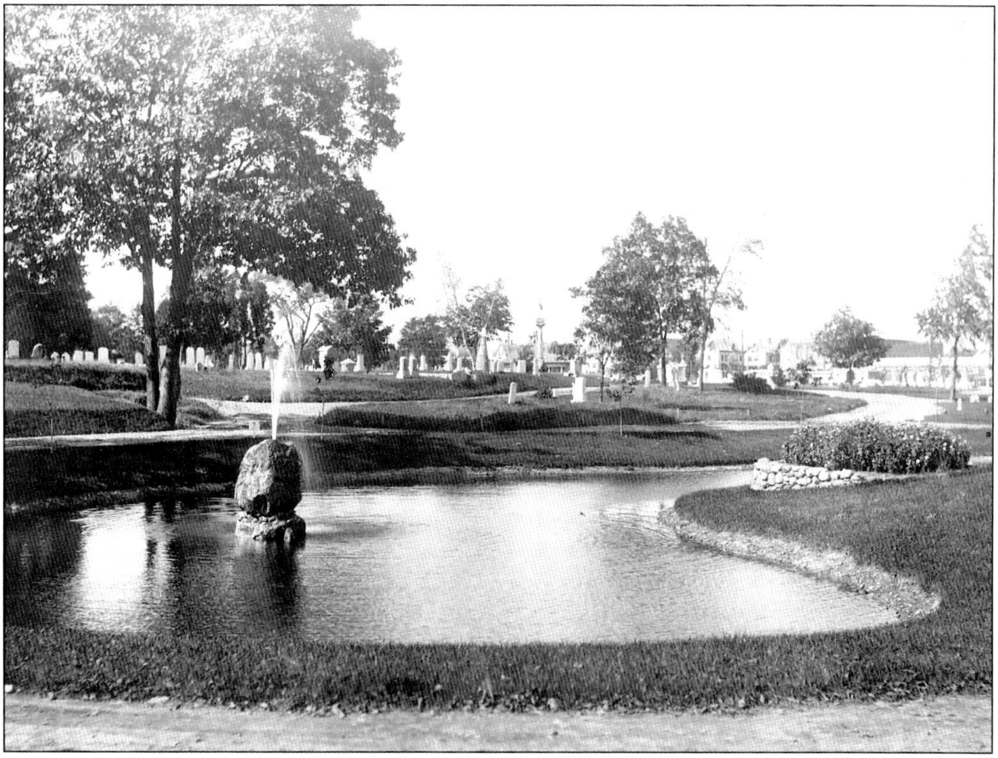

A 1902 view of the pond and fountain in Oak Grove Cemetery. Note the Cogswell Fountain in the center background. The Cogswell Fountain was relocated here from downtown for a very short period, was then moved to Slater Park at Newport Avenue, and now stands proudly in its original location in Hodgson Park, at the Main Street Bridge .

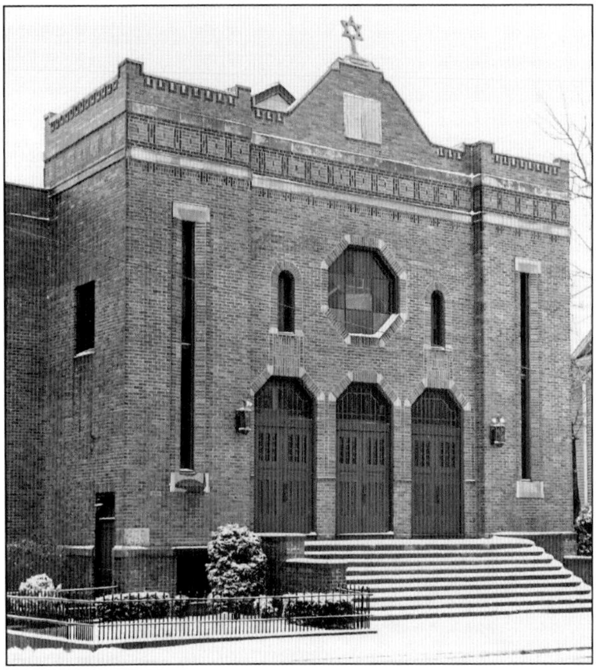

The Congregation Owahe Shalom constructed this synagogue in 1920, at what was then the center of the Jewish Community on the corner of High and Jackson Streets. By the 1970s, the Jewish Community had migrated to the Oak Hill section of Pawtucket and in 1981 the cornerstone was placed in their new synagogue on East Avenue. The old building was sold to the Cape Verdean Congregation, and was first used by them in 1979. It was renamed The Immaculate Heart of Mary Cape Verdean Roman Catholic Church. This photograph was taken in 1995. (*Times*.)

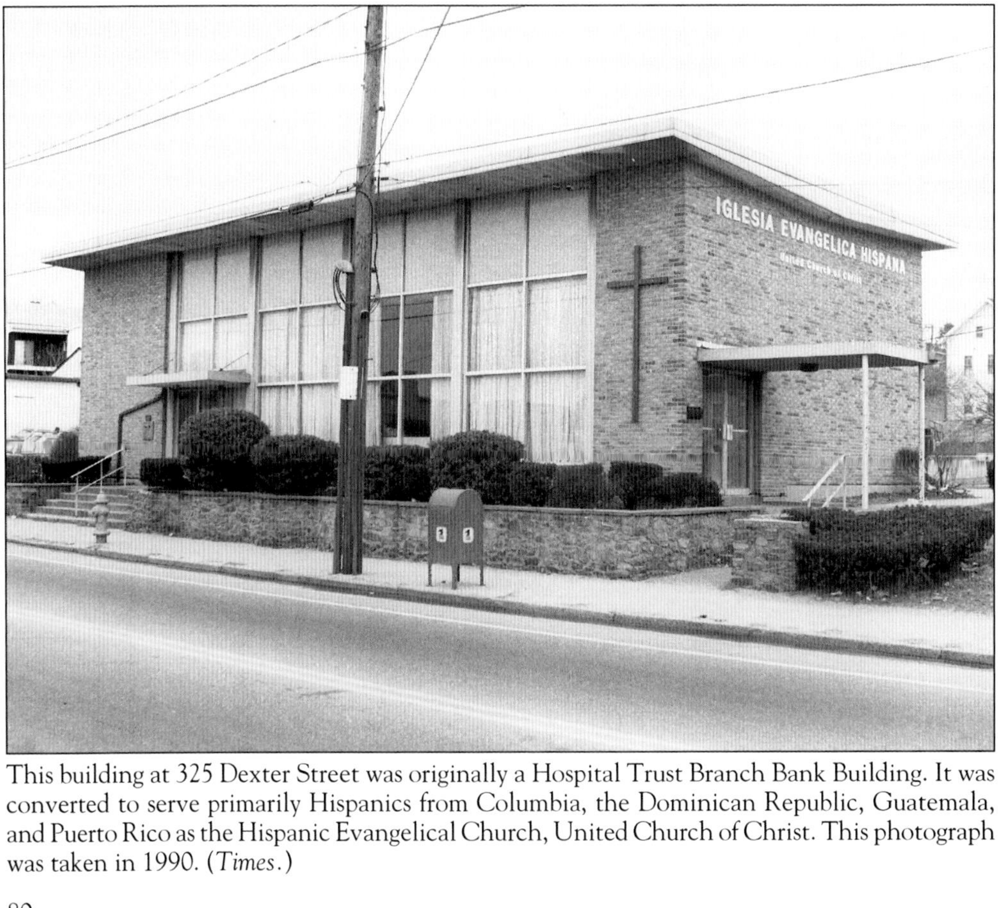

This building at 325 Dexter Street was originally a Hospital Trust Branch Bank Building. It was converted to serve primarily Hispanics from Columbia, the Dominican Republic, Guatemala, and Puerto Rico as the Hispanic Evangelical Church, United Church of Christ. This photograph was taken in 1990. (*Times*.)

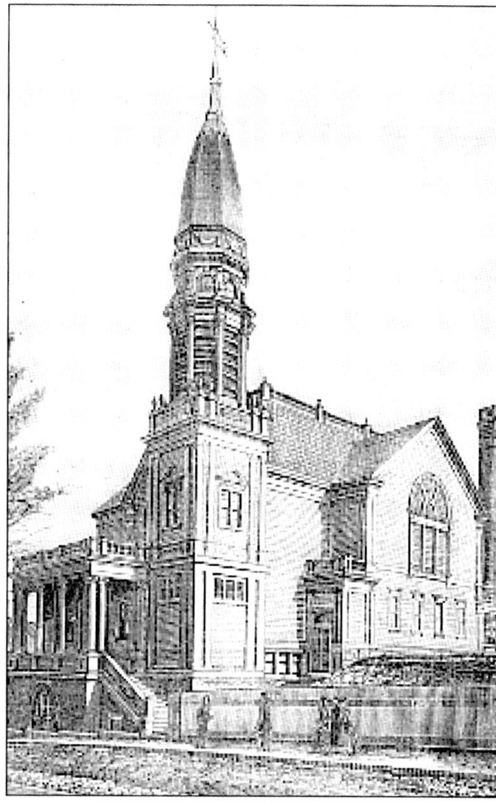

This was the original Park Place Congregational Church, which burned down in 1935. The cornerstone was laid in September 1894, and was located on Park Place Hill, just to the rear of the present Downtown Parking Garage. The first services were held in July 1885. This view was taken a year later, in 1886.

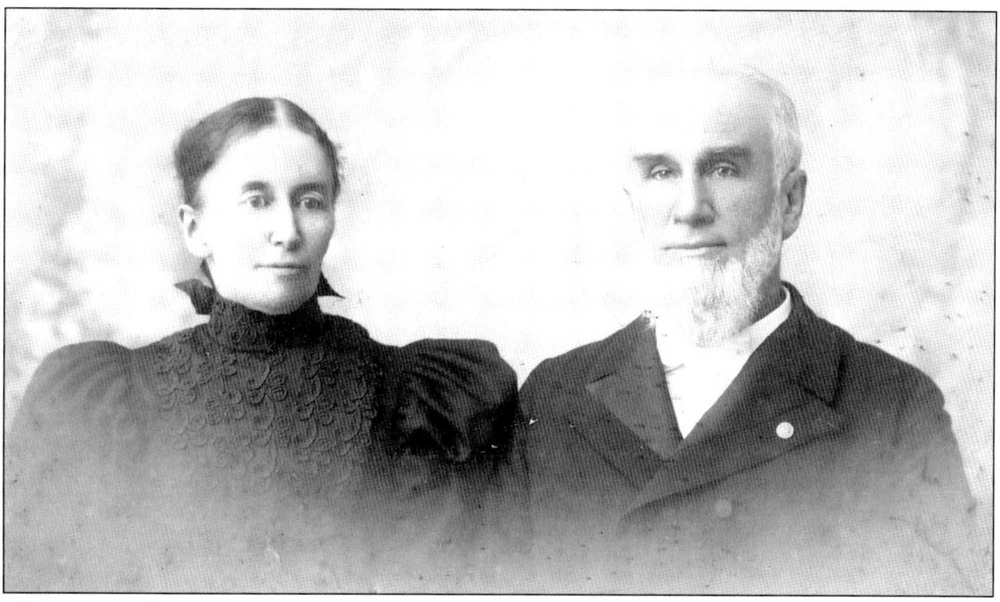

The Reverend and Mrs. Joseph J. Woolley, seen here in a photograph taken by Pawtucket photographer Frederick Bebby, c. 1886. Reverend Woolley, born in 1832, was pastor of the Pawtucket Congregational Church from 1871 to 1882, and pastor of Park Place Congregational Church from 1882 until his death in 1906. Woolley married Mary Ferris in 1861. She died in 1905.

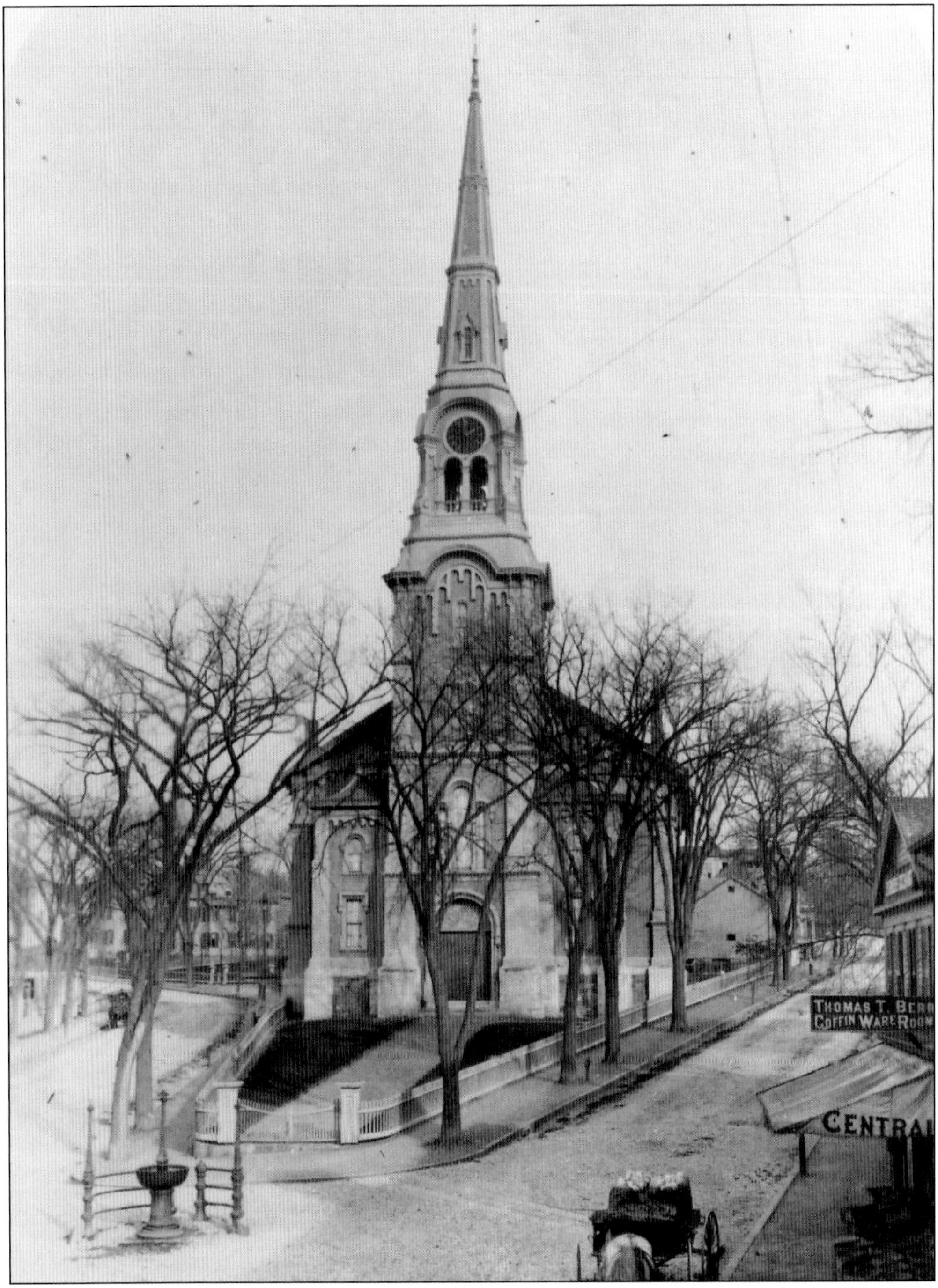

An 1880 view of the Pawtucket Congregational Church at the junction of Broadway and Walcott Street. This building was designed by John Stevens of Boston and built in 1868. It replaced the original church destroyed by the "Great Fire of 1864." At the junction is a Henry F. Jenks water fountain. Along Walcott Street can be seen George Crawford's market and Thomas T. Berry's mortuary. The spire of the church was blown down in the 1938 hurricane.

Hiker Monument honors those who served in the Spanish-American War. The monument was originally in the park, at the junction of Broadway and Cottage Street, but was removed to the junction of Cottage, Spring, and Grove Streets, in order to make way for the construction of Interstate Route 95.

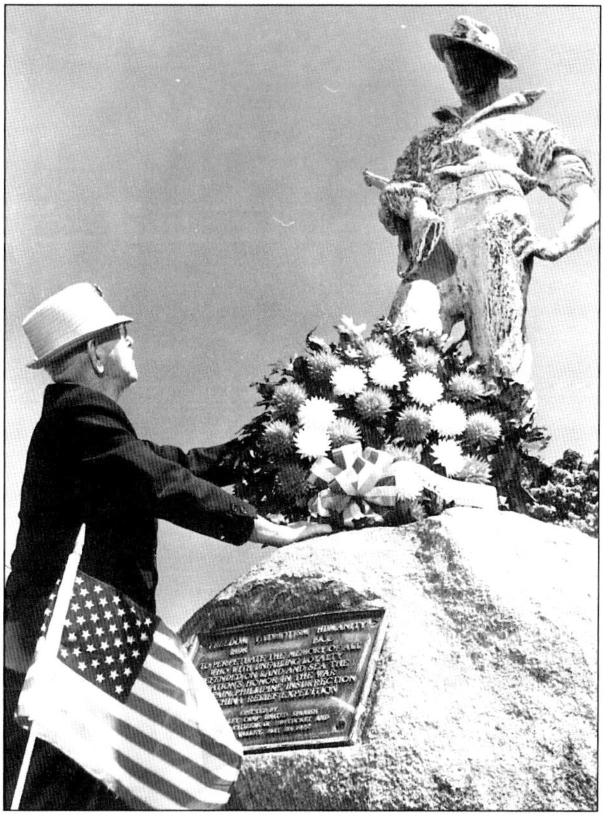

St. Edward's Roman Catholic Church at 308 Lonsdale Avenue, near Weeden Street, *c.* 1911. The church, an offshoot of St. Mary's Parish, was established on April 27, 1904, under Reverend Edward Carrigan, and held services in St. Jean Baptiste Hall in Woodlawn. They quickly purchased this building, formerly the Woodlawn Baptist Church, and materially altered and improved it. Its congregation laid the cornerstone to its current church, at the corner of Weeden and Hancock Streets, in 1937.

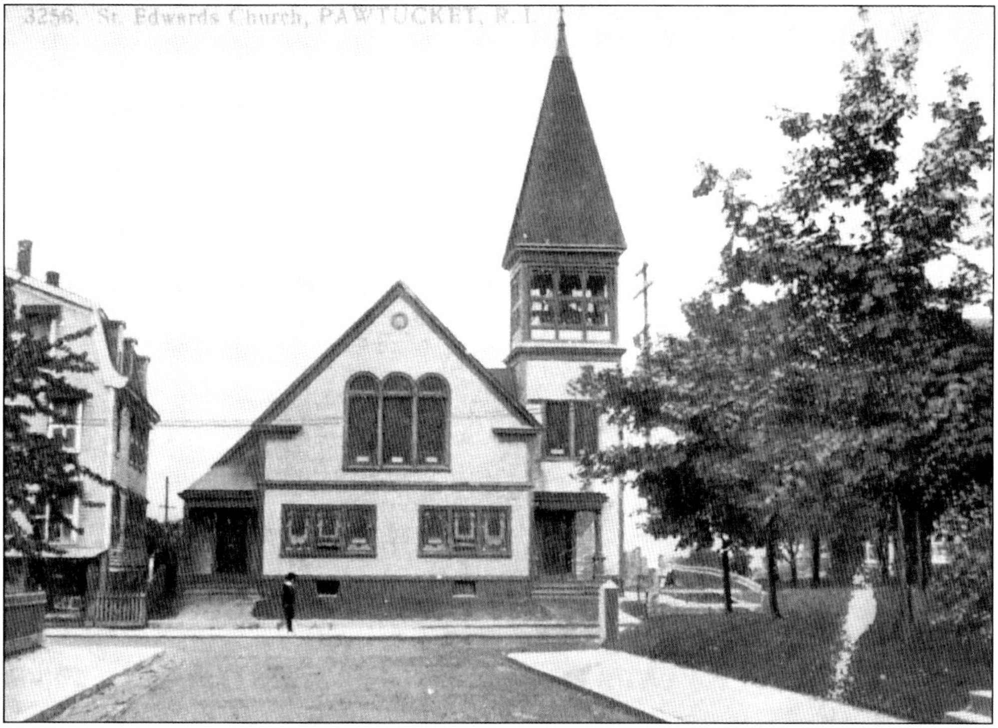

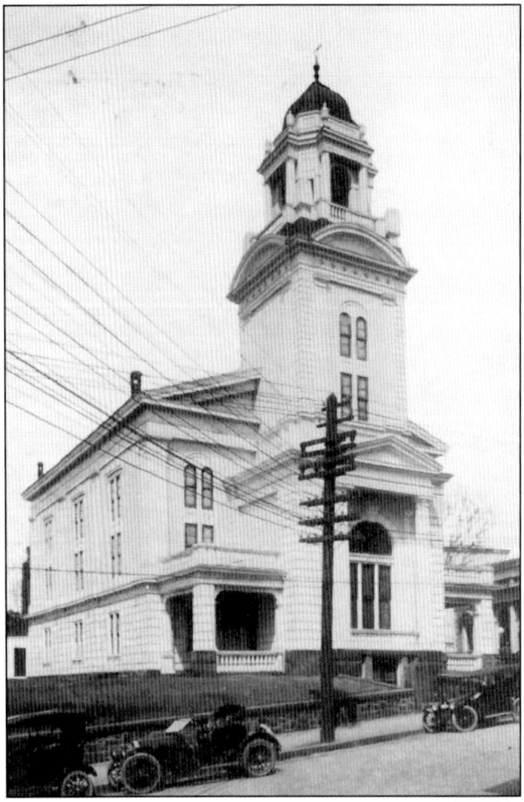

The First Baptist Church, at the corner of High and Summer Streets, c. 1920. This was the second edifice of the First Baptist Society. It was built in 1842, and designed by Providence architect John Holden Greene. This church building was destroyed by fire and torn down in 1957, so the congregation moved to its current church building on Cottage Street.

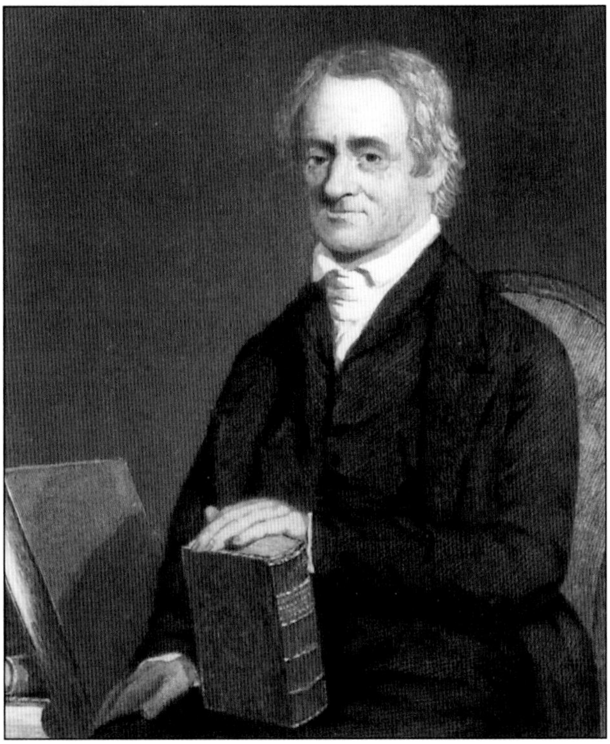

Reverend David Benedict (1779–1874), first pastor of the First Baptist Church, Pawtucket. He was Pawtucket's major historian and the author of a number of published histories of the Baptist denomination as well as a book defining all religions.

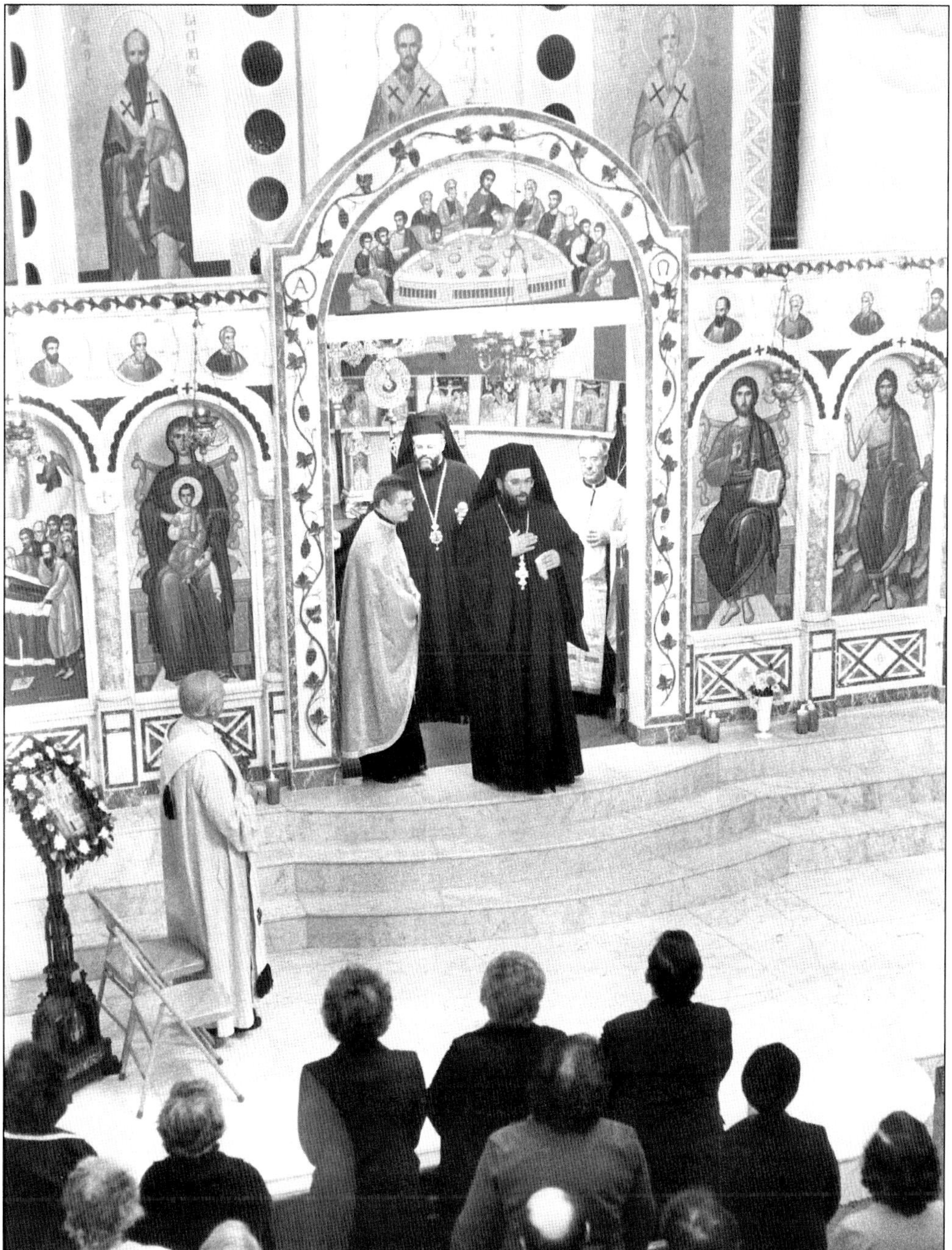

Reverend Vasilios D. Flionis (seen in the foreground, on the steps), being installed as the pastor of the Assumption Greek Orthodox Church, Pawtucket, on August 19, 1984. The church, at 99 Walcott Street, was built in 1967 and designed by Christopher Kantianis. (*Times*.)

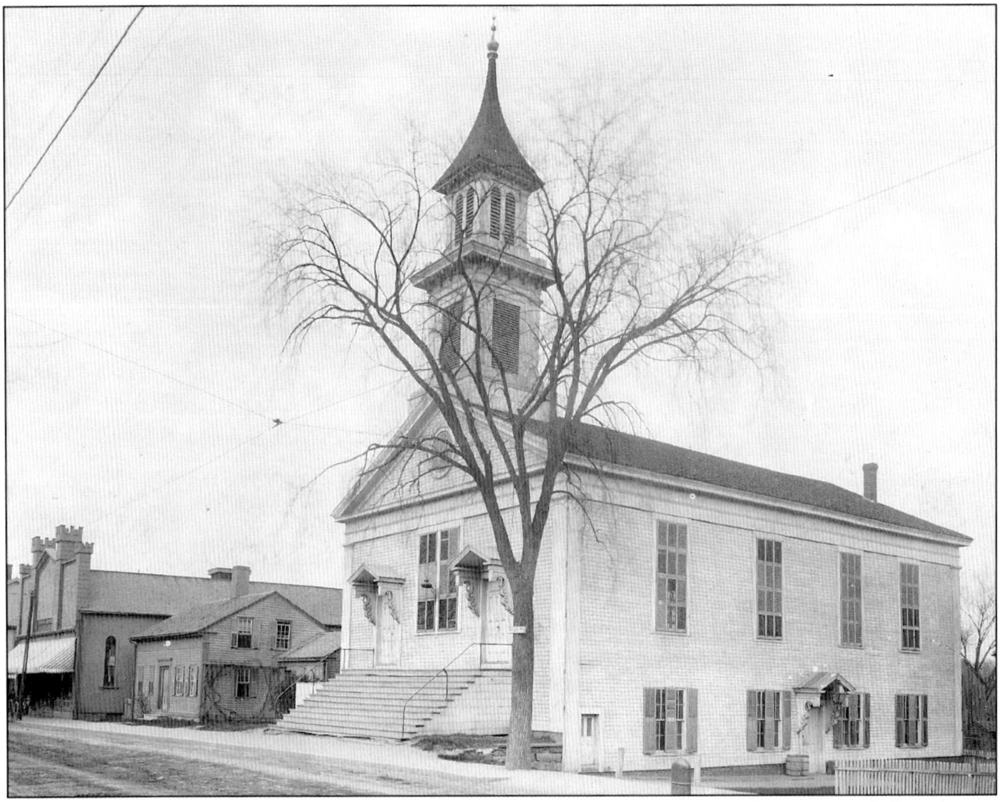

An 1880 view of the second church building of the First Methodist Church, built in 1842 on High Street opposite the corner of North Union Street. (Pawtucket Public Library.)

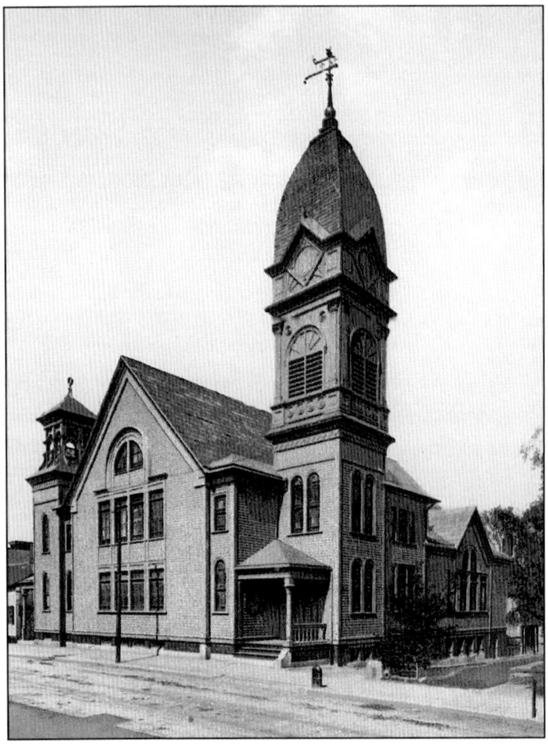

An early 1900s view of the third building, erected on the site of the second, in 1895. This church was demolished on February 17, 1967. At that time, the congregation made plans to consolidate with two other Methodist churches to form the Wesley Methodist Church, in Saylesville Highlands, Lincoln, Rhode Island, in 1963.

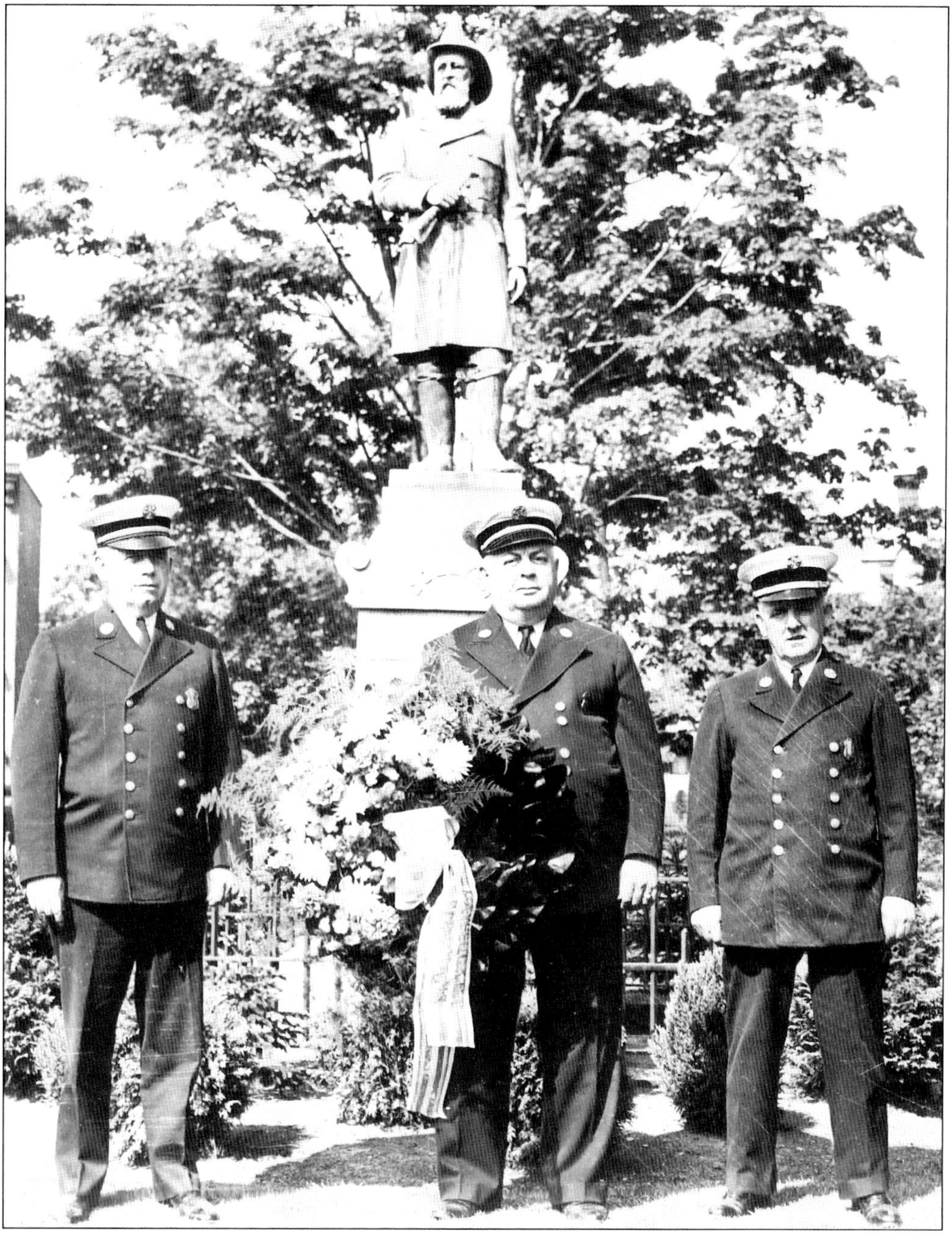

Pictured here are, from left to right: William T. Connolley, the deputy chief of the Pawtucket Fire Department; Napoleon Taupier, the chief; and James F. McCaffrey, the deputy chief. They are laying a wreath at the Collyer Monument in Collyer Park, at the junction of Main Street and Mineral Spring Avenue, in 1937. Samuel S. Collyer, appointed in 1874, was Pawtucket's first fire chief. He was killed on July 7, 1884, at the corner of Mineral Spring Avenue and Lonsdale Avenue. While responding to a fire, his two-wheeled horse hose cart overturned after striking a stone post at the corner of the sidewalk. (Pawtucket Public Library.)

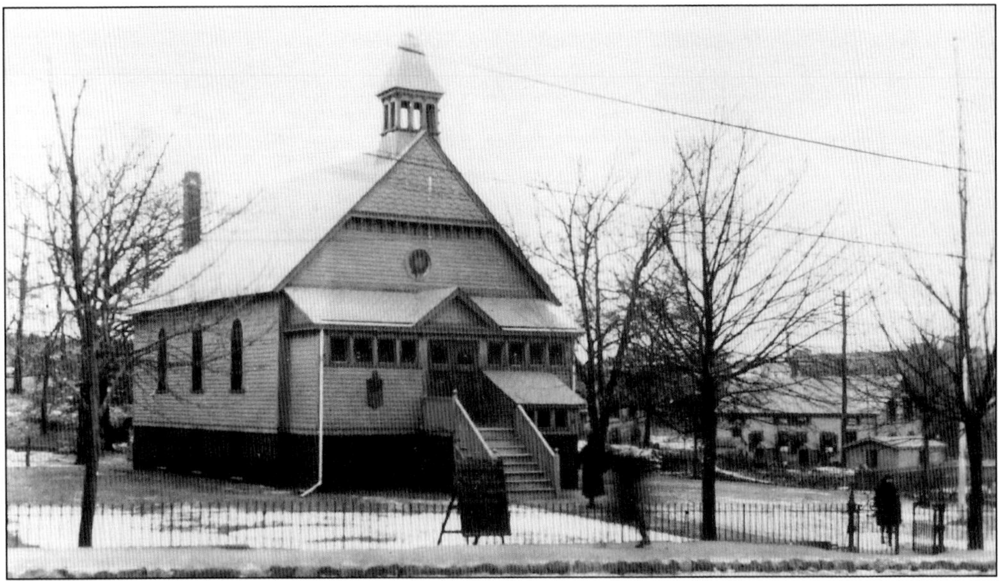

This chapel was built by W.F. and F.C. Sayles in the spring of 1886 as the Lorraine Chapel Sunday School. In April 1897 the Lorraine Manufacturing Company presented the building to the Weeden Street Congregational Society. In 1905, this society erected a new church at the corner of Smithfield and Owens Avenues, and changed their name to the Smithfield Avenue Congregational Church. The old building was sold in 1910 to the Rhode Island Episcopal Convention, remodeled and otherwise improved, and was re-dedicated in January 1907 as St. Luke's Episcopal Chapel. In 1992, the building was a private dwelling, at 557 Weeden Street.

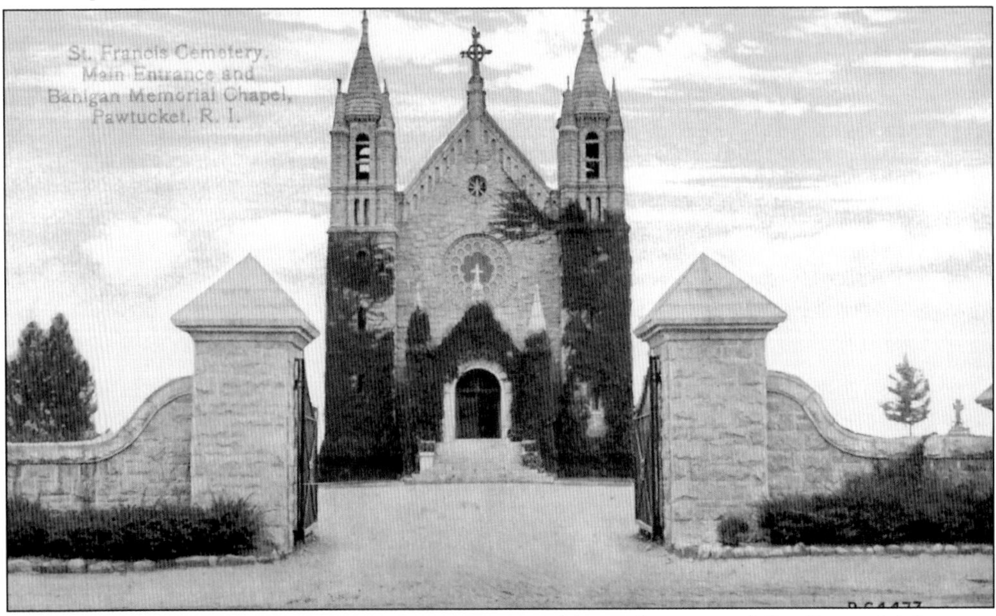

Through the gates of St. Francis Cemetery one could see the original St. Bernard Mortuary Chapel. The chapel was designed and erected by Joseph Banigan in 1898 at a cost of $100,000. A new and larger chapel of the same name was built on the old foundation in 1973, and it incorporated modern lighting, heating, and seating, as well as the stained glass windows from the old chapel.

Six

MAKING CONTACTS

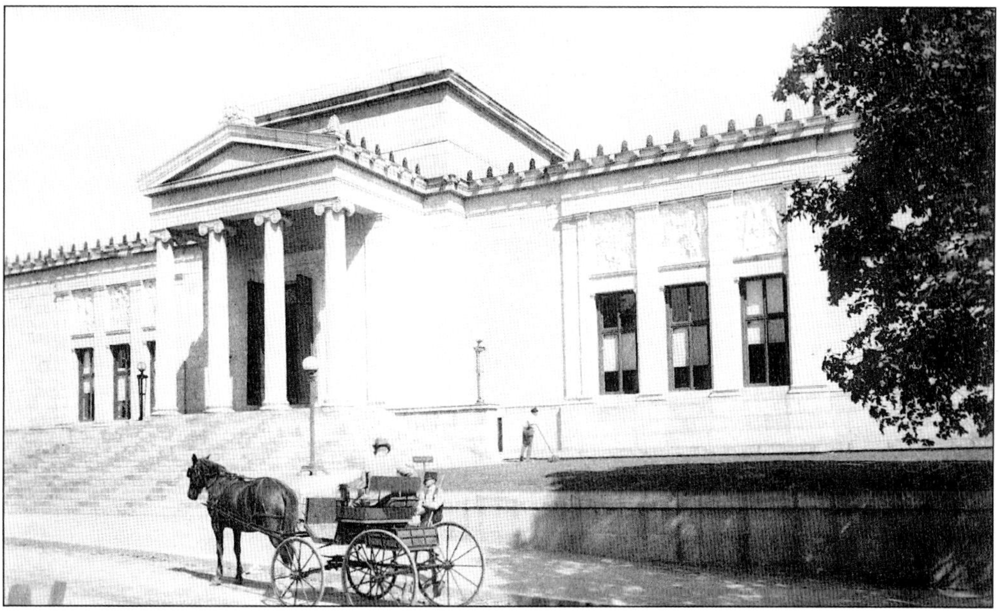

Frederick Clark Sayles, first mayor of Pawtucket, gave the land and money for the construction of the Deborah Cook Sayles Public Library, seen here c. 1906. The cornerstone was laid in 1899. The architects of the building were Cram, Goodhue, and Ferguson of Boston, under the direction of Sayles. It is a granite Greek Revival building, fronted by a portico of four Ionic columns—an exact copy of the doorway of the Erechtheion, in Athens, Greece. It is an open-shelf library, with room for fifty to seventy thousand books.

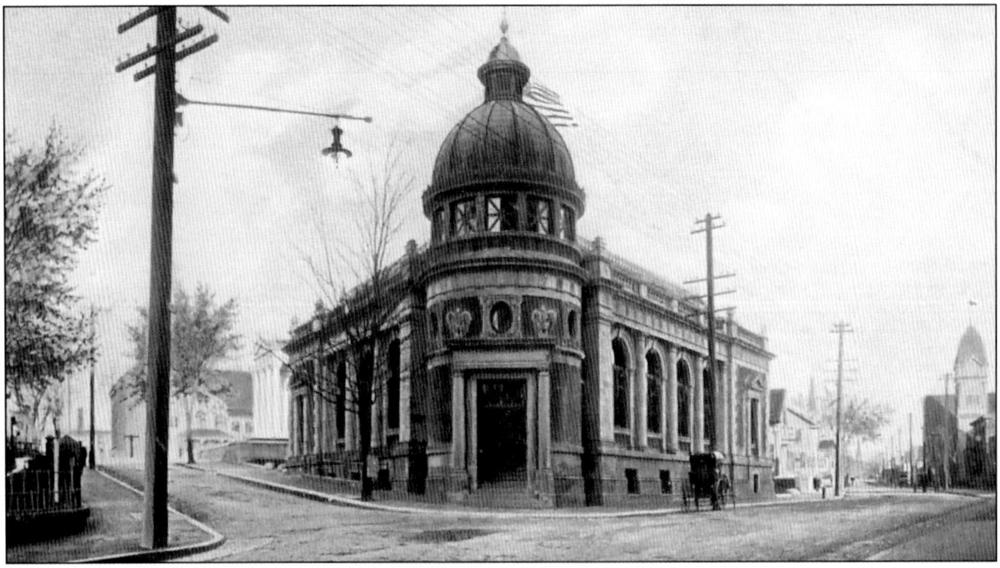

The old Pawtucket Post Office was designed by architects William Martin Aiken and James Knox Taylor and built in 1896–97. This photograph shows the post office c. 1908. It was hailed, in its day, as the most handsome structure in the city. From 1933 to 1967 it served as the Welfare Building. It was converted to the Pawtucket Public Library Annex in 1981–82, and dedicated as the Gerald S. Burns Wing in 1985.

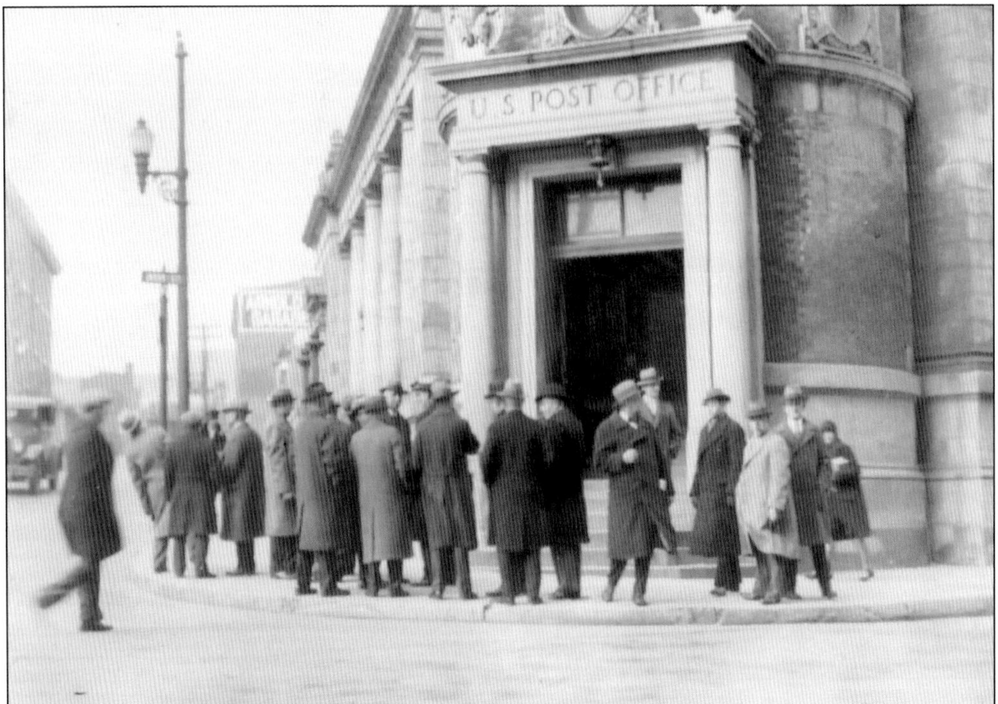

The February 1928 jury visit to the Pawtucket Post Office, from which "yeggs" had removed stamps worth $254,200 in the largest stamp theft in history. "Pawtucket Johnnie" Connelly was convicted.

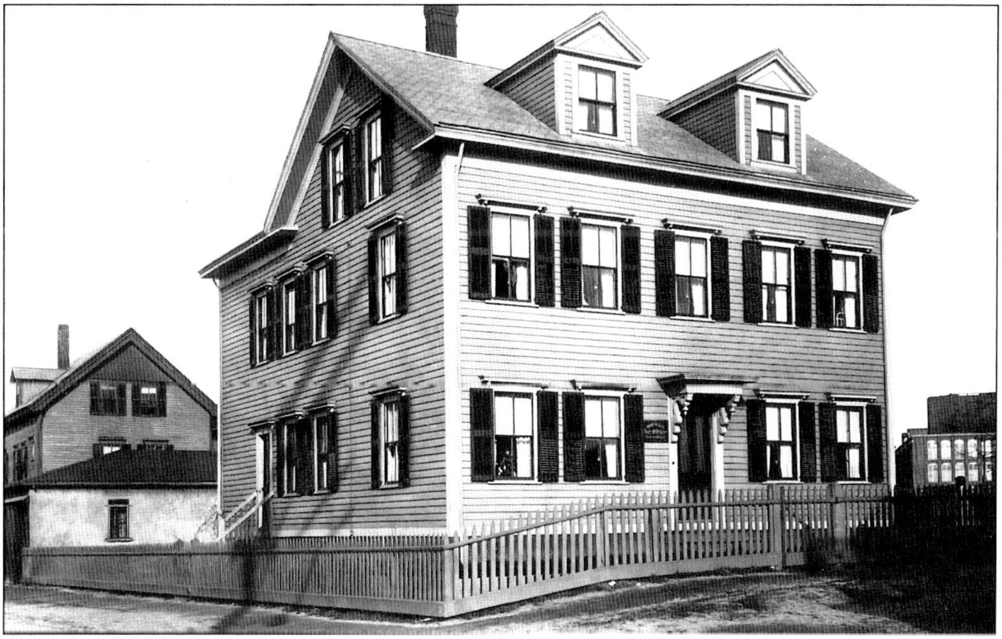

The Pawtucket Day Nursery's new seventeen-room home opened on Thornley Street on January 18, 1921. Begun in 1892 at the instigation of Reverend Frederick W. Hamilton of the Universalist Church, it provided day-care for "deserted wives' and widows' children" while the mothers were at work. Earlier, it had smaller homes on Capital Street and a few doors away on Thornley Street. In 1972, it was replaced by a bright new nursery, just a few feet from this older building at 25 Thornley Street.

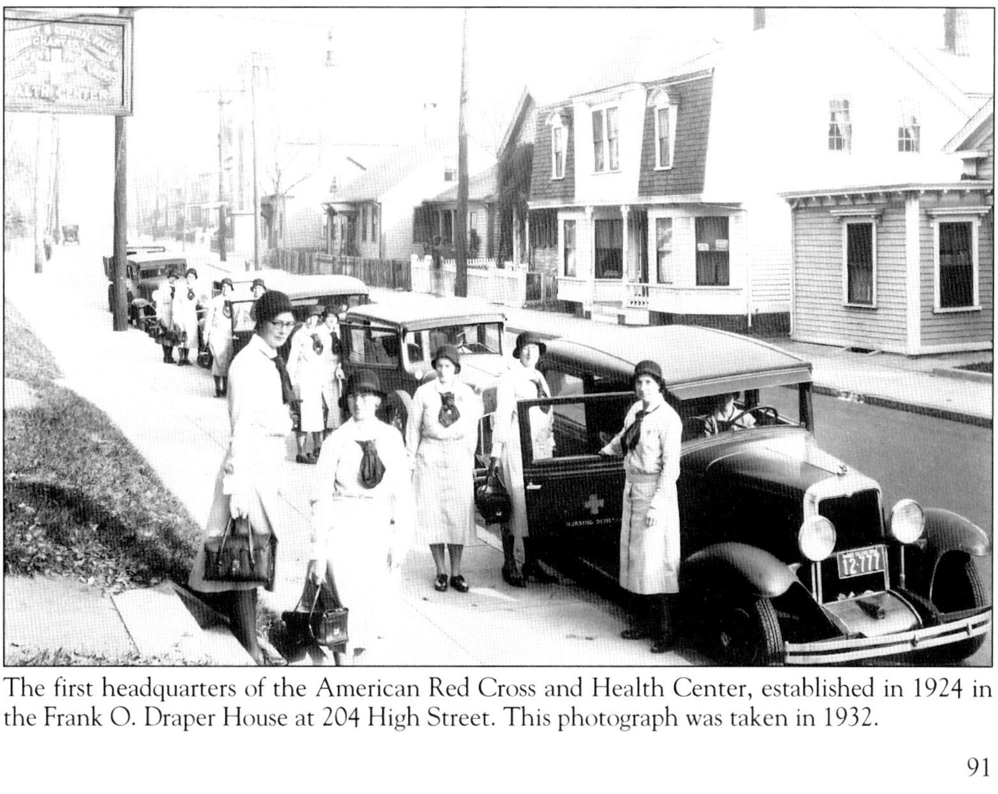

The first headquarters of the American Red Cross and Health Center, established in 1924 in the Frank O. Draper House at 204 High Street. This photograph was taken in 1932.

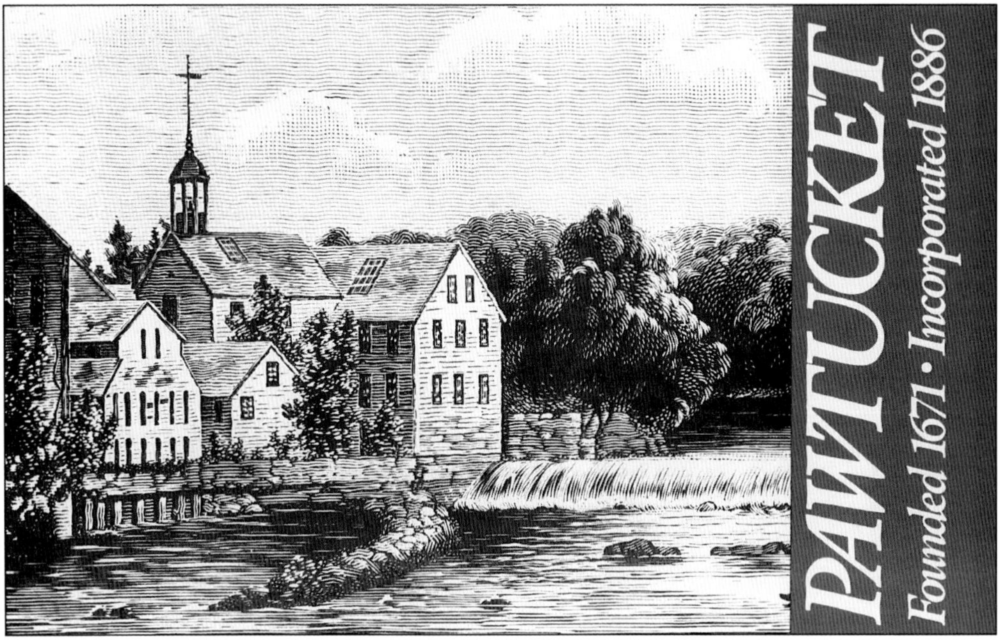

A reproduction of the official City of Pawtucket flag. It was adopted by the city council on October 6, 1974, and it shows the Old Slater Mill, its dam, and the tail race.

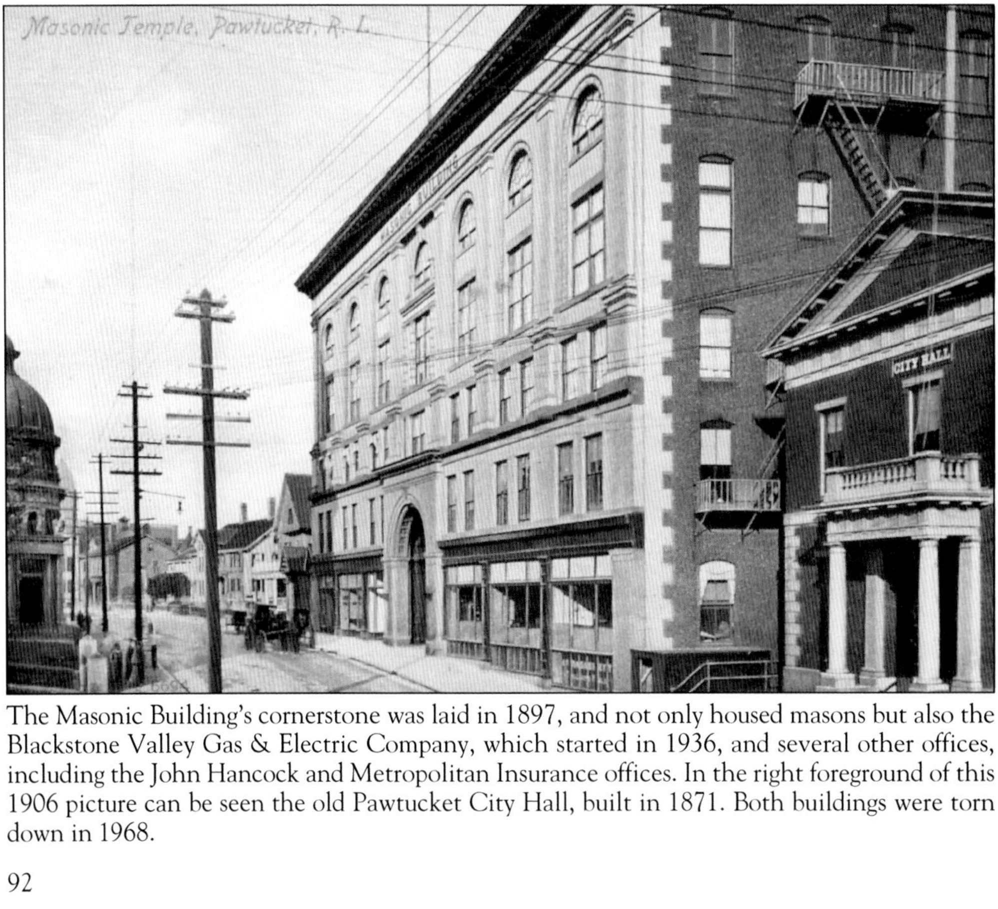

The Masonic Building's cornerstone was laid in 1897, and not only housed masons but also the Blackstone Valley Gas & Electric Company, which started in 1936, and several other offices, including the John Hancock and Metropolitan Insurance offices. In the right foreground of this 1906 picture can be seen the old Pawtucket City Hall, built in 1871. Both buildings were torn down in 1968.

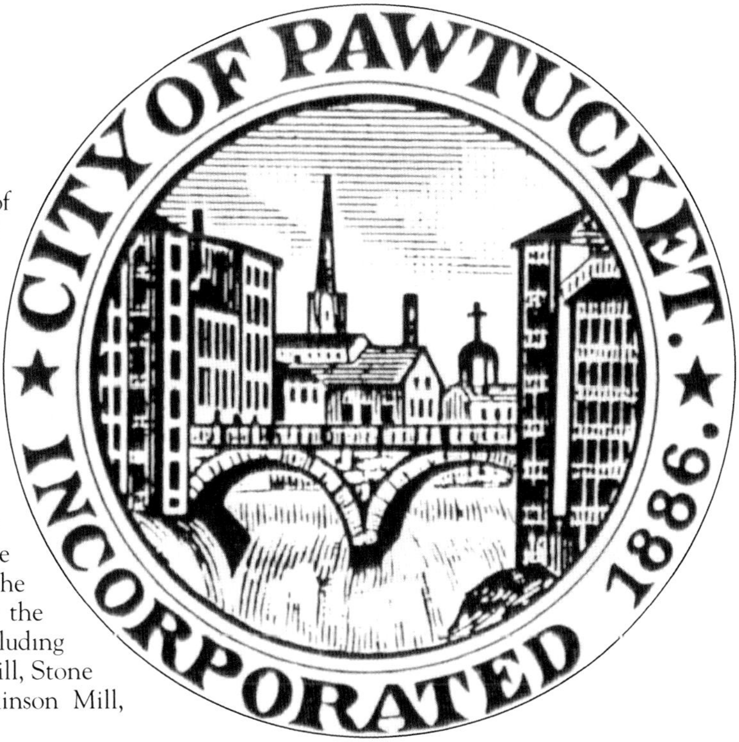

The seal of the City of Pawtucket, adopted at the time of the incorporation of the city in 1886. It was taken directly from the seal of the former consolidated Town of Pawtucket, but with changes to the wording to reflect the town's new status as a city. The engraving depicts the falls at Pawtucket with the Main Street Bridge and the surrounding old mills including the New Mill, Yellow Mill, Stone Mill, Slater Mill, Wilkinson Mill, and others.

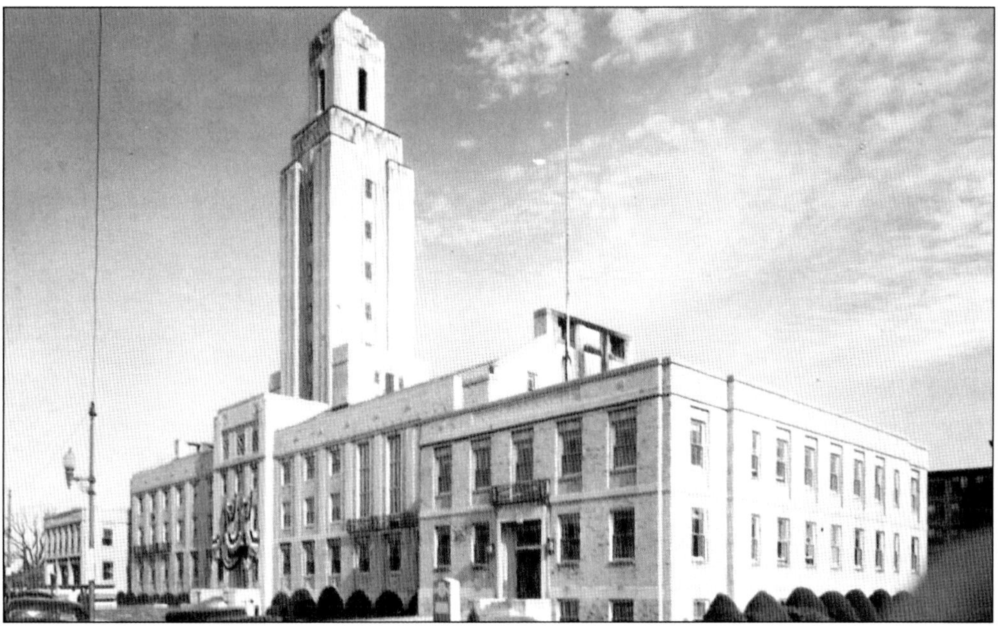

Pawtucket's current city hall, completed in 1936, was designed to consolidate all departments of city government under one roof, including the police and fire departments. It was the first project in Rhode Island to be undertaken under the National Recovery Act, with PWA funds. A tomahawk and a weathervane surmount the tower in honor of Alderman Kenney, who was instrumental in proposing the elaborate design of the building and who used the tomahawk as his political campaign symbol.

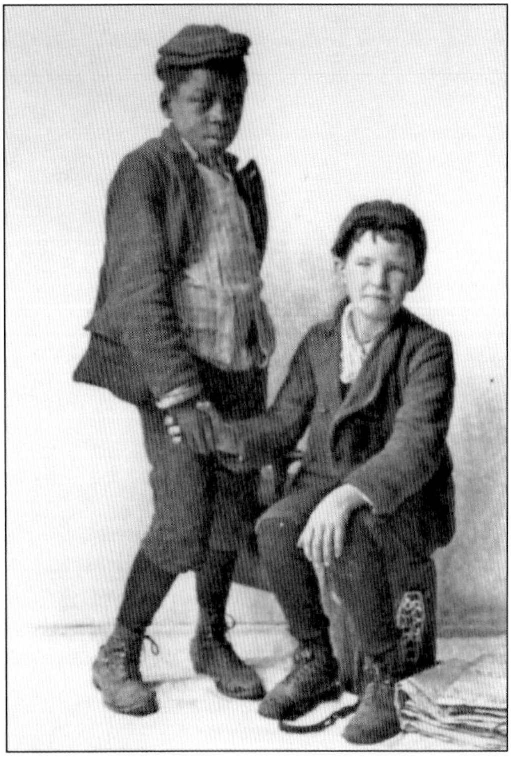

This illustration of a shoeshine boy and a paper boy was the logo on the stationery of the Pawtucket Boys Club in 1905 (today, it is correctly called the Pawtucket Boys and Girls Club).

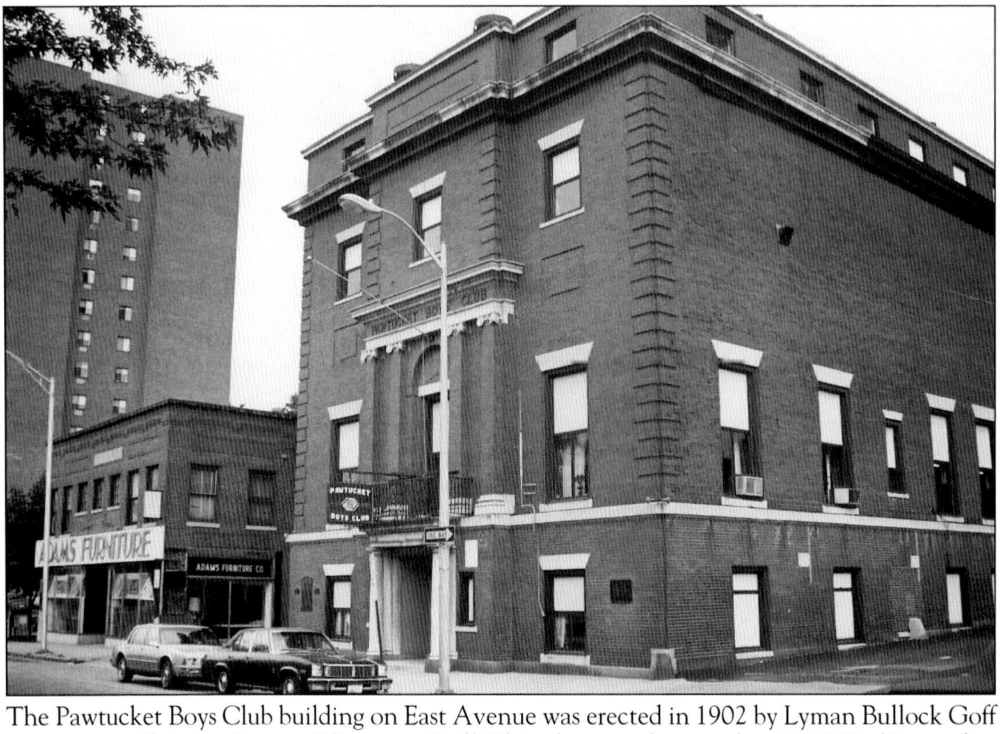

The Pawtucket Boys Club building on East Avenue was erected in 1902 by Lyman Bullock Goff in memory of his son, Lyman Thornton Goff. This photograph was taken in 1970. (Pawtucket Public Library.)

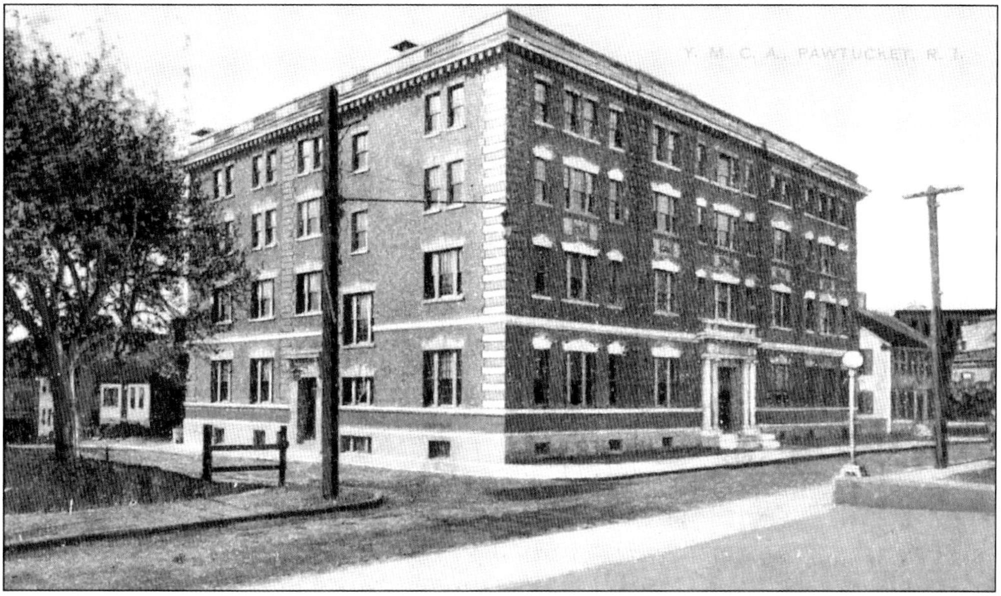

In 1907, the Pawtucket/Central Falls YMCA, begun in 1889, opened this new building to the public. Located at the corner of Summer and Maple Streets, it incorporated dormitories, a reading room, a parlor, a game room, a swimming pool, a gymnasium, and a bowling alley. It remains the home of the YMCA today.

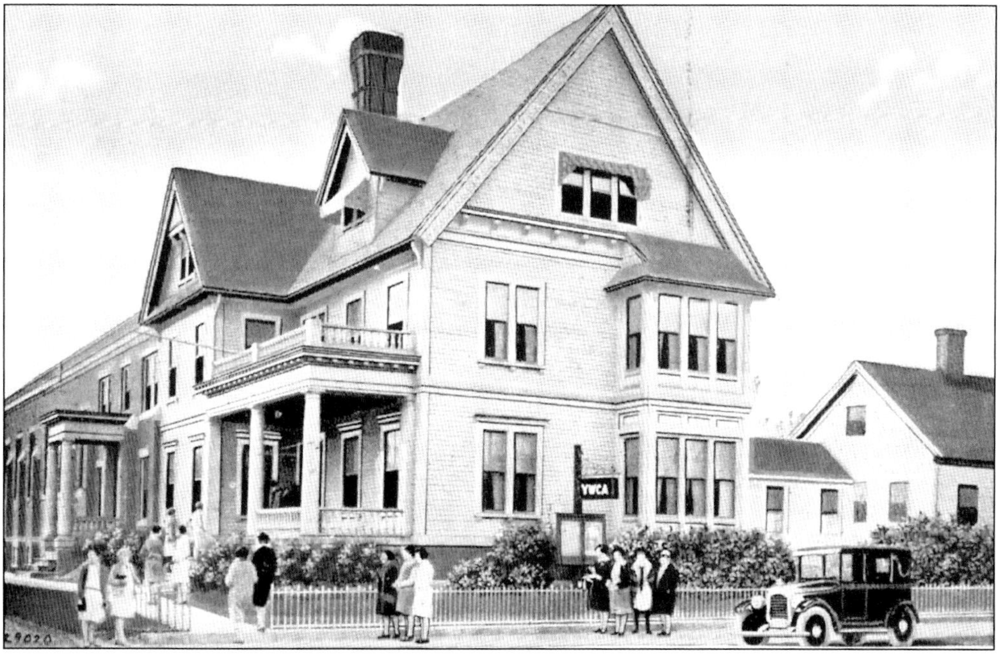

The YWCA, located on Broad Street south of Nickerson Street, pictured here c. 1906. This picture shows the original home, the "Victorian," built c. 1880 and bequeathed to the organization in 1915, and also its extension, added in 1916 and housing a gymnasium, a swimming pool, meeting rooms, classrooms, and offices. The extension was removed in 1992 to construct a new learning center. Today, the "Victorian" houses the YWCA offices and the Coalition Against Domestic Violence.

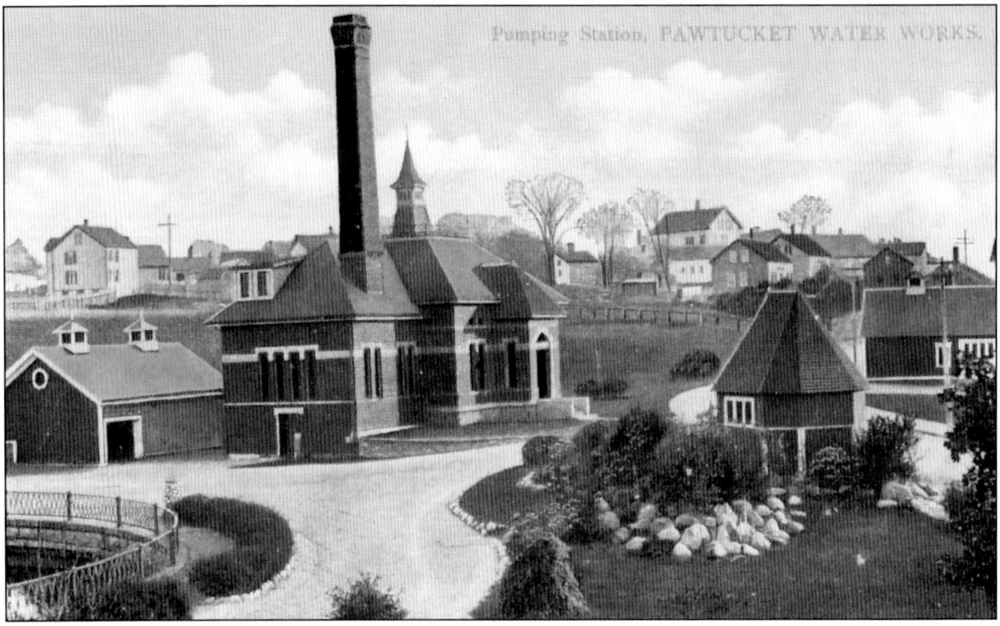

A turn-of-the-century view of Pumping Station One was built in 1878 on Branch Street. It was later used for the department's accounting division. It has been named an American Water Landmark by the American Waterworks Association.

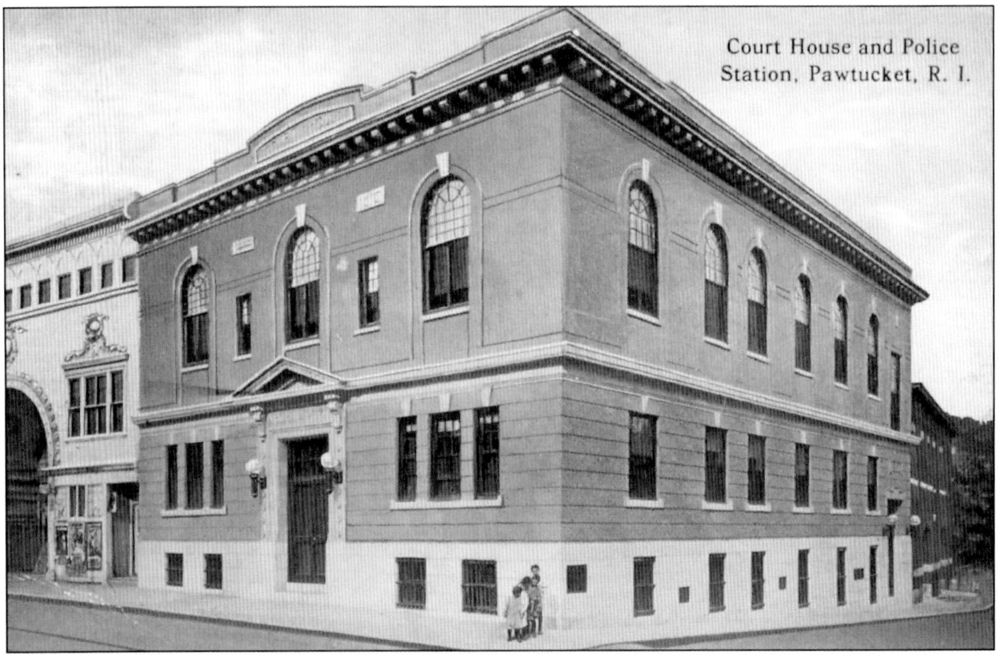

The brick court house/police station was built in 1869 at 87 North Main Street (now Roosevelt Avenue) as a fire station. It was altered in 1875 and an addition was made in the rear in 1890 to serve as a stable. It is pictured here c. 1921. During our times, the Blackstone Valley Historical Society occupied the second floor and the traffic division made traffic and street signs in the rear. To the left is the short-lived Crown Theater, which was occupied for years by the Stafford Mills Remnant Store run by the Greenwoods. The building was razed in 1968.

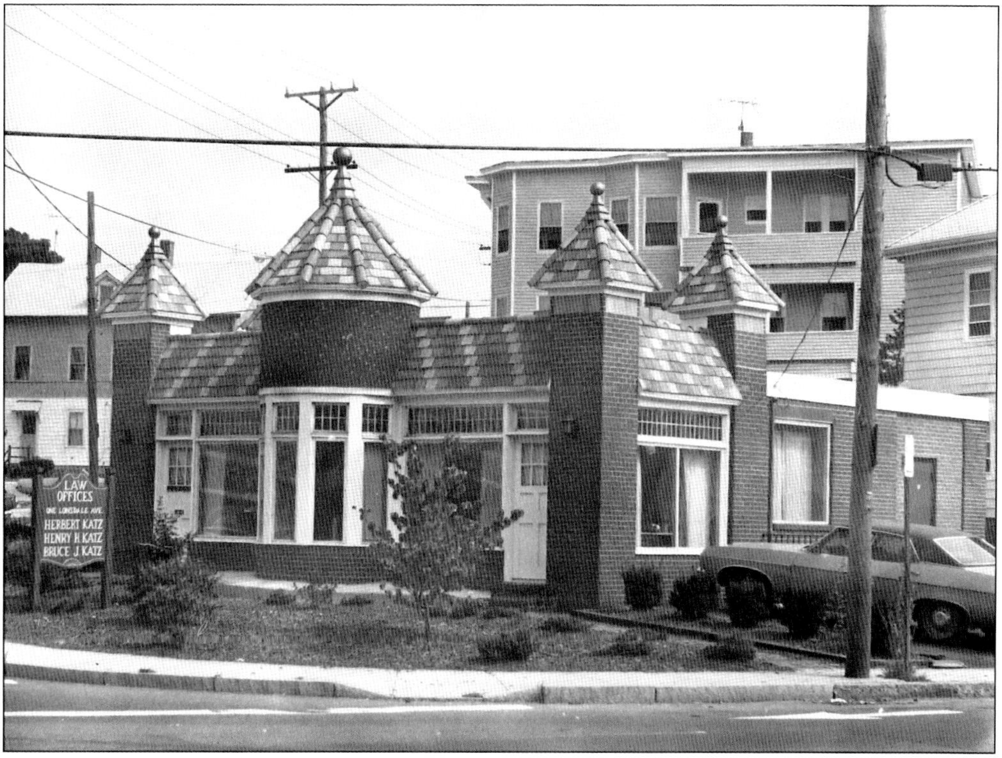

Art's Auto Supply and gasoline station was built in 1928, at the corner of Main Street and Lonsdale Avenue, and continued operation until 1978. It is seen here in 1979, the same year that it was converted to office space for the law firm of Katz, Butler & Katz. (*Times*.)

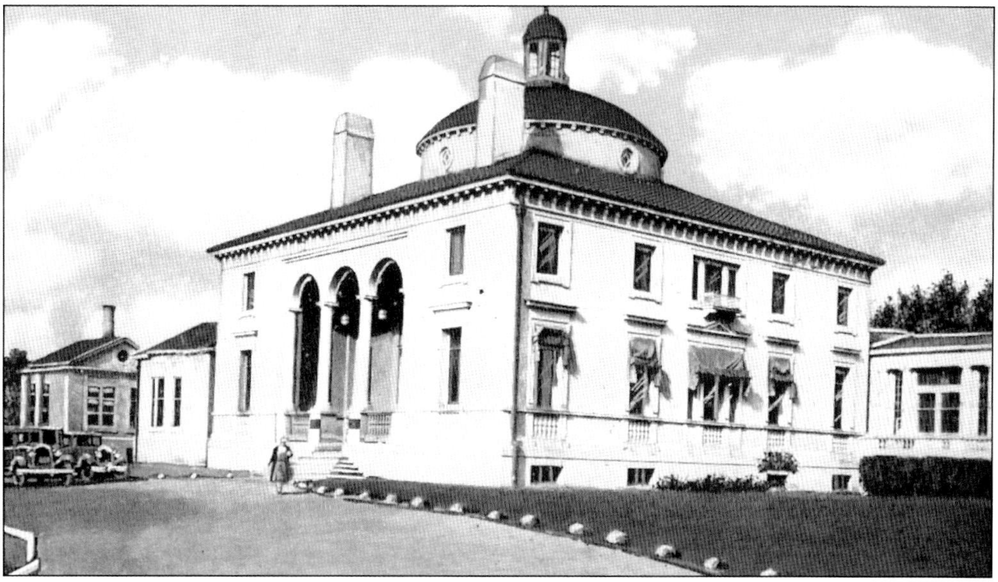
On October 10, 1910, the Memorial Hospital opened its doors. It was built on the site of the old Dunnell Homestead on Prospect Street, as a memorial to Mary Wilkinson Sayles. The hospital has been enlarged and modified several times and is known today as the Memorial Hospital of Rhode Island. It is seen here *c.* 1920. (Pawtucket Public Library.)

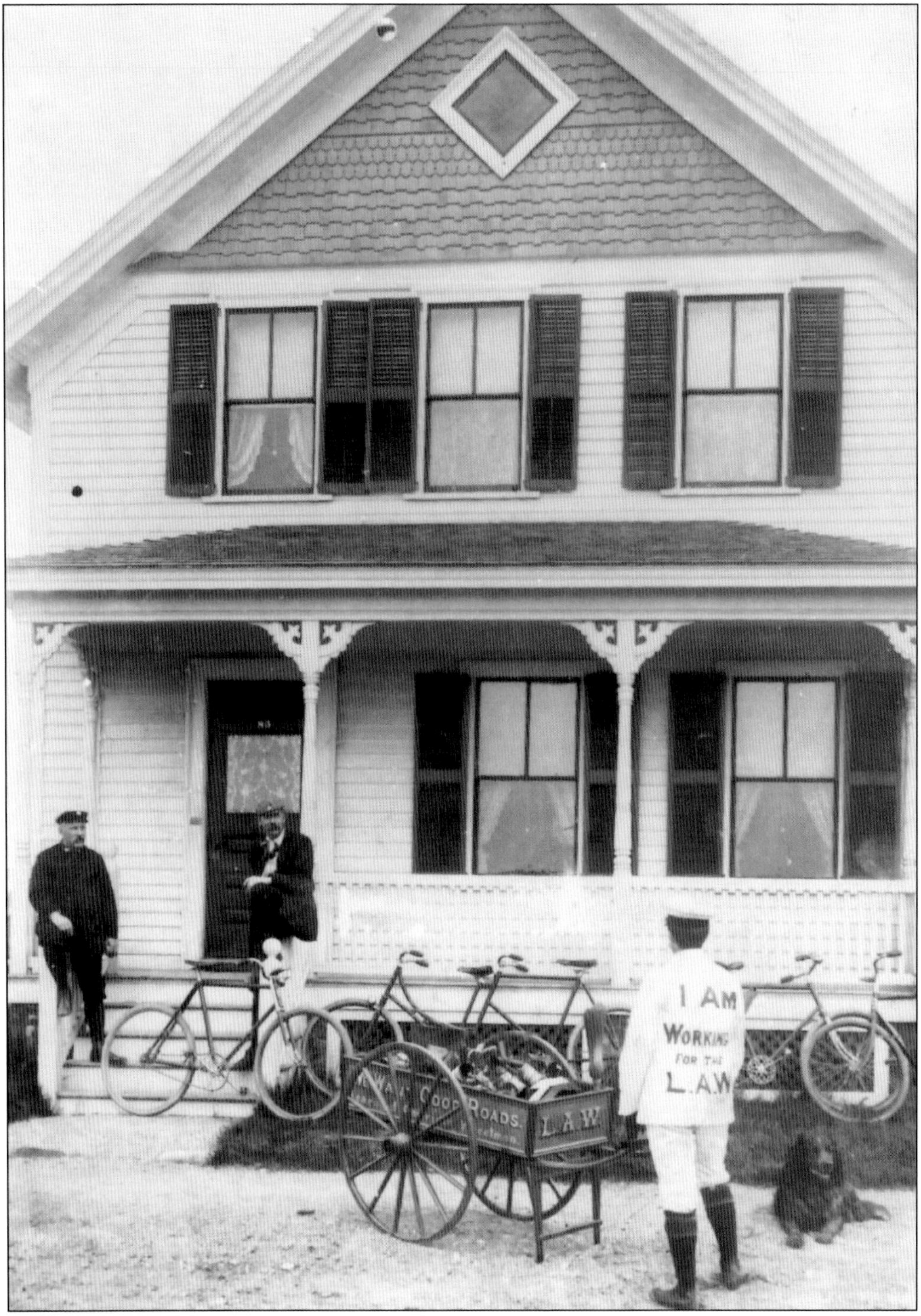

Robert A. Kendall (left) and A.M. Sanborn (middle), of the League of American Wheelmen (LAW), on the front steps of the John E. Palmer House at 109 Coyle Avenue. The wheelbarrow contains trash the LAW worker has collected in support of the Better Roads Plank at the 1906 Democratic and Republican Conventions.

Seven

MOVING WATER

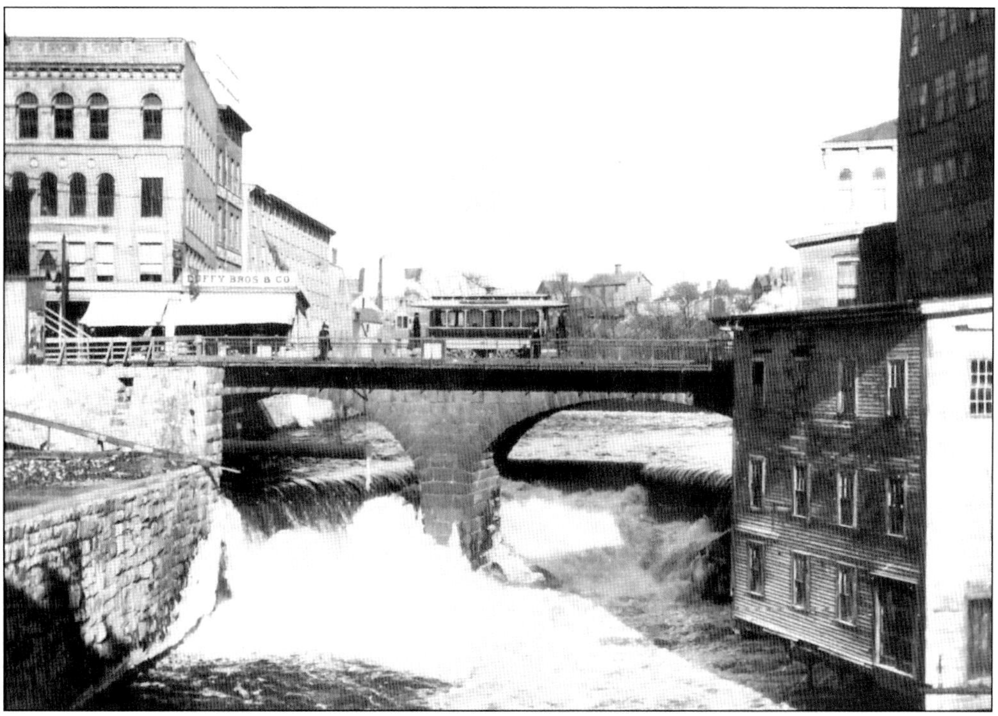

Pawtucket Falls, at the Main Street Bridge, c.1897. Above the bridge is Duffy Brothers & Co., electricians and hardware, the predecessors of today's William K. Toole Company. Duffy Brothers & Co. was run by Edward C. and Francis J. Duffy, and William K. Toole.

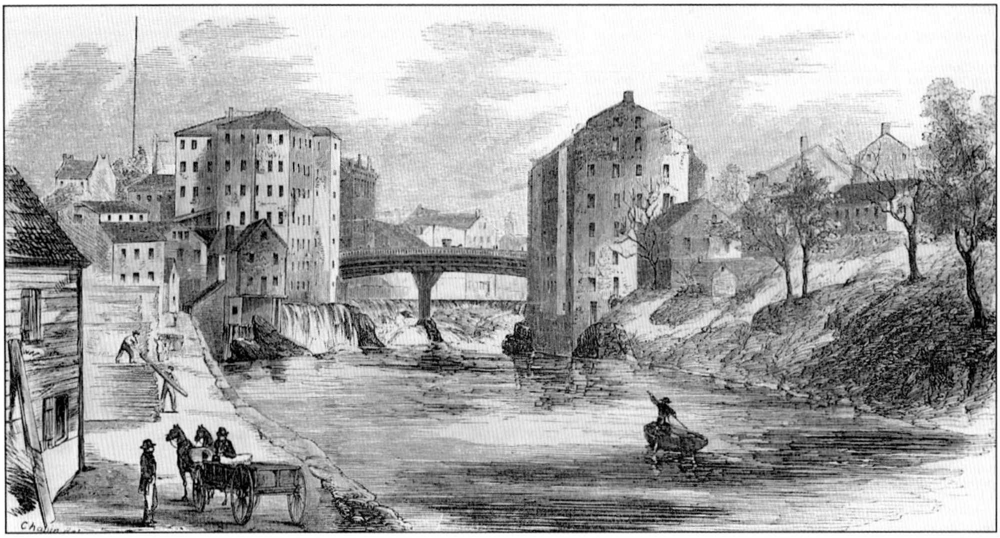

An engraving from *Ballou's Pictorial Drawing-Room Companion*, June 23, 1855.

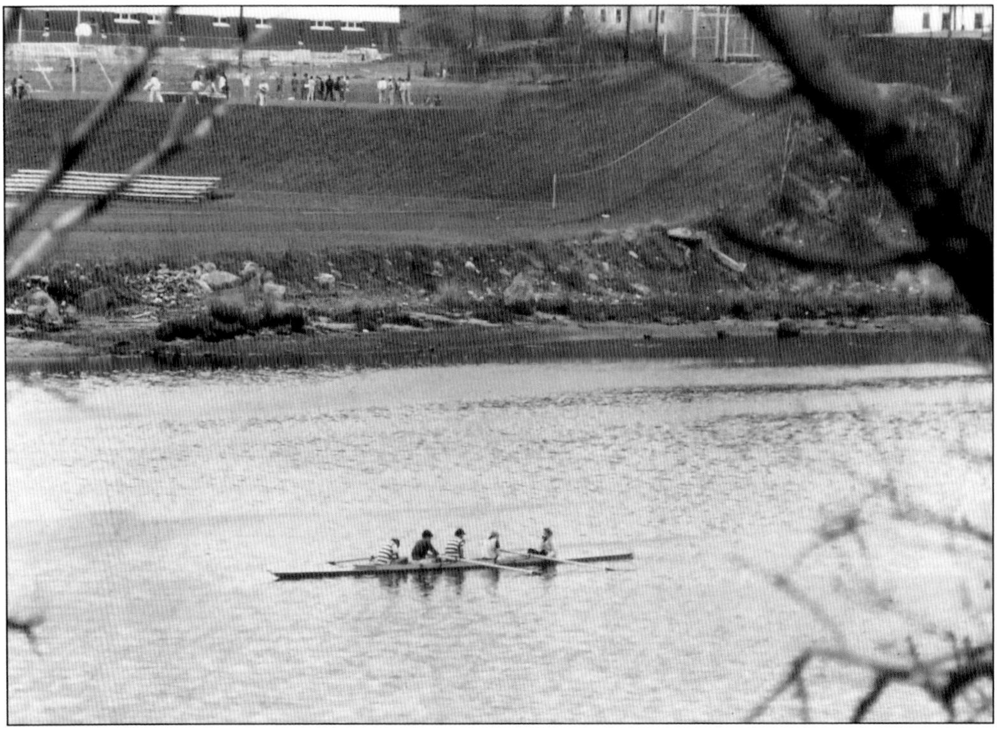

A recent view of a Brown University crew, practicing on the Pawtucket River, near Max Read Field and the Varieur Elementary School, off Pleasant Street. (Pawtucket Public Library.)

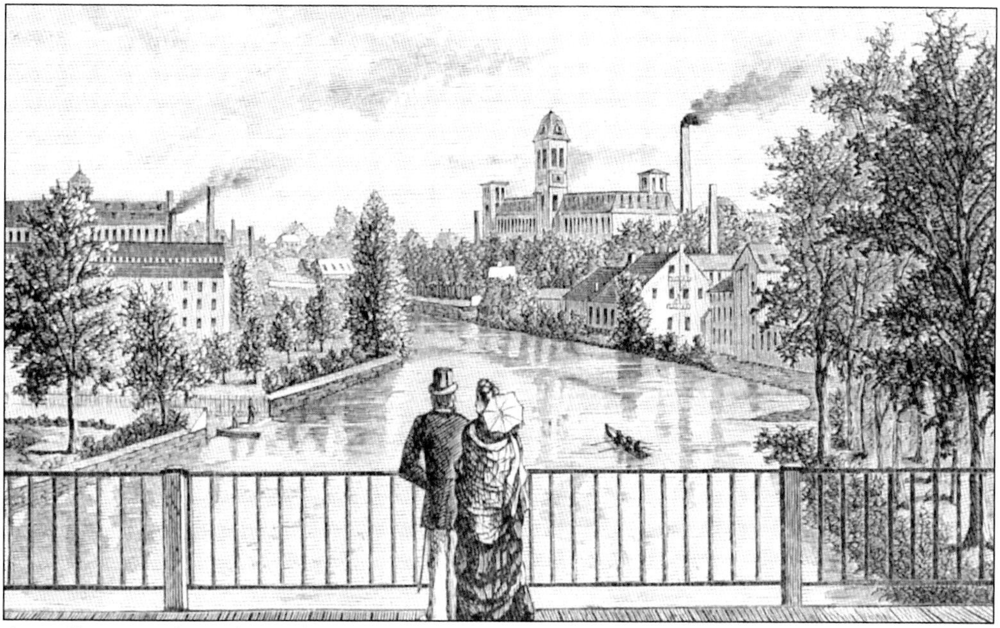

A strolling couple in the early 1880s, looking north from the Exchange Street Bridge over the Blackstone River. The Green & Daniels Mill is in the center background.

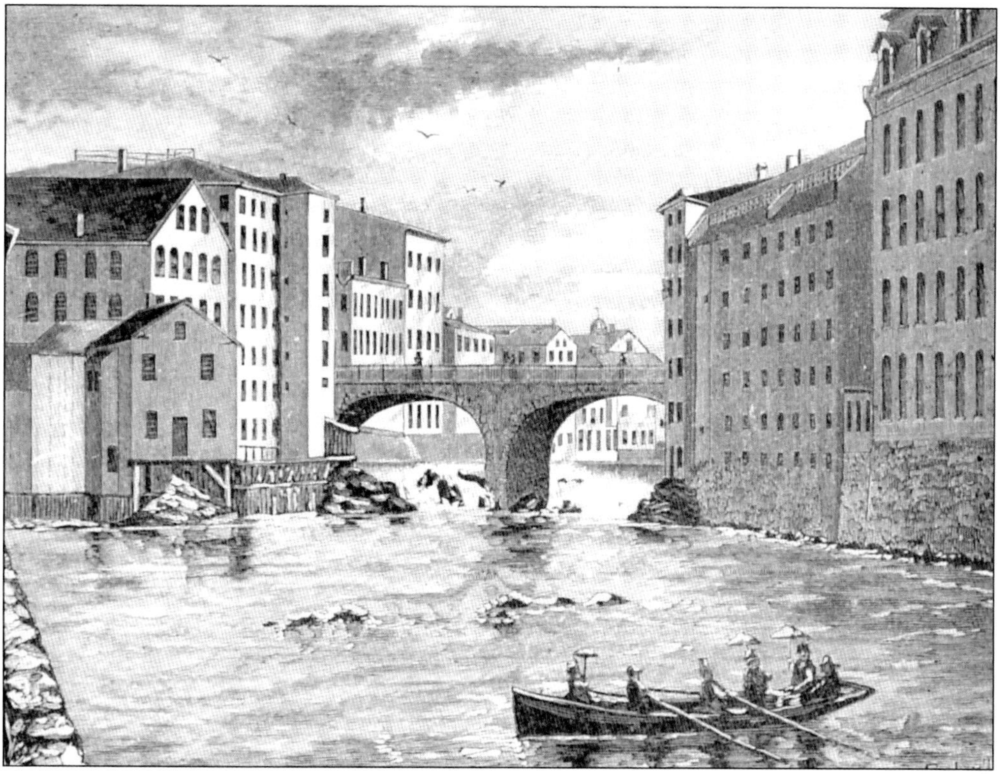

Boating and fishing were common on the Pawtucket River, below the Main Street Bridge. Here, the ladies are seen enjoying a river outing while protecting their fair skin by holding parasols above their heads.

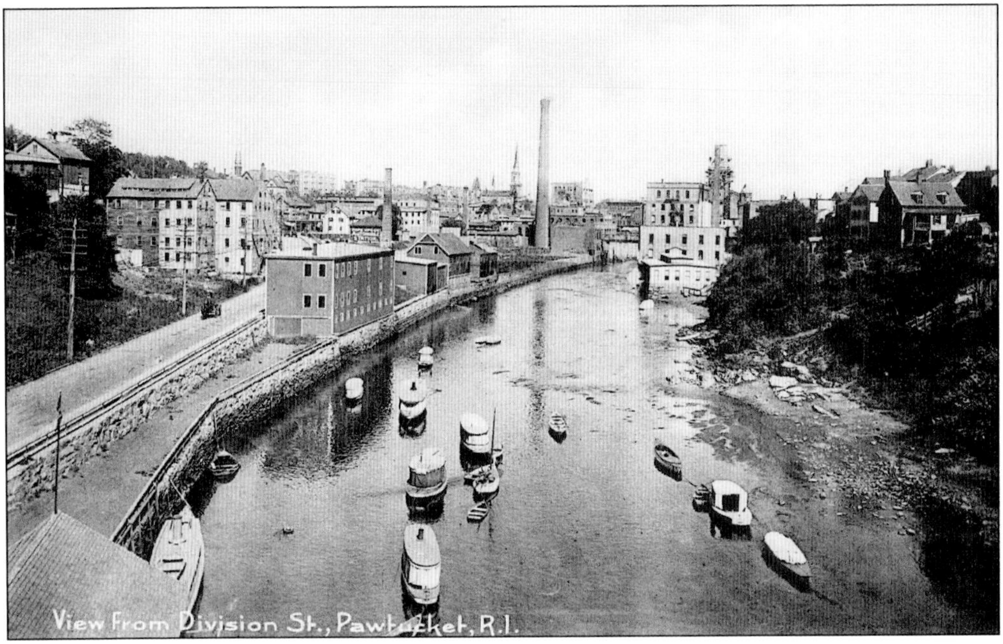

The Pawtucket River, north of the Division Street Bridge, *c.* 1900.

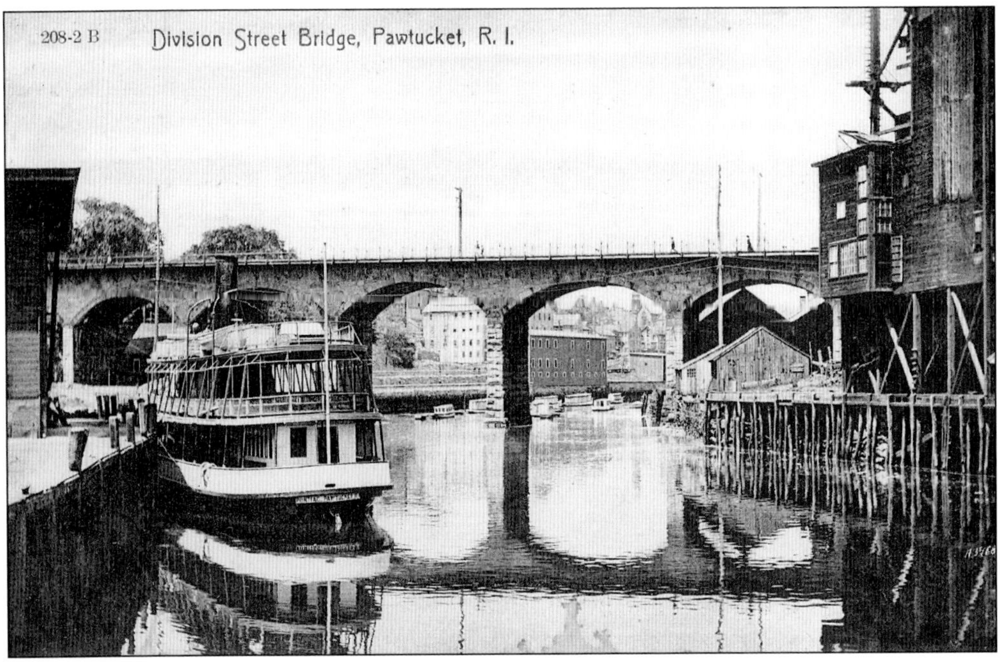

The Pawtucket River, south of the Division Street Bridge, *c.* 1900. The excursion steamer *Pontiac* (formerly the *Pioneer*) is at her pier.

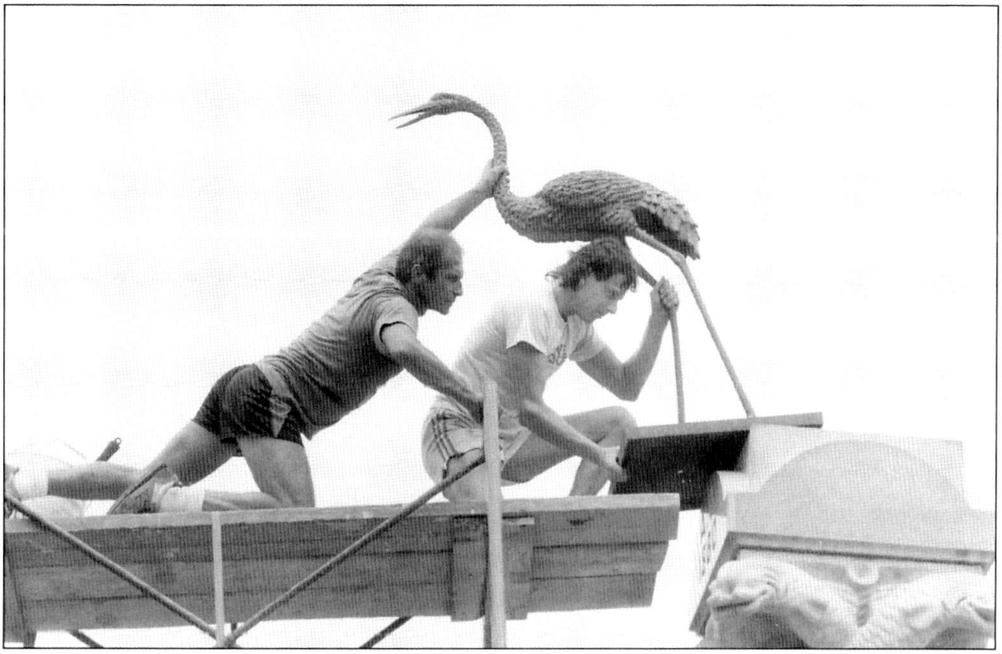

Anthony Sciolto (left) and John Lewis, of Sciolto Monuments, placing the heron on top of the Cogswell Fountain in Hodgson Rotary Park, Pawtucket, on July 31, 1991. Note that the crystal starfish has not yet been installed in the bird's beak. (*Times.*)

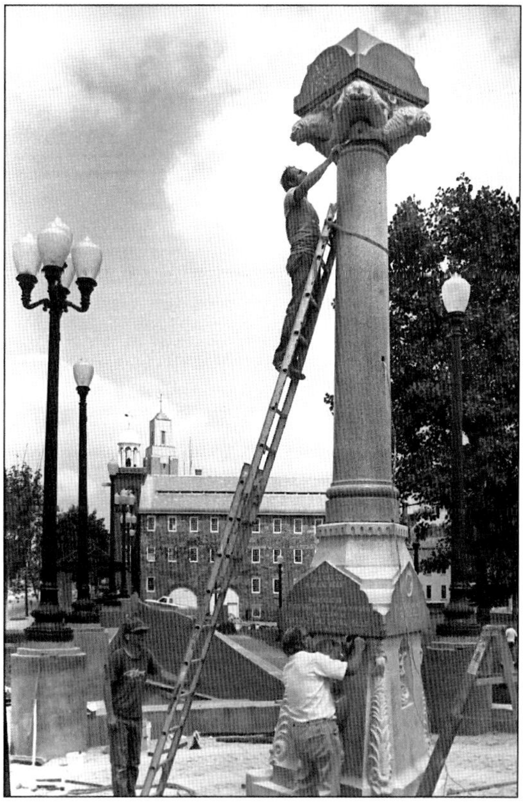

Monument renovator Anthony Sciolto (on ladder) puts the finishing touches on the relocated Cogswell Fountain, at the corner of Roosevelt Avenue and Main Street, in 1991. (*Times.*)

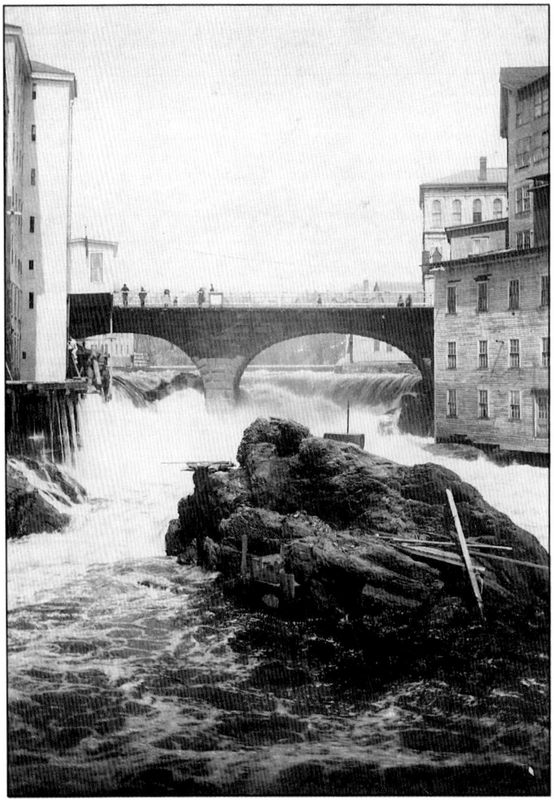

An 1880s freshet roaring under the Main Street Bridge. The New Mill can be seen on the left and the Yellow Mill is on the right. The Nahum Bates Block is visible across Main Street, in the background to the right.

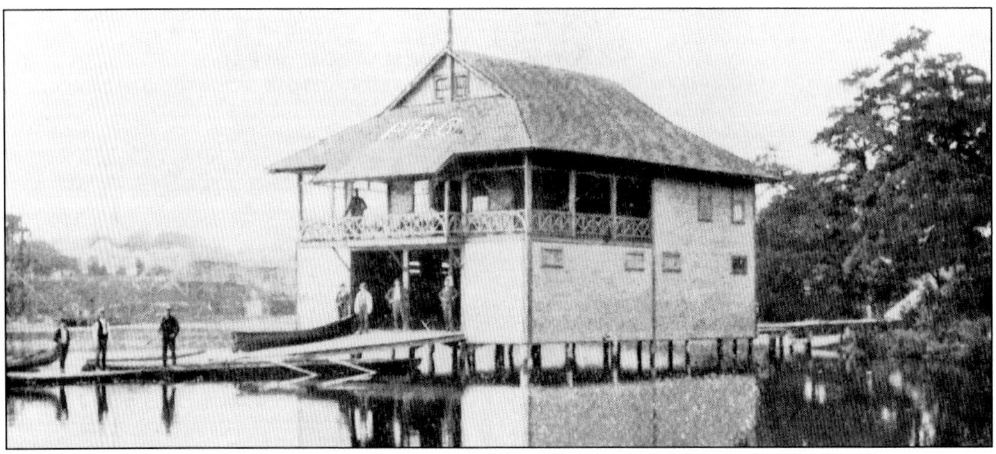

A 1891 photograph of the Pawtucket Boat and Athletic Club, located off School Street just north of the current location of the Old State Pier.

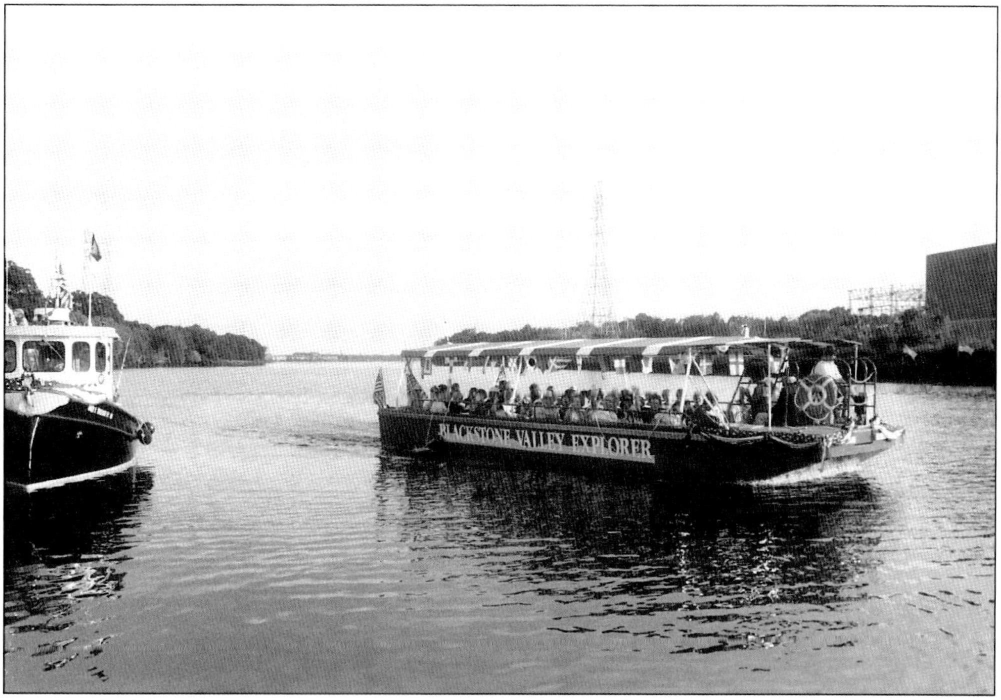

The Blackstone Valley Tourism Council's *Blackstone Valley Explorer*, launched August 19, 1993, takes sight-seers north on the Pawtucket River from the Old State Pier to view the Falls at Pawtucket. This photograph was taken in 1994. (*Times*.)

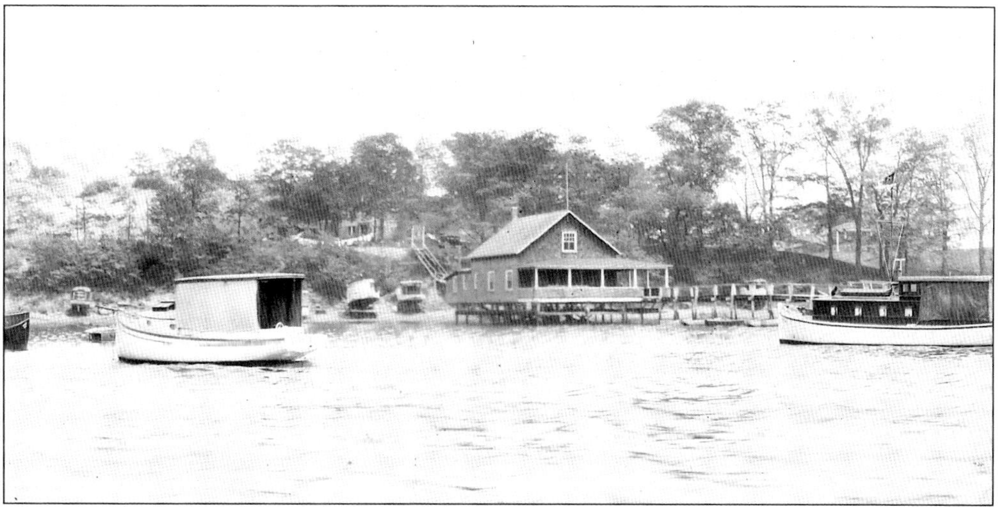

In 1914 the Pawtucket Motor Boat Club, organized in 1911, built this clubhouse at the foot of Bishop Street (which no longer exists) at Bishop's Bend. On the right is Lewis Fleming's *Joyce Edna*. Along with the clubhouse, the *Joyce Edna* was smashed to splinters by the 1938 hurricane. On the left is a converted cat boat, belonging to Arthur Salsbury.

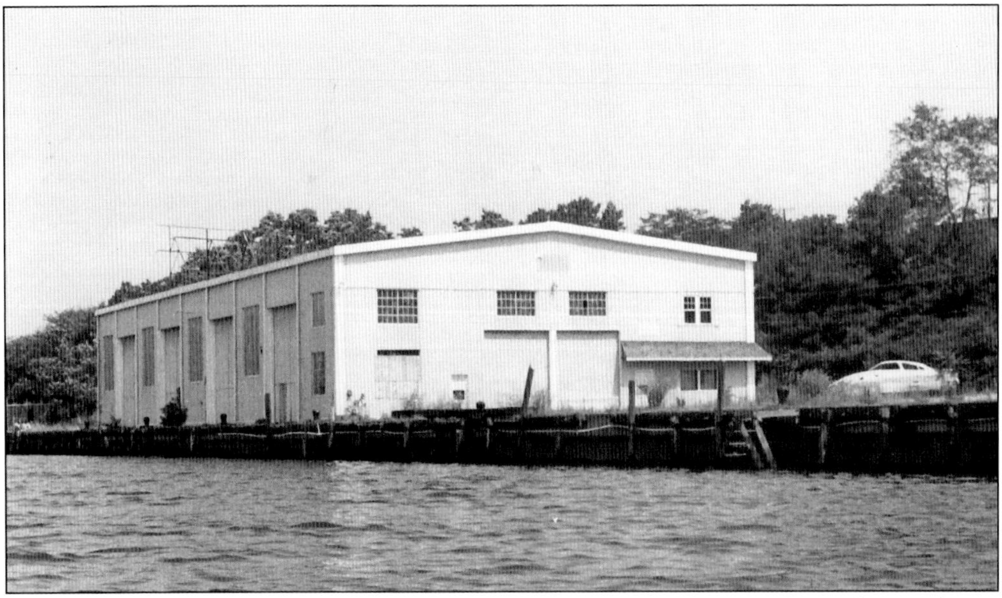

The Old State Pier, off School Street. This view, from the early 1980s, shows the warehouse built in 1919 by the Blackstone Valley Transportation Company, for the steamboat freight of their Pawtucket/New York shipping business. At the time of this photograph, Bill Parent was readying the building to be the center of his new marina. (*Times*.)

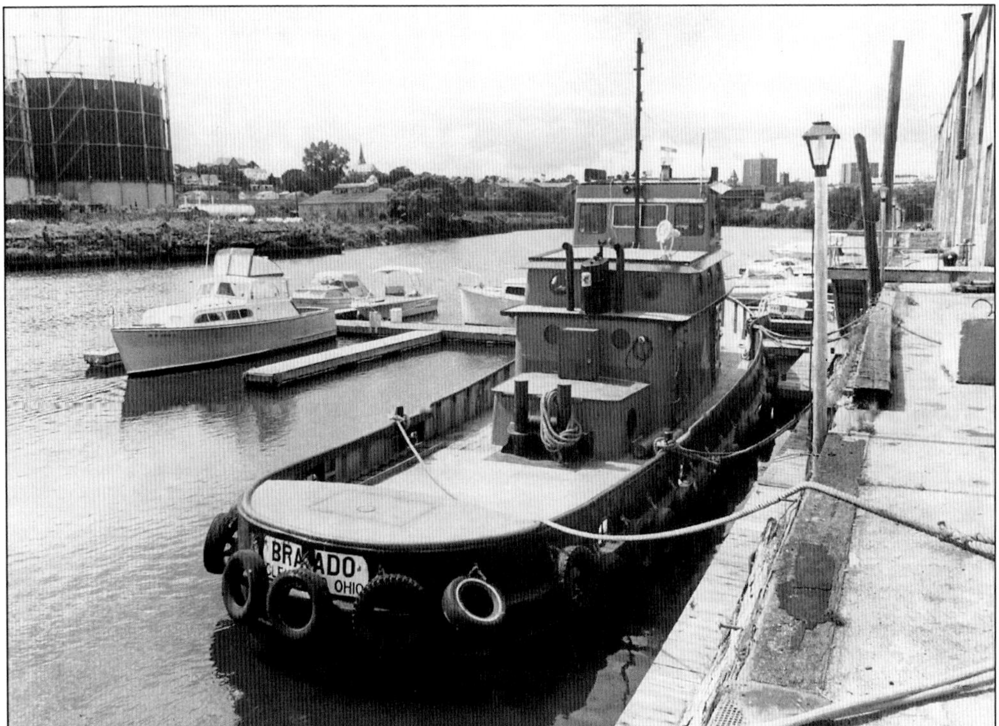

Well under way by the time this photograph was taken in August 1981, Parent's Marina demonstrates some of the sixty boats of all sizes that docked at the Old State Pier. The tug boat *Bravado* is in the foreground. (*Times*.)

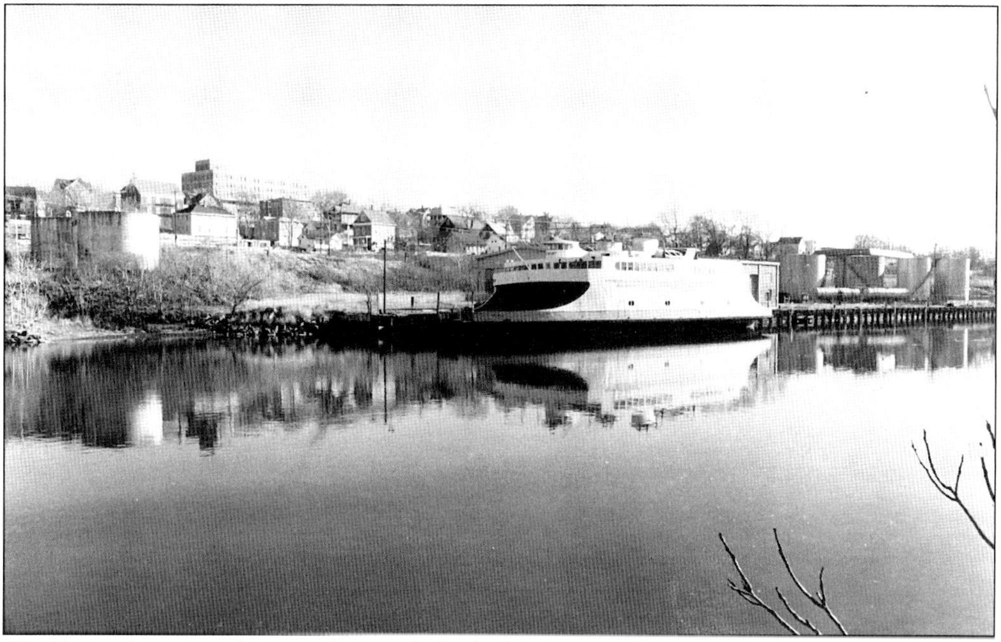

This December 1972 photograph records the high-water mark of a noble experiment, *The Ferry*. The retired ferryboat *Newport* arrived at Pawtucket's Old State Pier in August 1969 to be used as a much-needed youth center. The experiment was over by 1974, and the ferry is now a floating restaurant in Portland, Maine. (*Times*.)

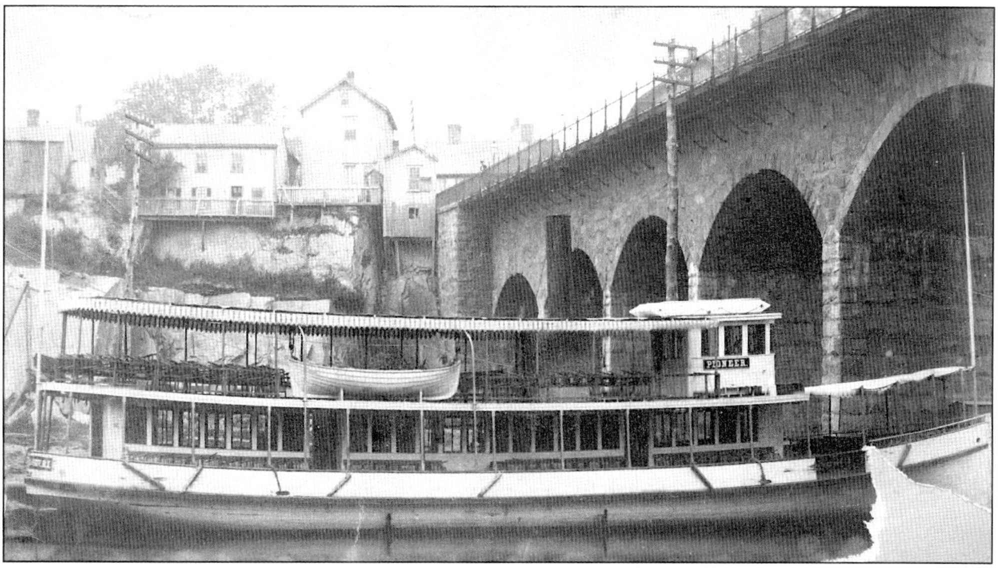

The *Pioneer* passes under the Division Street Bridge in the 1890s. In 1883, Moncrief, McClay and Company built this vessel, the second steamer of the Pawtucket Steamboat Company to bear the name Pioneer. She was the mainstay of the fleet, steaming the river and the bay until 1917. Her name was changed to *Pontiac* in 1902.

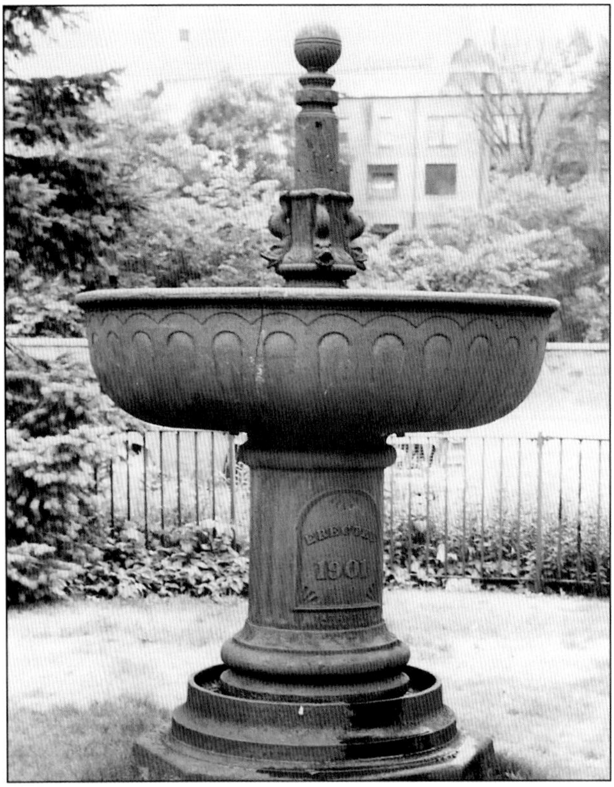

A Captain Henry F. Jenks water fountain, cast in Pawtucket. Shown here in its original location on Pine Street in the back of Union Wadding, it was later moved to the yard at the Old Slater Mill. It remained in storage for many years at Slater Park, and now graces the Park's Armistice Boulevard entrance.

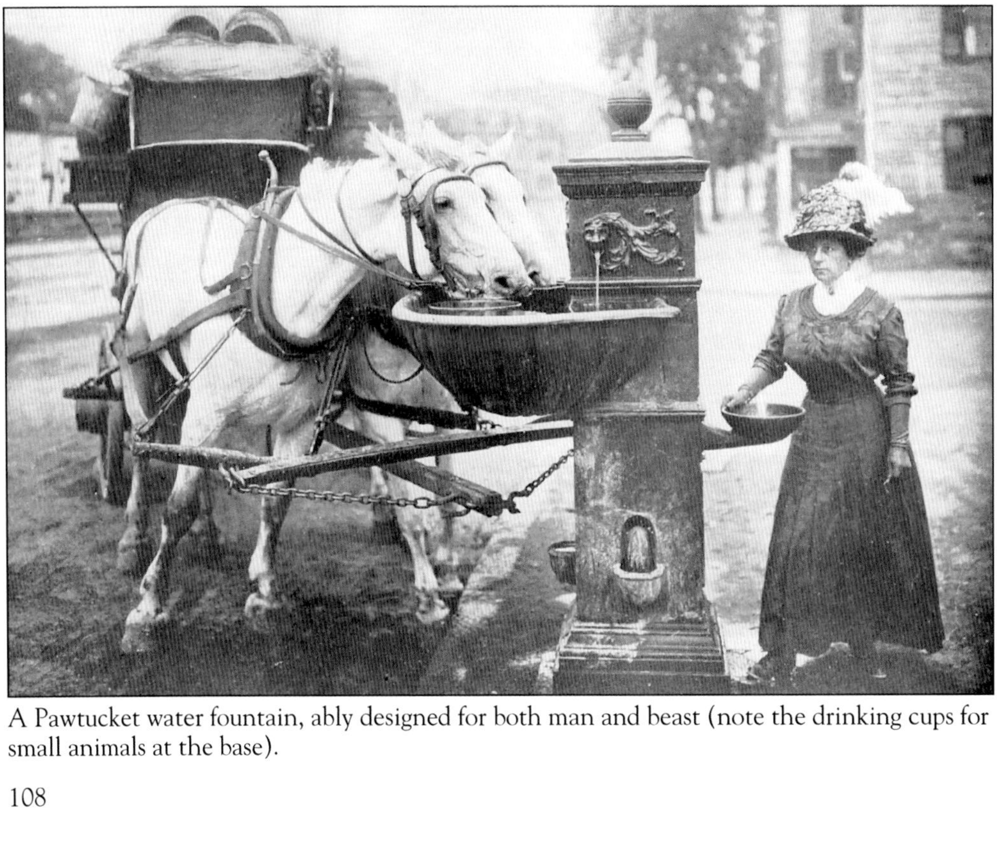

A Pawtucket water fountain, ably designed for both man and beast (note the drinking cups for small animals at the base).

Eight

Having Fun

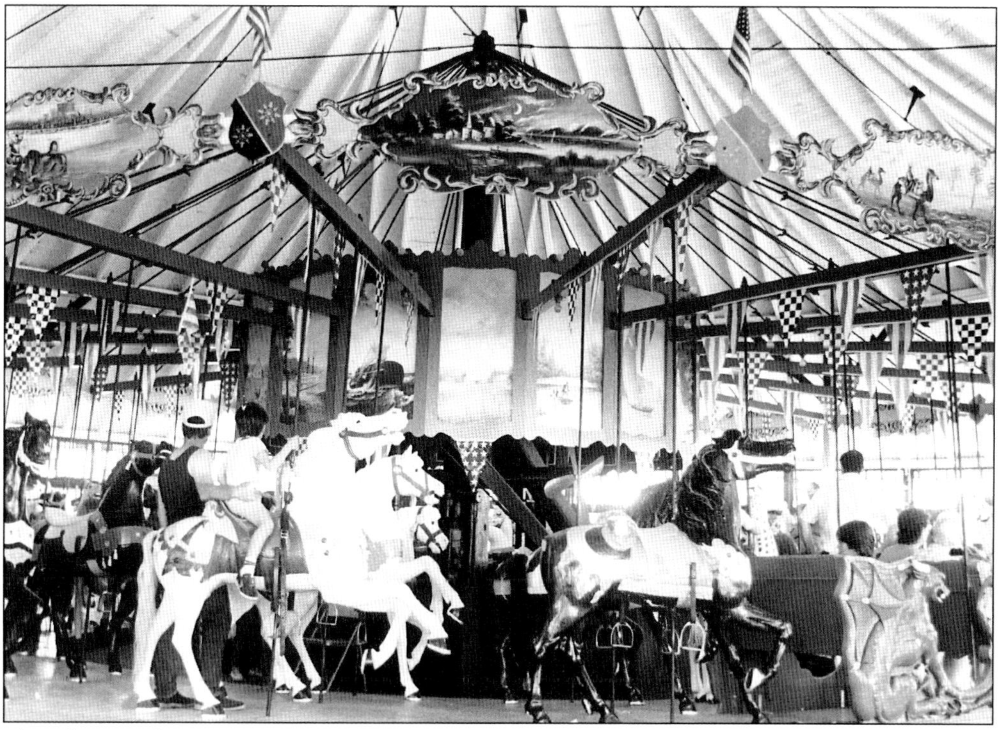

The Slater Park Carousel, located adjacent to the Daggett House, is considered one of the best-designed carousels in the world. It is among the earliest ones built by Charles I.D. Loof, whose workshop was in East Providence at Crescent Park. It was brought to Slater Park in 1910, and completely restored in 1971, through a grant from the National Trust for Historic Preservation. It has been in continuous summer-use ever since. (*Times.*)

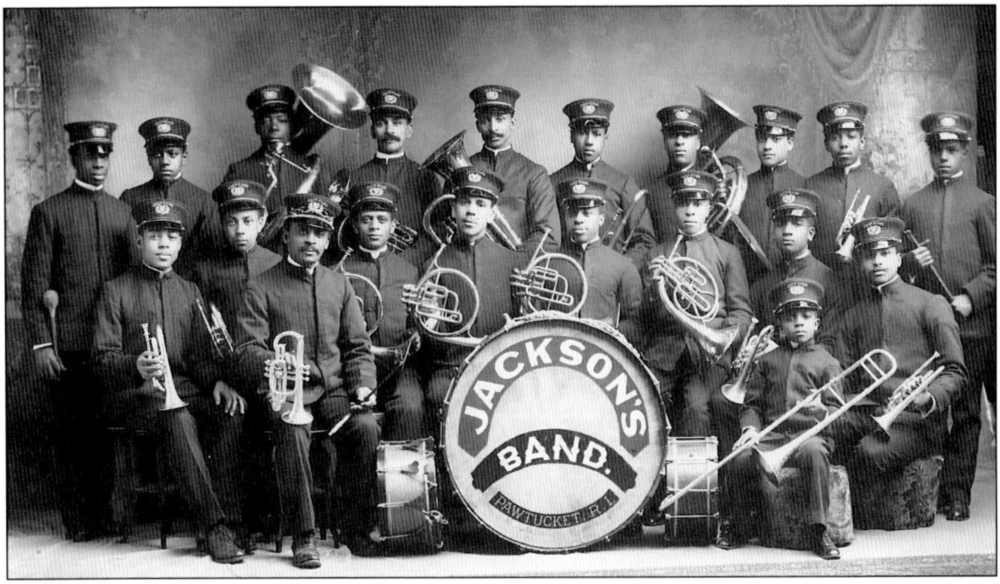

On September 27, 1903, Professor Ellis T. Jackson, cornet soloist and band master, organized a band whose members could hardly read a note or even make a sound on an instrument. The Jackson Band headed the Police Association parade the following June. They met in the Cottrell Block, at what was then 355 Main Street. The officers were Frank Grimes (president), Solomon Edwards (vice president), and John Davis (treasurer). This photograph was taken in 1905.

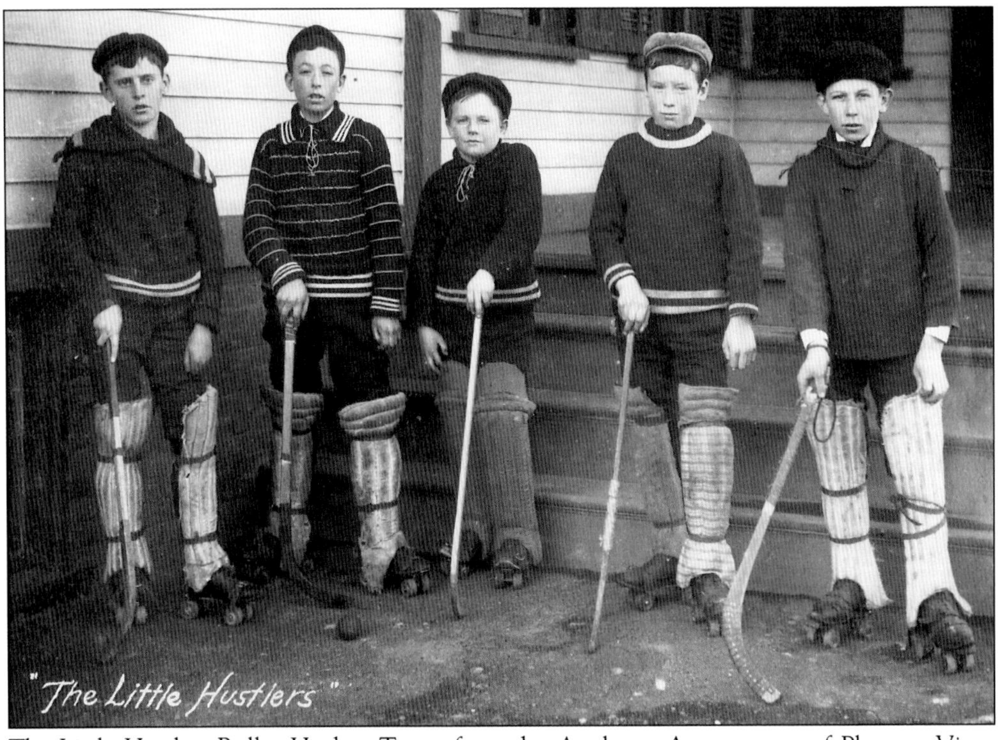

The Little Hustlers Roller Hockey Team, from the Appleton Avenue area of Pleasant View, c. 1898. Those pictured include John Andrew Teeden (left) and John Hodgert (third from left).

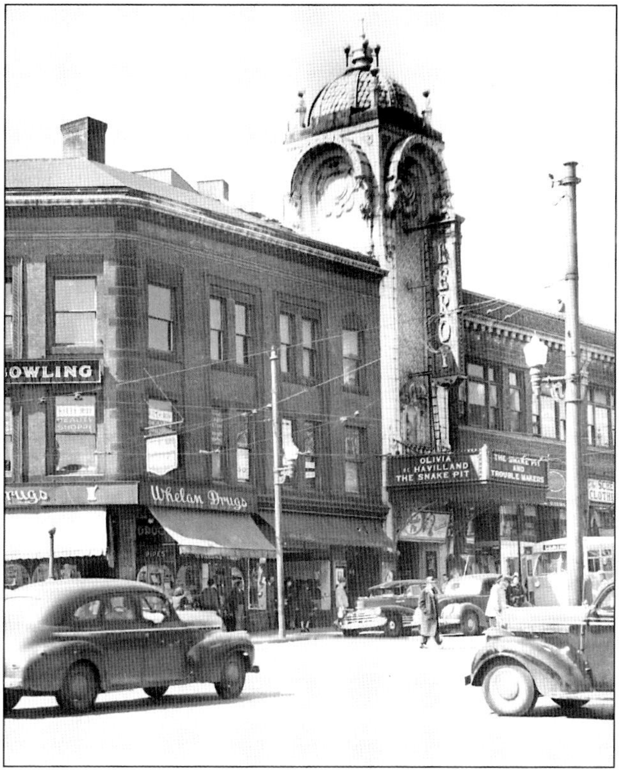

Described as "a Million Dollar Theater" when it opened on April 1, 1923, the Leroy premiered to a full house watching silent movies. In the late 1920s, Will Rogers entertained audiences with a two-hour monologue. The 2,700-seat Leroy was erected as a lasting tribute to Leroy Payne, who died in France in World War I. It boasted the largest Wurlitzer organ in New England, which was so complex that few organists could play it. Movie operations ceased in October 1973. (*Times*.)

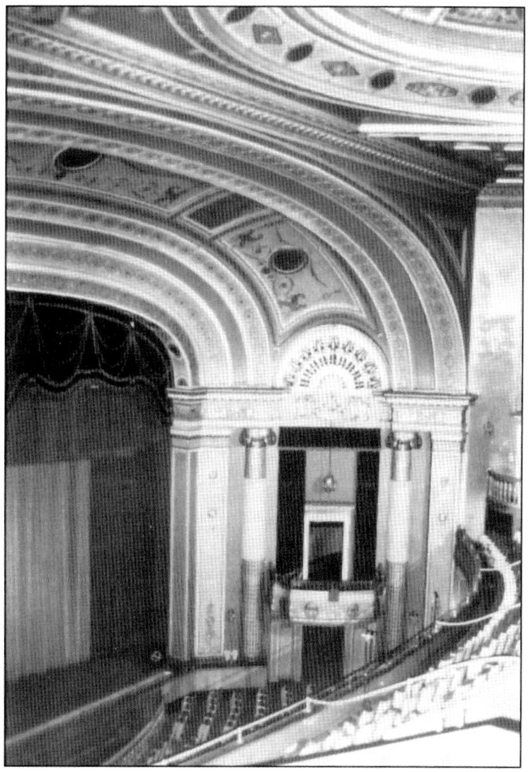

A view from the first balcony of the Leroy Theater. The interior of the building remains virtually unchanged and in fairly good condition.

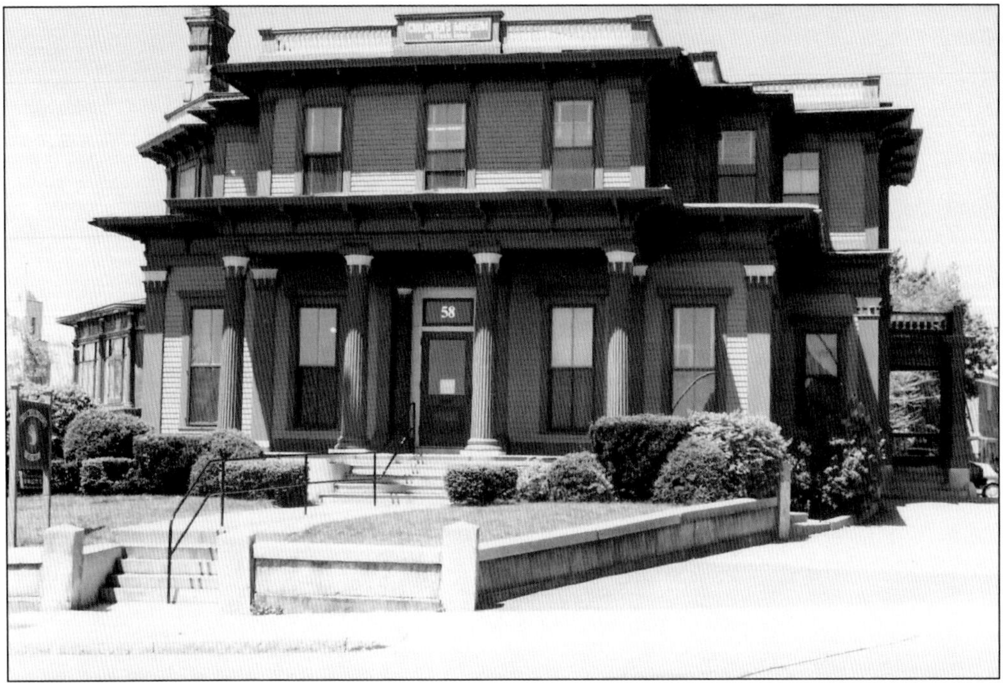

The Pitcher-Goff Mansion, built in 1840 and remodeled in 1881, at 58 Walcott Street. Everyone from far and wide knows the building as the Children's Museum. In 1943, Lyman B. Goff's daughter, Mrs. Kenneth Wood, deeded the property to the Pawtucket Congregational Church, which then leased it to the American Red Cross and the Boy Scouts of America. Today it is leased to the Children's Museum of Rhode Island (see p. 125).

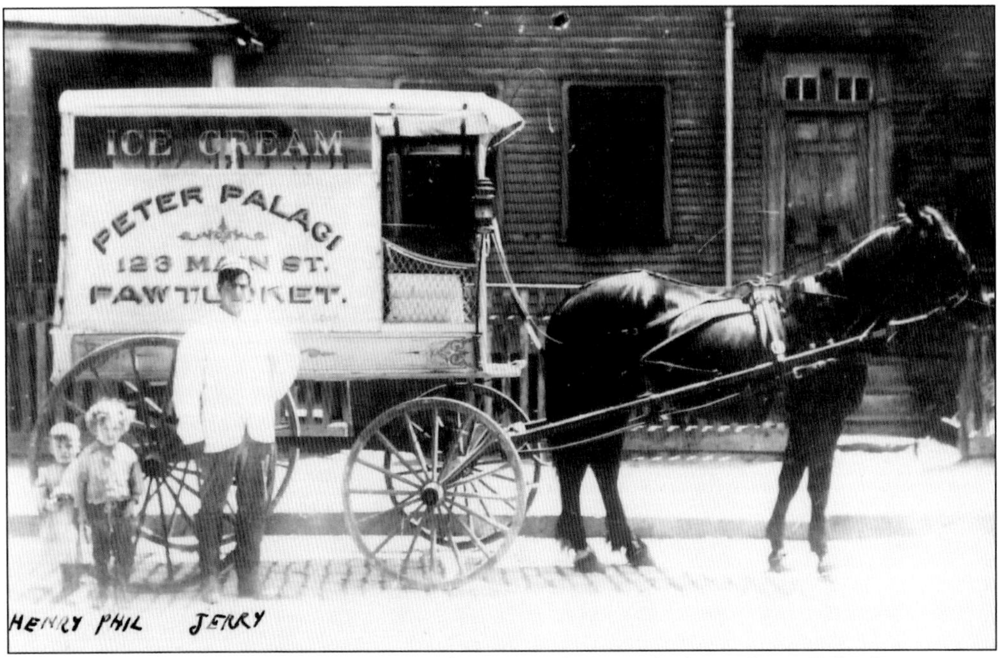

Peter Palagi was a legend in Pawtucket. This 1907 photograph shows Peter Palagi's ice cream wagon. Pictured here are, from left to right, Henry Palagi, Phil Palagi, and Jerry Lucchesi.

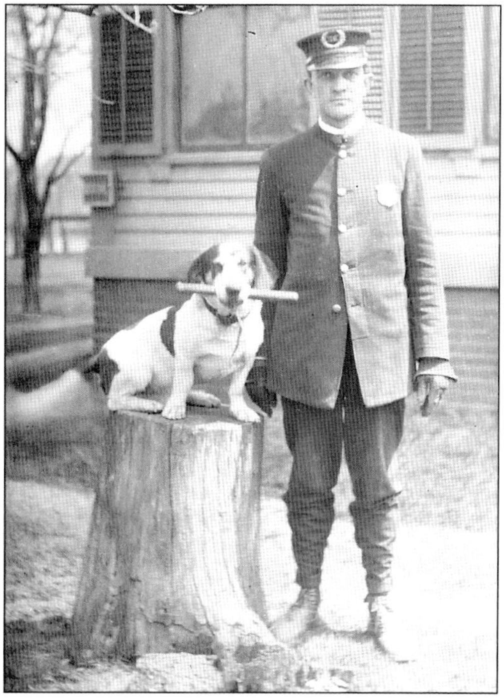

Dr. William J. Graham's dog Buster, with his pal, officer William J. Laird, outside the doctor's house at 577 Smithfield Avenue. Buster and Laird walked "the beat" together, with Buster carrying his own billy club attached to his collar. Laird lived at 12 Gooding Street. This photograph was taken c. 1911 (see p. 126).

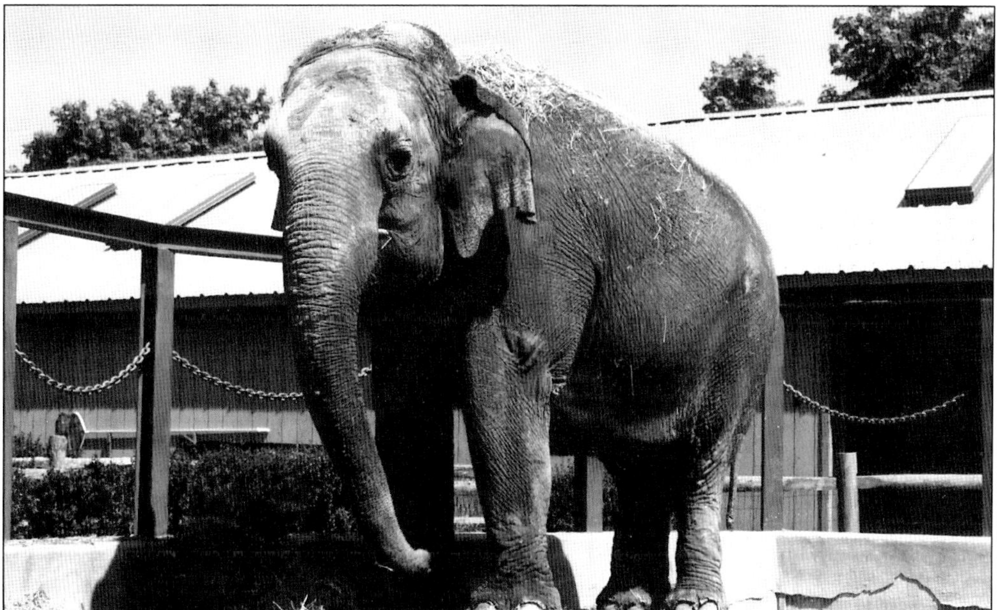

Fanny, Pawtucket's beloved elephant. She was born somewhere in Asia and was acquired by the Ringling Brothers Barnum & Bailey Circus. Pawtucket purchased the approximately four-year-old Fanny in 1958, for about $10,000. For a time, she made her home in the lower level of the Slater Park Boat House, and was later housed at the former Prospect Street Fire Station. In 1984, a house was built for her at the Slater Park Zoo. In June 1993, Fanny was sent, amid the tears of many Pawtucket well-wishers, to her new and more natural home, the Black Beauty Ranch in Murchison, Texas, when the Slater Park Zoo closed.

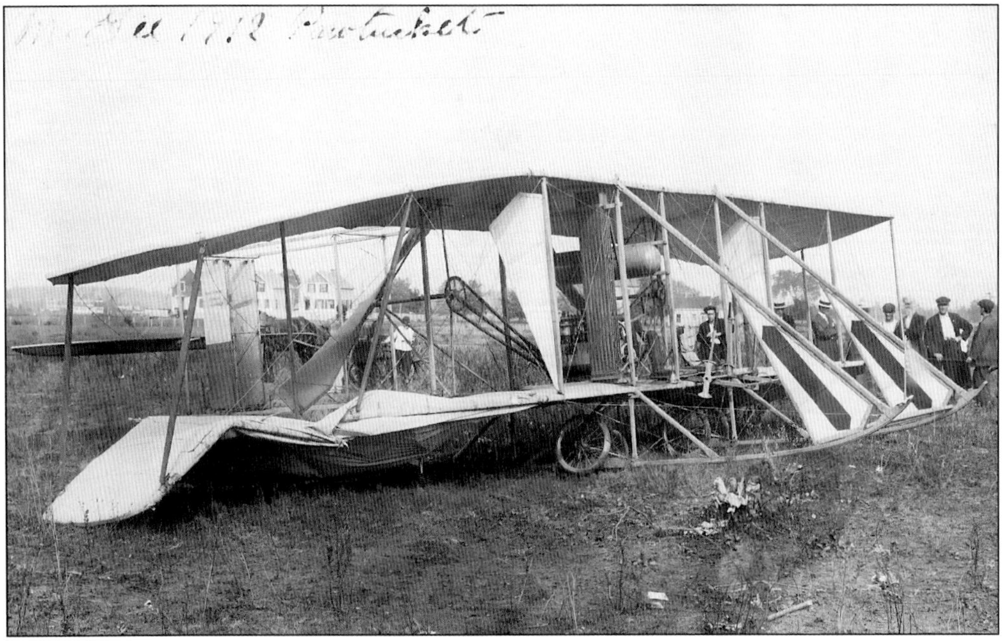

A plane flown by Jack McGee, pictured in 1912.

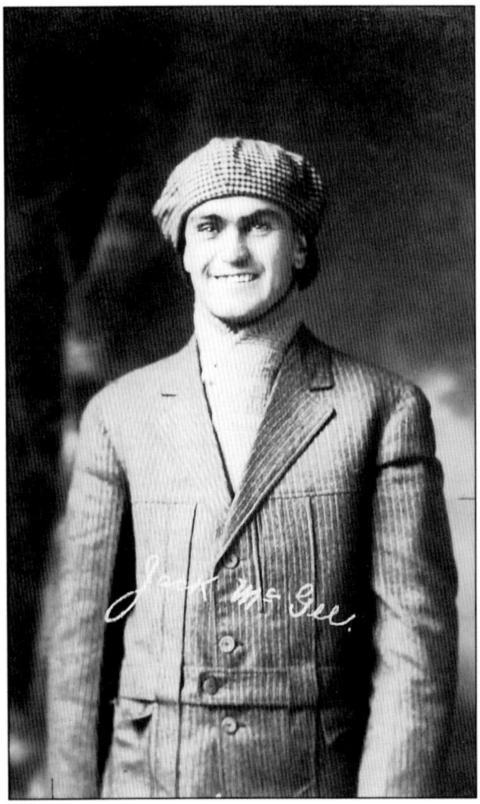

A photograph of the celebrated Pawtucket aviator John "Jack" McGee. He was born in 1885, and began his flying career in 1911. With courage and a disdain for danger, he created a legend by flying those flimsy machines of wire and fabric. In 1919, he died while piloting a test plane which crashed in the waters of Greenwich Bay, off Cowessett, Rhode Island.

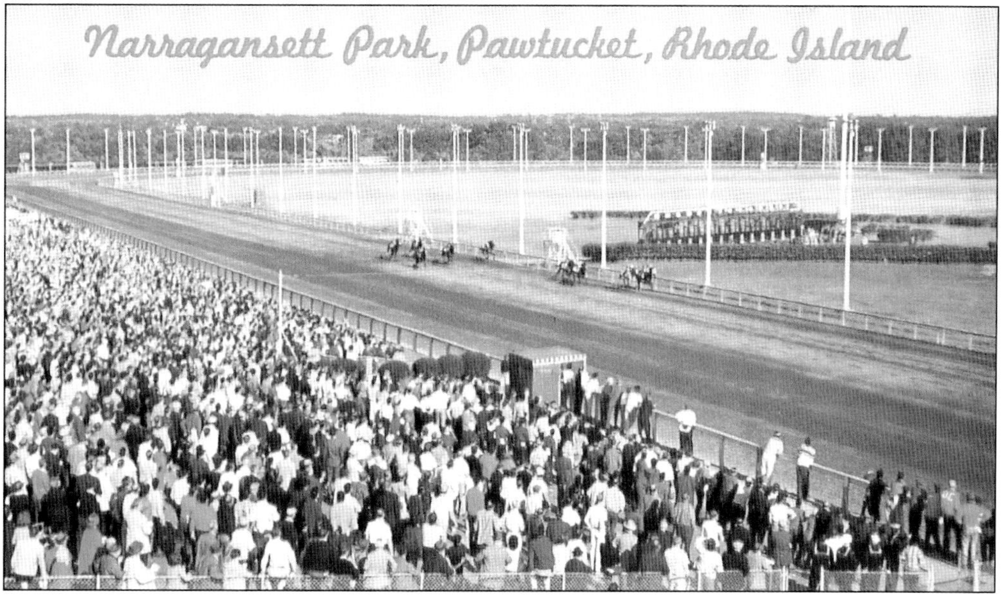

The Narragansett Park Race Track, *c.* 1940s. Fast-working entrepreneur Walter O'Hara began the construction of Narragansett Park in June 1934. Opening day was August 1, 1934, and there were 37,281 avid patrons on hand. James E. Dooley was president from 1934 to 1963. His son, Judge J. Alden Dooley Sr., then ran "Gansett" until it closed in 1978. Some of the most famous racehorses of this century raced here, including Sea Biscuit, Bull Lea, War Admiral, and Coaltown. Whirlaway and Alsab ran in their famous match-race of September 1942.

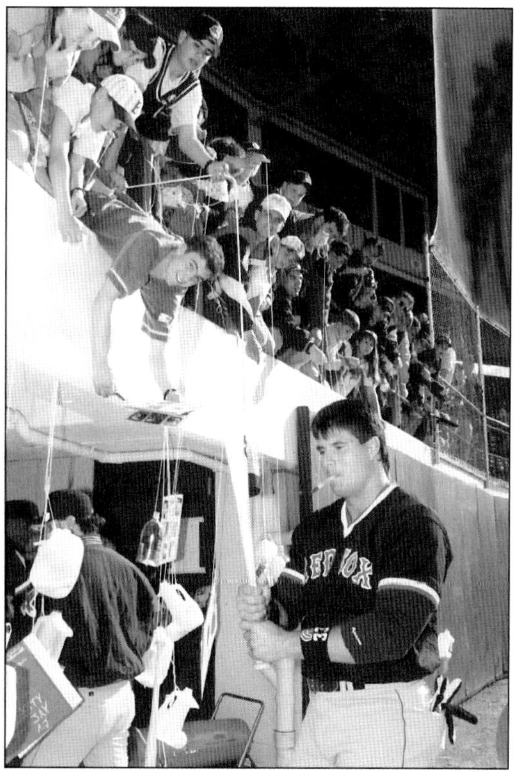

PawSox fans go fishing for autographs at McCoy Stadium, during the Boston Red Sox/Pawtucket Red Sox Annual Alumni Exhibition Game, in May 1995. BoSox slugger Jose Canseco obliges by signing for some of the PawSox faithful.

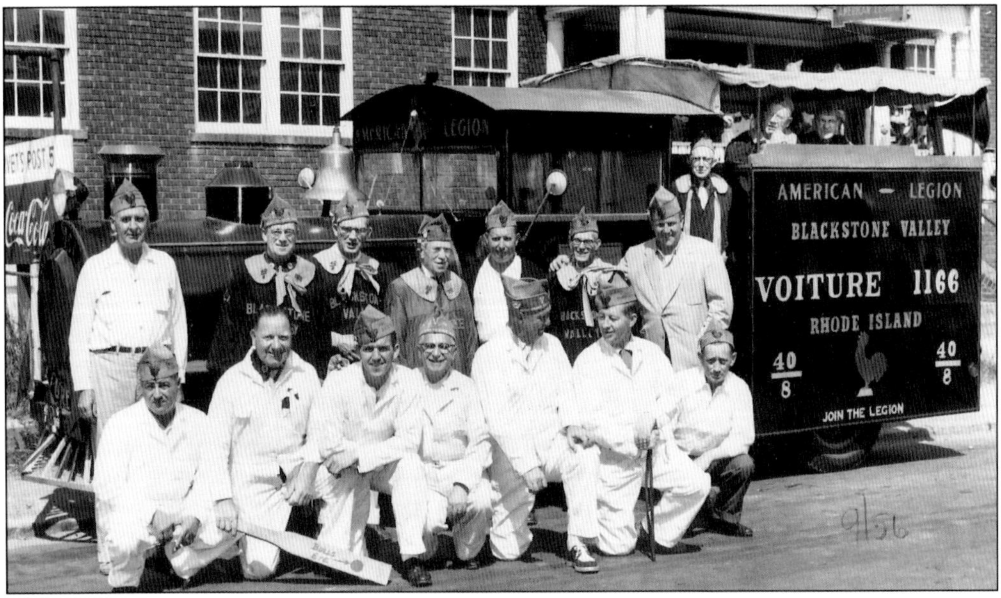

Members of the American Legion-Pawtucket Post's fun-loving arm, the Forty and Eight, outside the Novelty Park Club on Division Street, *c.* 1941. This mock-up engine pulled the Forty and Eight Voiture 1166, a railroad car shipped from France as a reminder of their World War I experiences. It was called Forty and Eight because it carried either forty soldiers or eight horses. Pictured here are: (front row) Gene Vanty, Jack Hutchinson, Henry Glodblatt, Frank Snow, Ed Carty, and John Finnegan; (back row) John Peacock, Jack Silverman, Ray Richards, Art Taylor, John Zurowski, and Jack Cassidy. Center, in the tender, is Roy Bowen. The others are unknown.

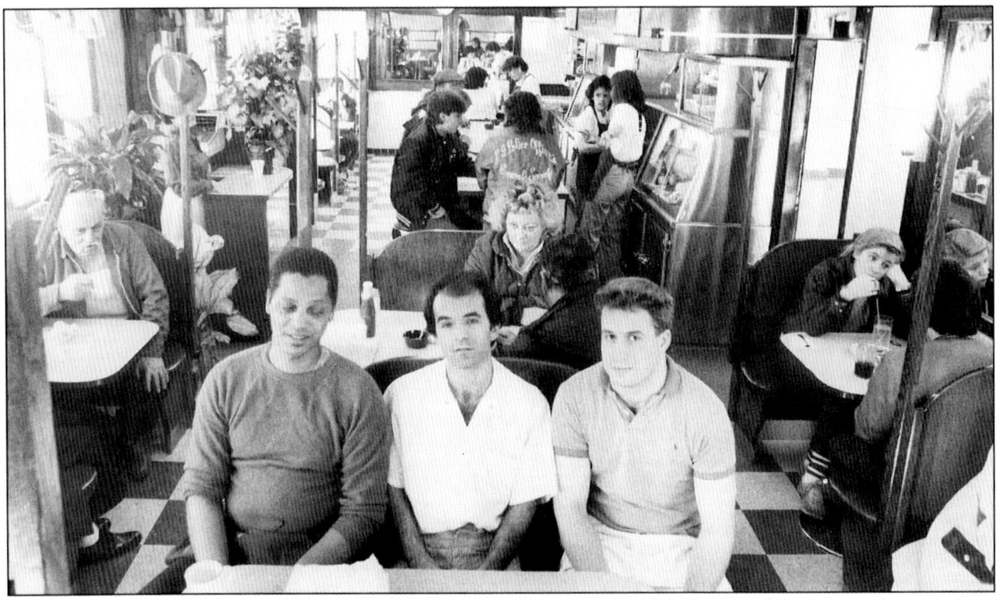

The interior of Pawtucket's historic Modern Diner, March 1985. Pictured here are, from left to right: (foreground) Craig Suide, Nick Demou, and John Lavall. The diner, formerly on Dexter Street near Main Street, was placed on the National Register of Historic Places, and moved to its current place of business on East Avenue. (*Times.*)

Nine

GOING HOME

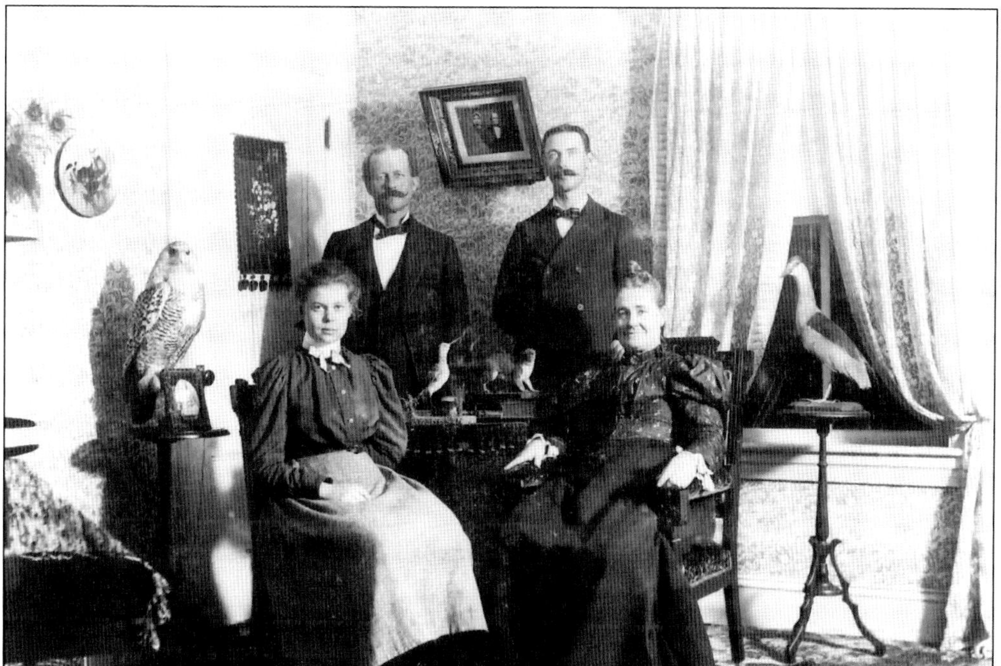

The Victorian parlor of the Samuel W. Slocum House at 47 Sanford Street in 1893. Pictured here are, from left to right: (front row) Eliza May "Lyle" (Slocum) Watjen and Eliza Jane (Short) Slocum; (back row) Samuel "Young Sam" Slocum (policeman) and Henry M. Slocum Sr.

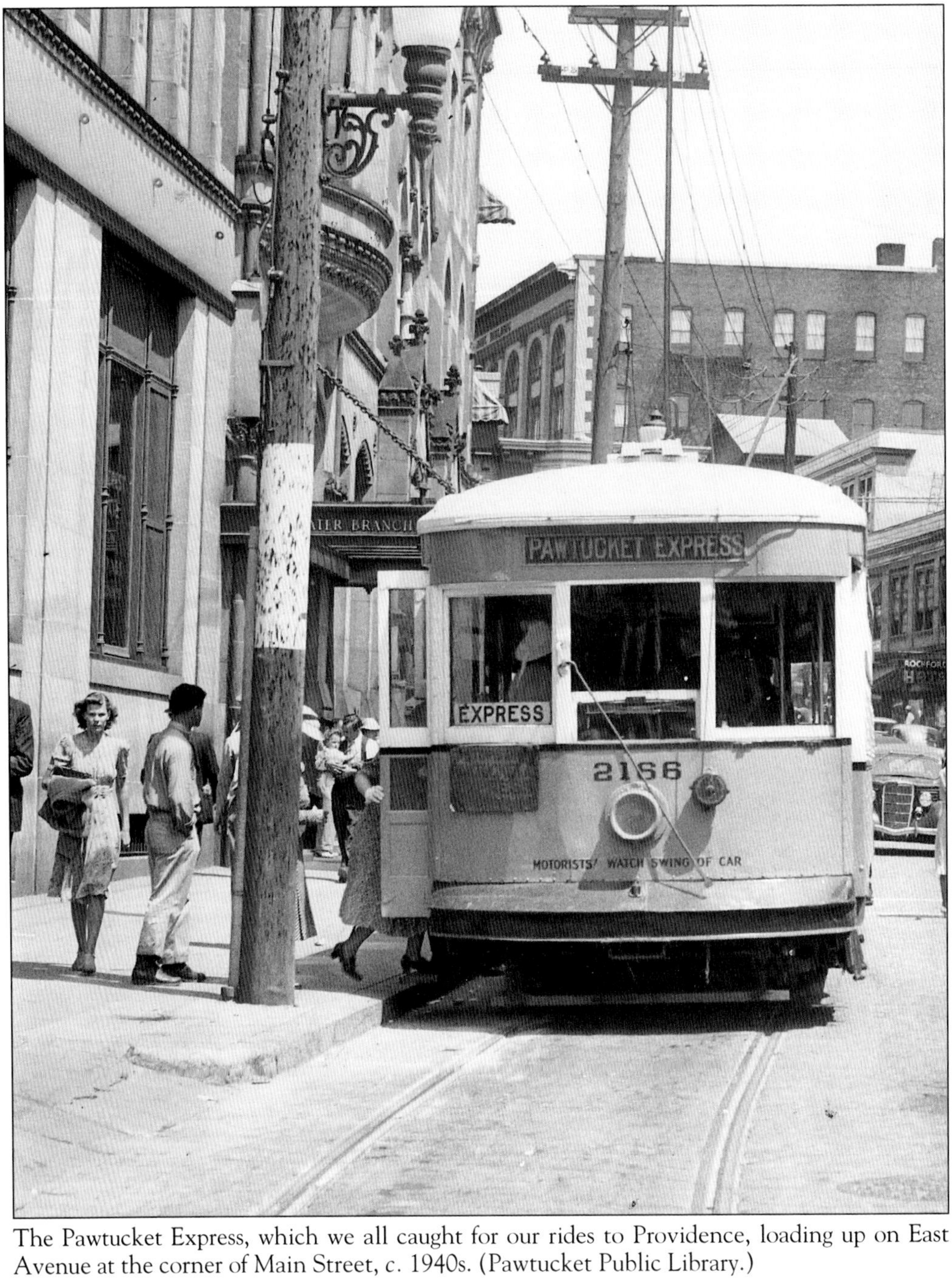

The Pawtucket Express, which we all caught for our rides to Providence, loading up on East Avenue at the corner of Main Street, *c.* 1940s. (Pawtucket Public Library.)

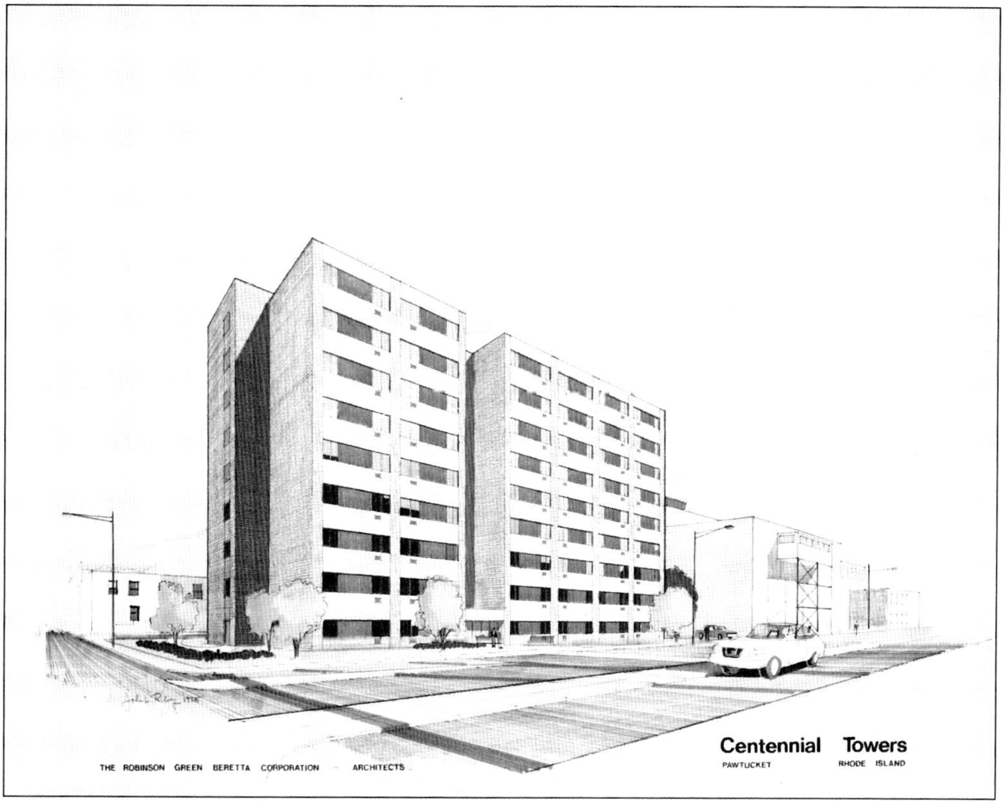

An artist's rendition of Centennial Towers.

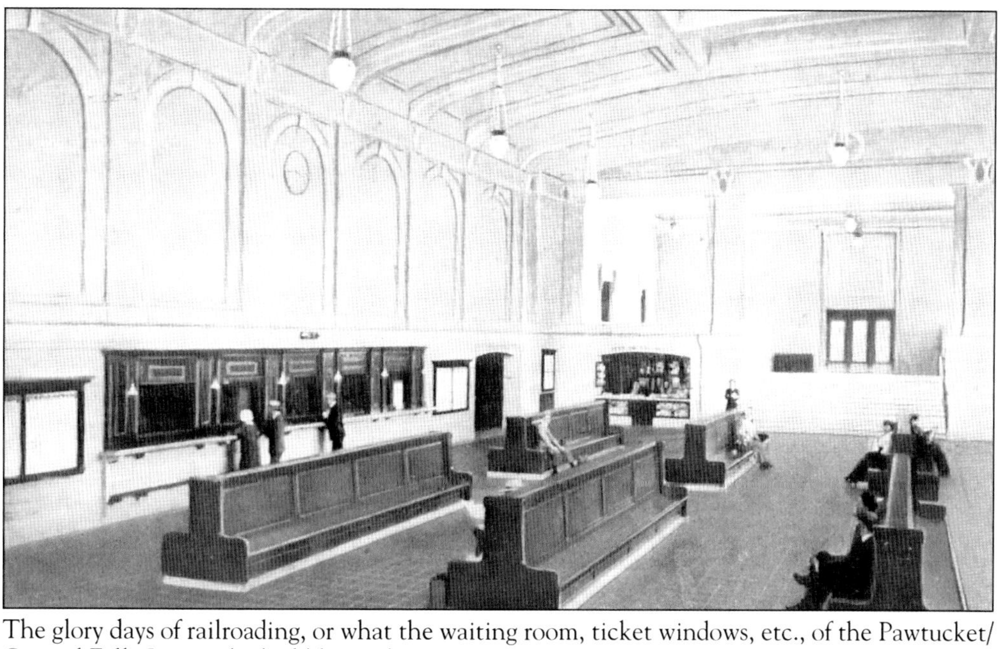

The glory days of railroading, or what the waiting room, ticket windows, etc., of the Pawtucket/Central Falls Station looked like in the 1920s.

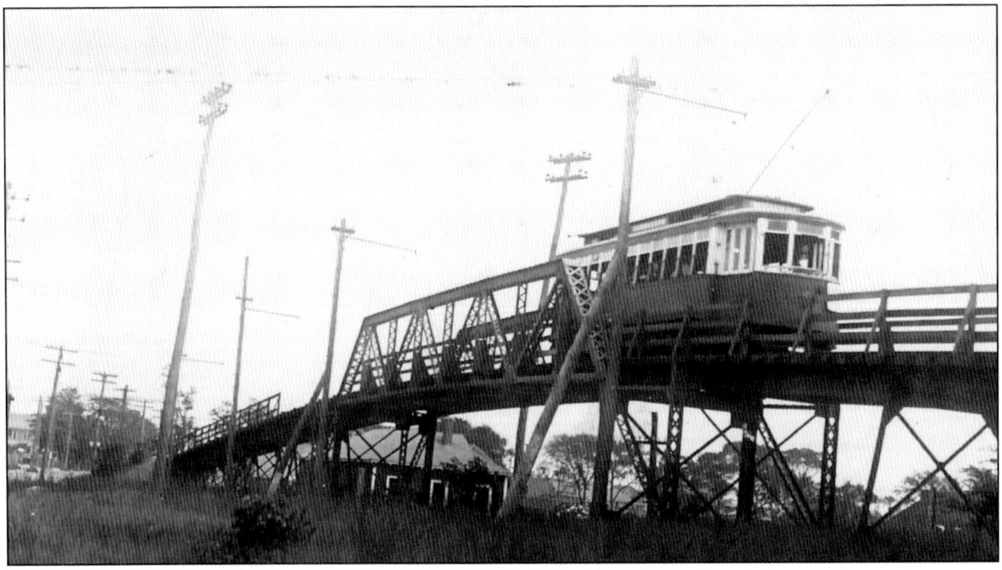

A trolley car crossing the famous trestle over the railroad tracks at Brook Street (now Armistice Boulevard), on its way to Slater Park (or Daggett Park as it used to be called), c. 1920.

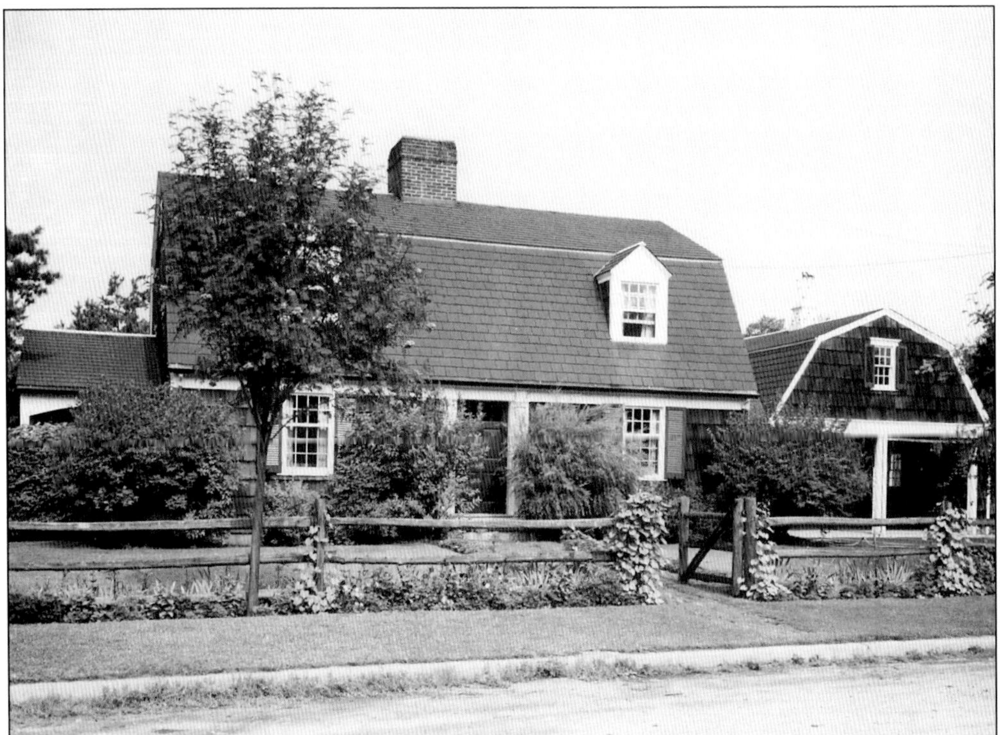

The home of Merrill Richardson, co-owner of New England Towel Supply, at 85 Pequot Road, Countryside, Pawtucket. The architects were Monahan & Meikle and the contractor was Harold C. England. Mr. Richardson's house was completed in June 1941.

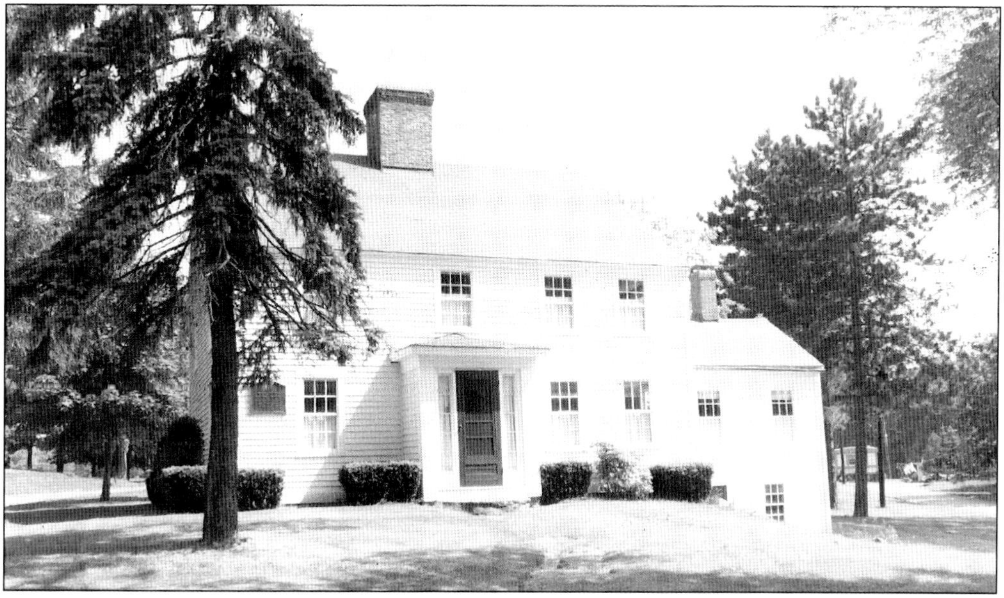

The Daggett House, built in 1685, is the oldest standing house in Pawtucket. Eight generations of Daggetts lived on this beautiful farm, now known as Slater Memorial Park. The house and land was purchased by the City of Pawtucket in 1894. The Daughters of the American Revolution leased the house in 1902 and began its restoration. Daggett House was opened to the public in September 1905. (Pawtucket Public Library)

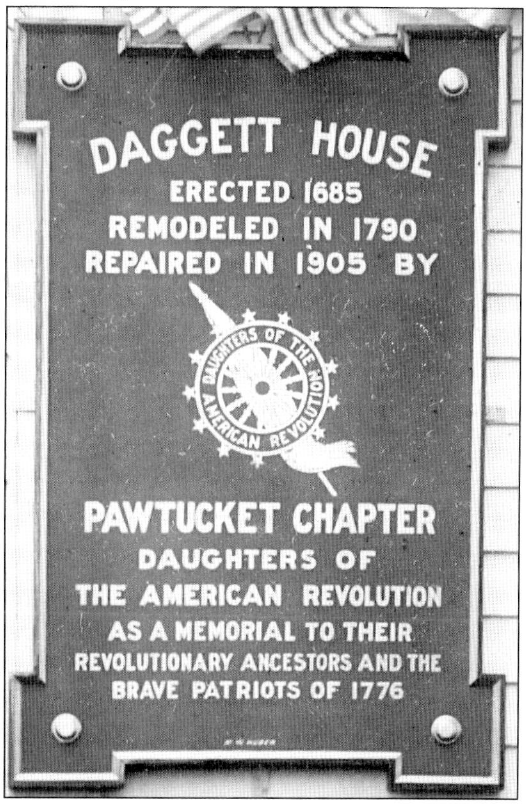

The plaque attached to the Daggett House in Slater Park in 1905. Tours of this historic museum are given by the Pawtucket Chapter of the Daughters of the American Revolution (DAR). This plaque is now missing.

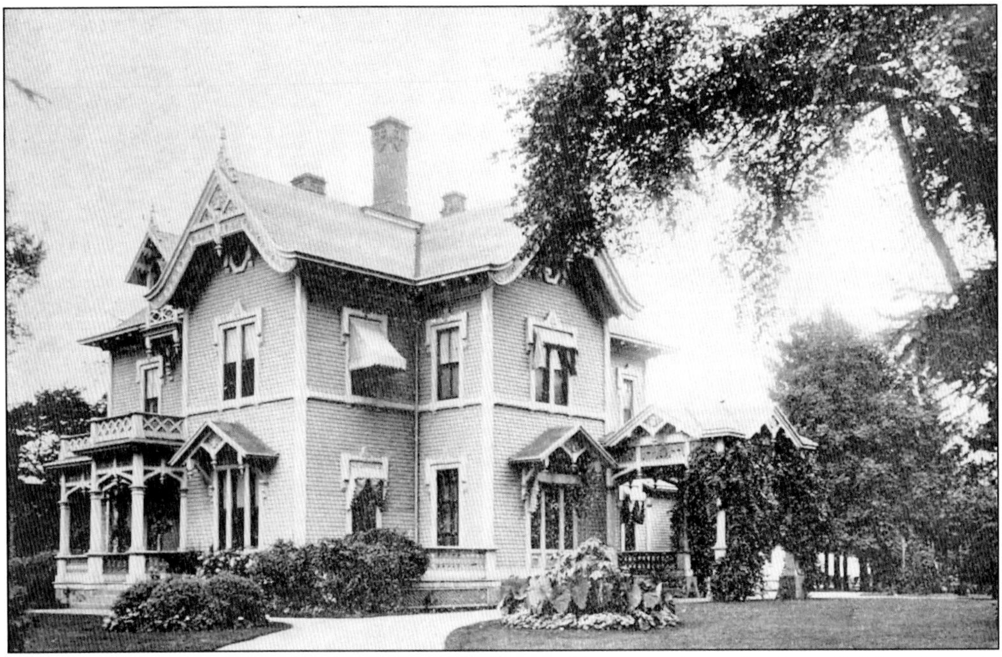

The Longely House, formerly the Simon W. Dexter Homestead, was built in 1882 and vastly improved by Mr. Longely. Formerly located at 87 Walcott Street, it was torn down in 1935, and replaced by Longely Court and the pre-World War II homes built there.

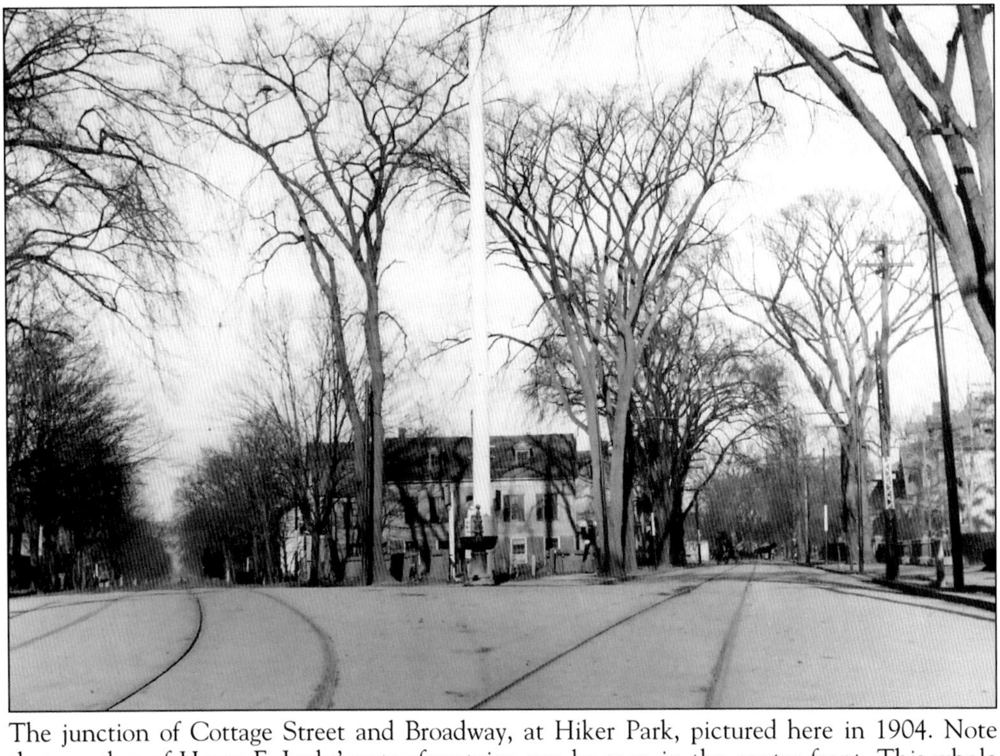

The junction of Cottage Street and Broadway, at Hiker Park, pictured here in 1904. Note that another of Henry F. Jenks' water fountains can be seen in the center front. This whole intersection was eliminated when I-95 was constructed. (Pawtucket Public Library.)

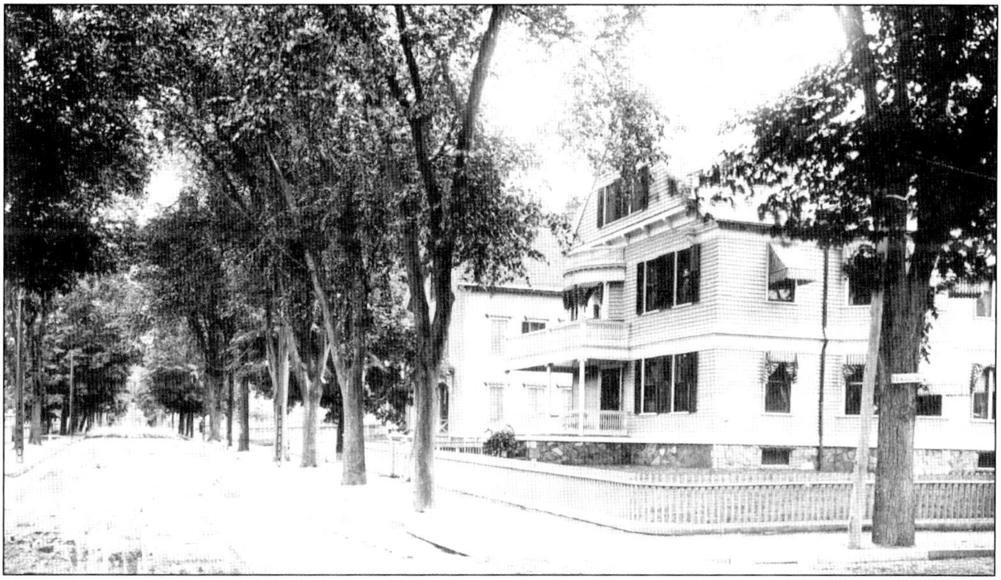

An 1896 view of the John Parmenter Hood Mansion at the corner of Cottage Street and Howard Avenue. Architect Albert Humes designed this late Victorian house c. 1891–92. Fire destroyed the house in 1979 and it was torn down soon after.

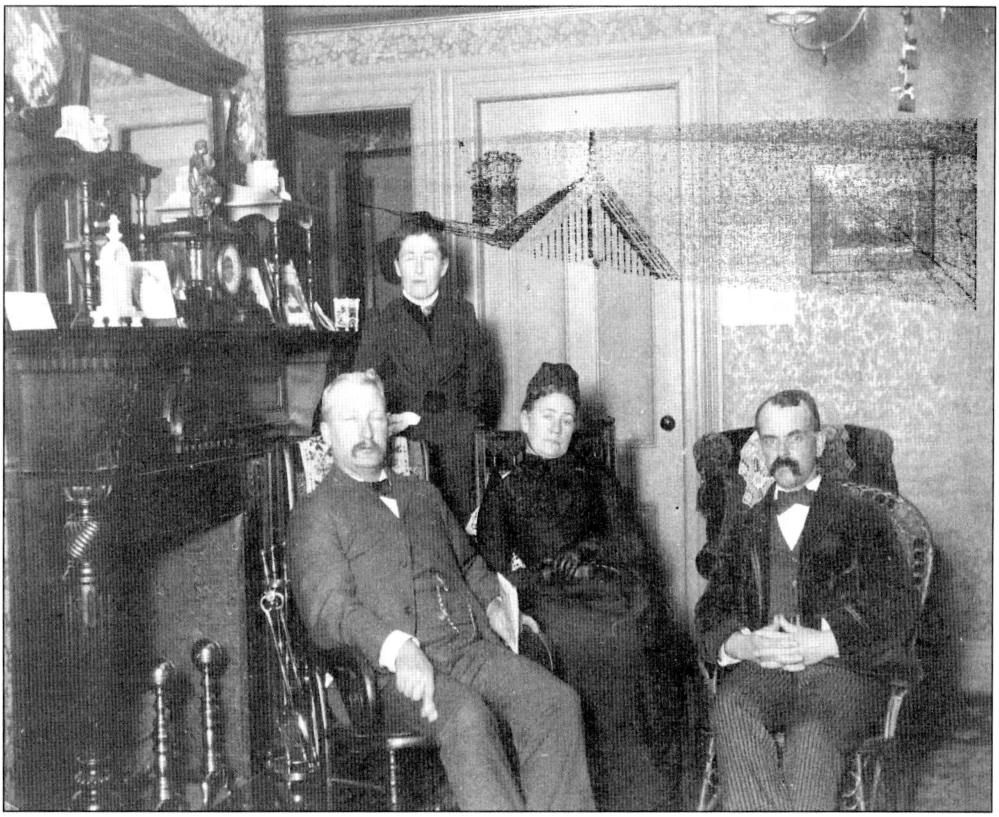

The residents of the John P. Hood Mansion. Vella Mathewson Hood is shown standing in the parlor, with John P. Hood at the right.

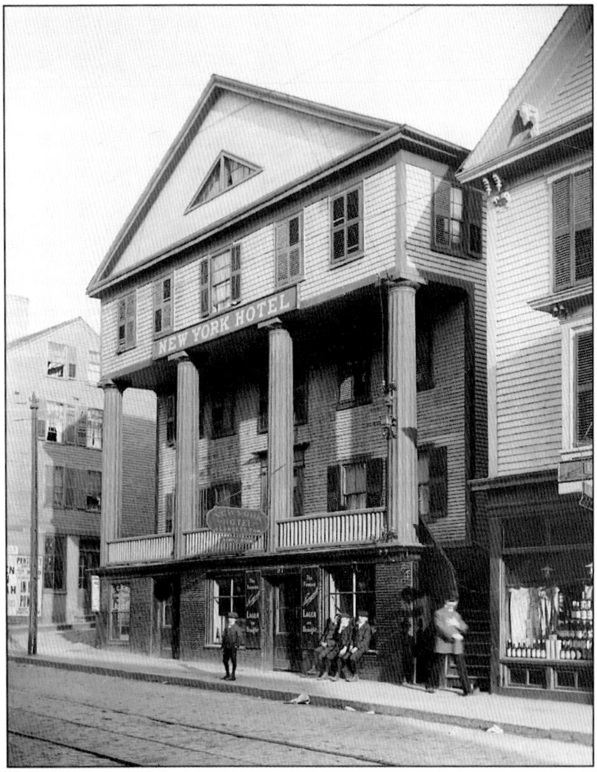

In 1904 the New York Hotel, run by Joseph Lonsett, was located on lower Broadway at Wing Lane (Wing Lane no longer exists). The hotel started *c.* 1925 as a boarding house run by Ebenezer Foster. It was successively known as the Mechanics Hotel (1838–1862), the Pawtucket Hotel (1862–1902), the New York Hotel (1902–1916), the Jackson Hotel (1916–1923), and the Jackson Lodgings (1924–1932). The building was torn down in 1935.

This 1871 photograph of the former Judge Pardon E. Tillinghast House, on Walcott Street, Pawtucket, shows the ornate style of Victorian Gothic architecture, which was popular from 1860 to 1890. Fancy towers and bay windows were typical of such houses. The house has been replaced by the parish house of the Pawtucket Congregational Church.

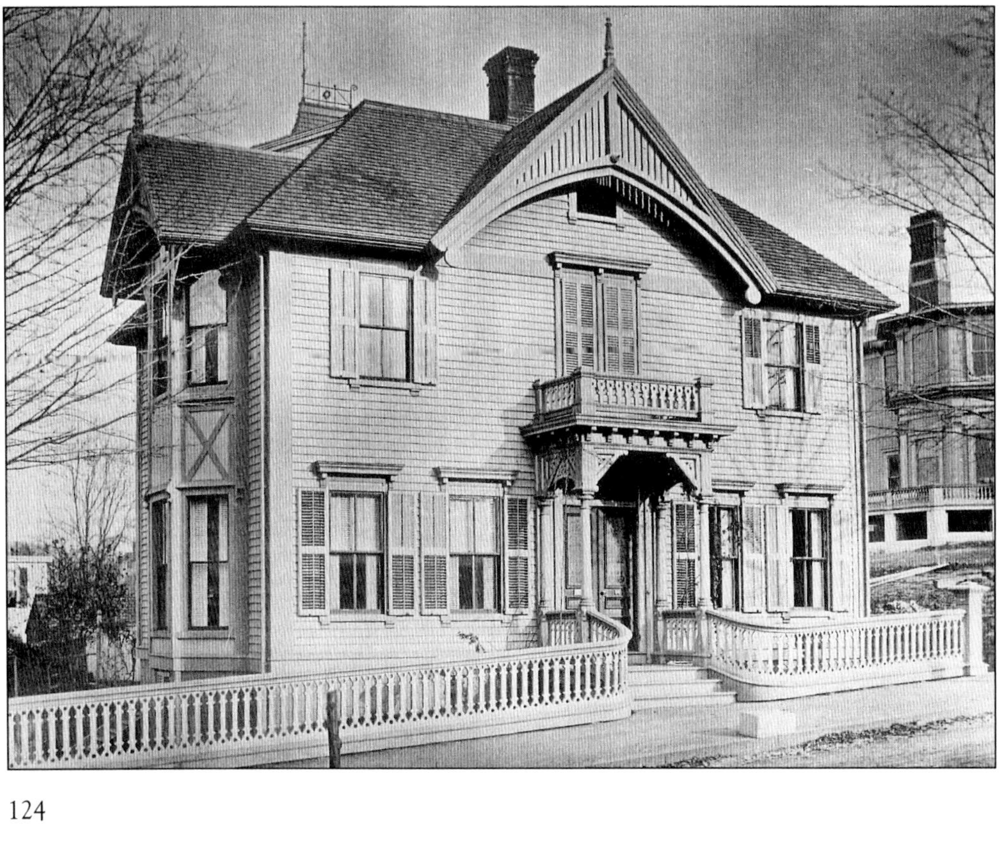

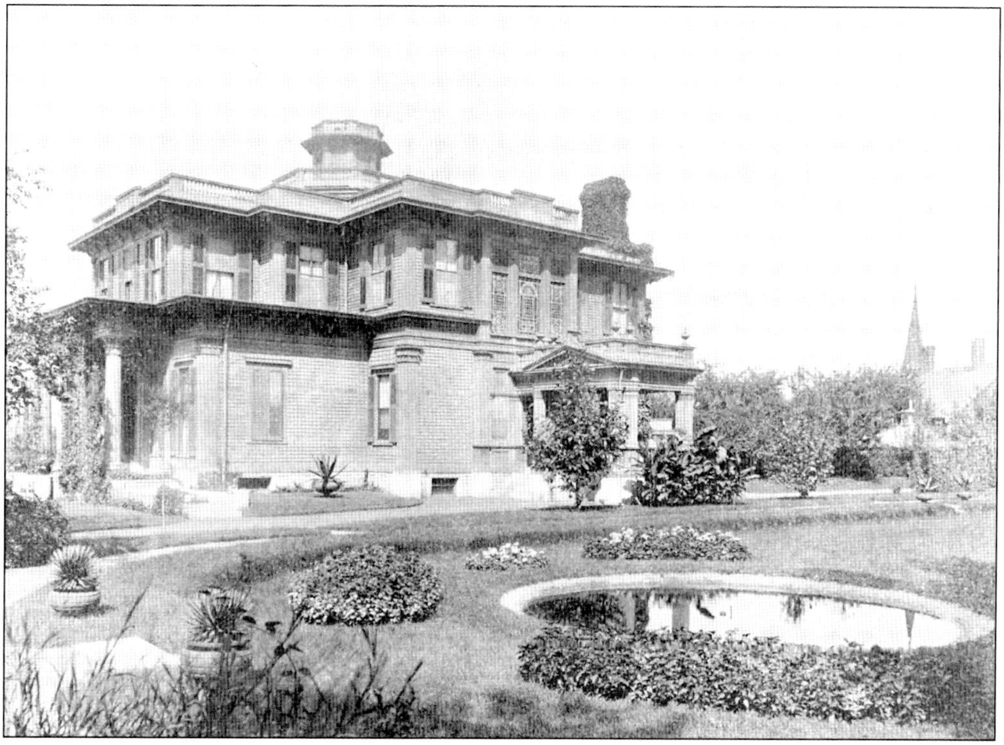

Express attention is given to the well-known and admired sunken gardens at the Colonel Lyman Bullock Goff Mansion. This view shows the gardens from the northwest corner of Summit Street at Walcott Street, where the land dropped off 5 or 6 feet to the pond below. The garden area is now a part of I-95 (see p. 112).

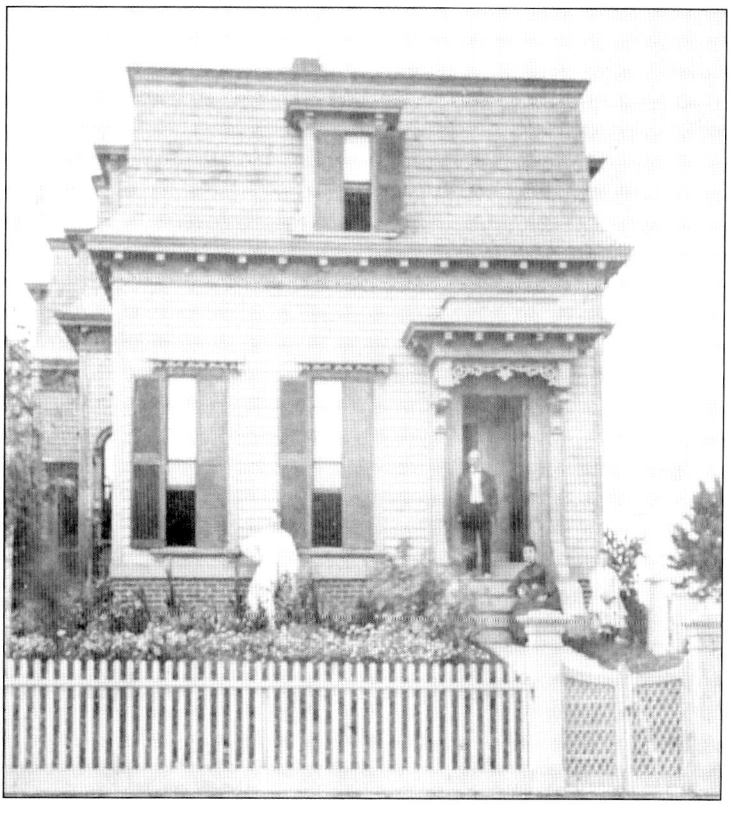

Built by William H. Bliss c. 1869, this house still stands at 168 Pine Street at the corner of Harrison Street.

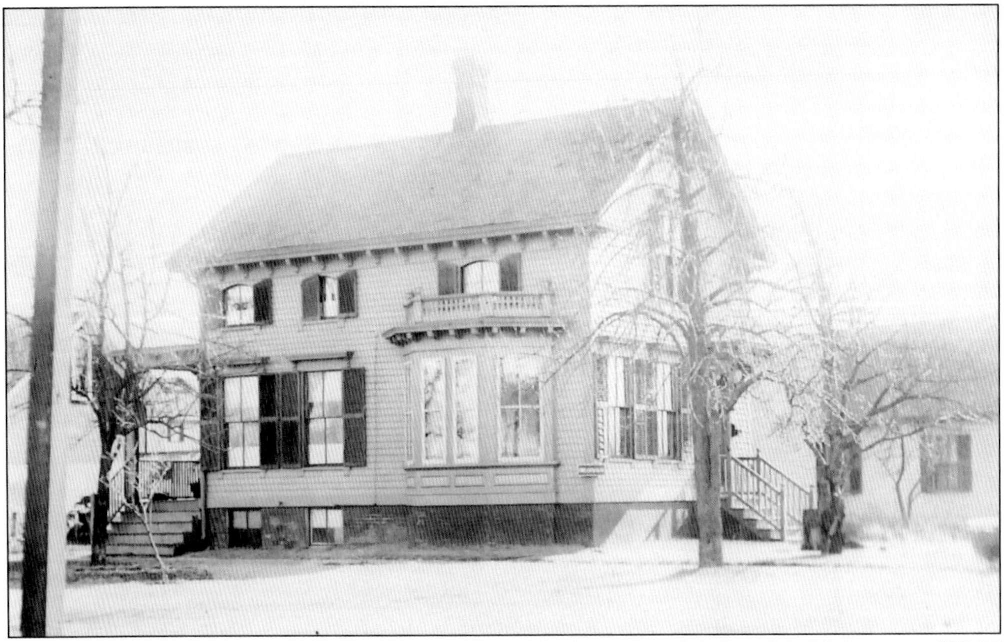

The home of Dr. William J. Graham, c. 1911. In this house, at 577 Smithfield Avenue, "Will" practiced medicine for twenty-six-and-a-half years, from January 1905 to September 14, 1931. In 1932, Dr. Graham moved to Foster, Rhode Island (see p. 113).

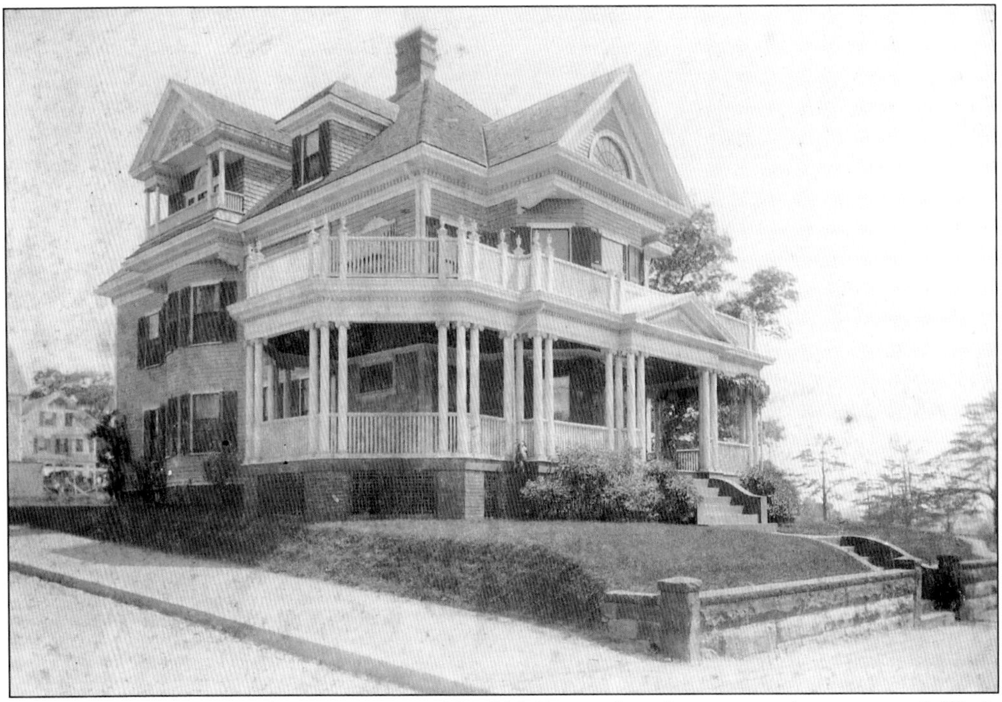

The George F. Cunningham House, at 330-332 Pawtucket Avenue at the corner of Clyde Street, was built in 1900 and is pictured here in the same year. Mr. Cunningham was a well-known champion roller polo player. He and his family lived at No. 330, and Robert A. Kendall was his first tenant, in No. 332 of this duplex house.

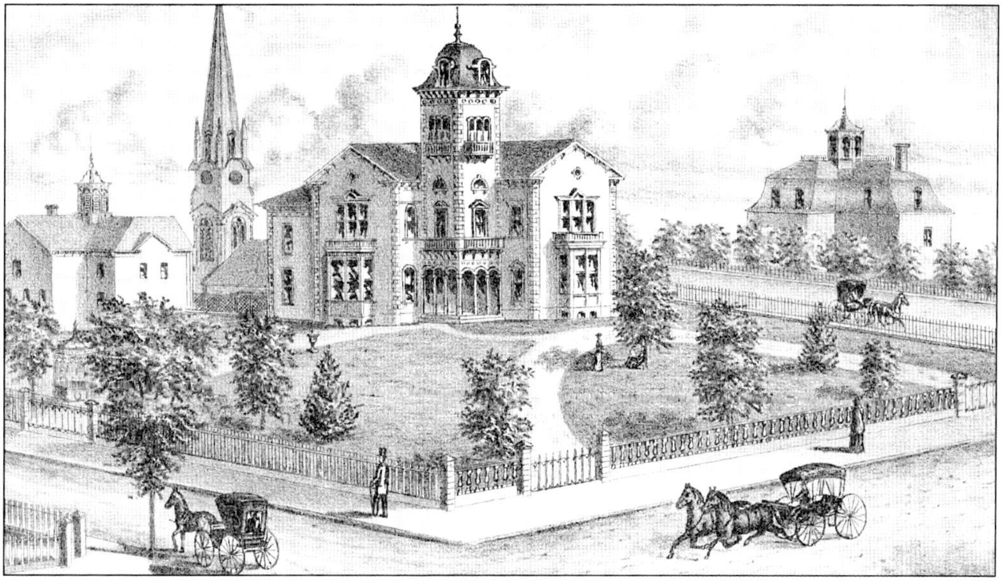

A c. 1887 view of the General Olney Arnold House, built in 1876 and located at the corner of Broad and Miller Streets, near Barton Street. Arnold was president of the First National Bank and treasurer of the Pawtucket Hair Cloth Company and Cumberland Mills Company. He lived here until his death in 1900. It was then converted to the Blackstone Hospital (1915–1919), the Hotel Georgian (1920–1930), the Hotel Slater (1935–1945), and the Hotel Arnold (1946–1962). The building was eventually demolished, and in 1966, the John F. Kennedy Housing for the Elderly and the Handicapped was built on the site.

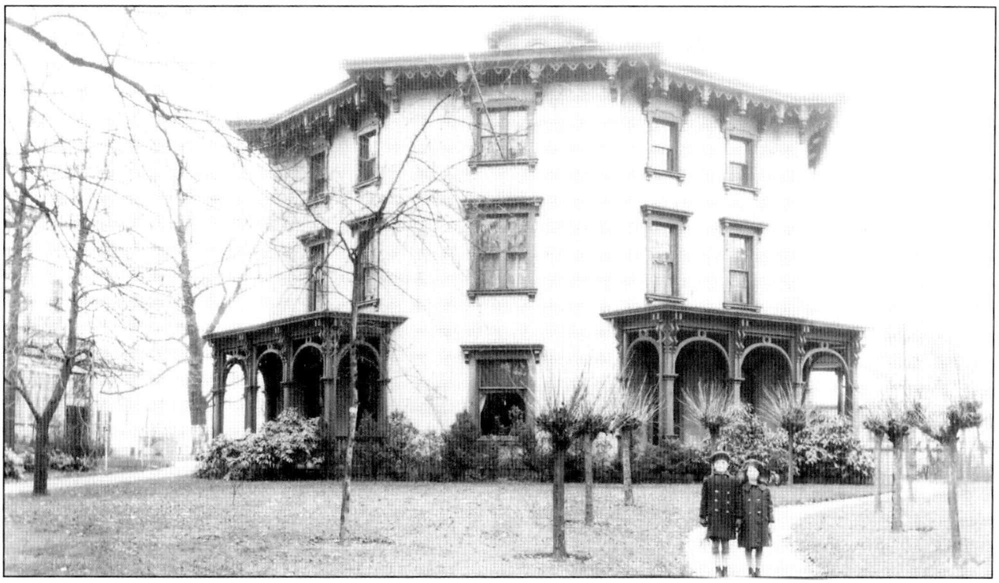

In 1856 Jesse S. Thornton built the Octagon House at 42 Park Place. Octagon houses were a phenomenon in the 1850s. We remember this most notably as the Adam Sutcliff Home. After Adam Sutcliff's death in 1919, his daughter June (Mrs. Thomas F. Morris) returned with her children to live with the children's grandmother and Uncle Marcus Sutcliff. The house was torn down shortly after 1955. June Morris' children, pictured here, are George E. Morris (left) and his sister June F.S. (Morris) Russell.

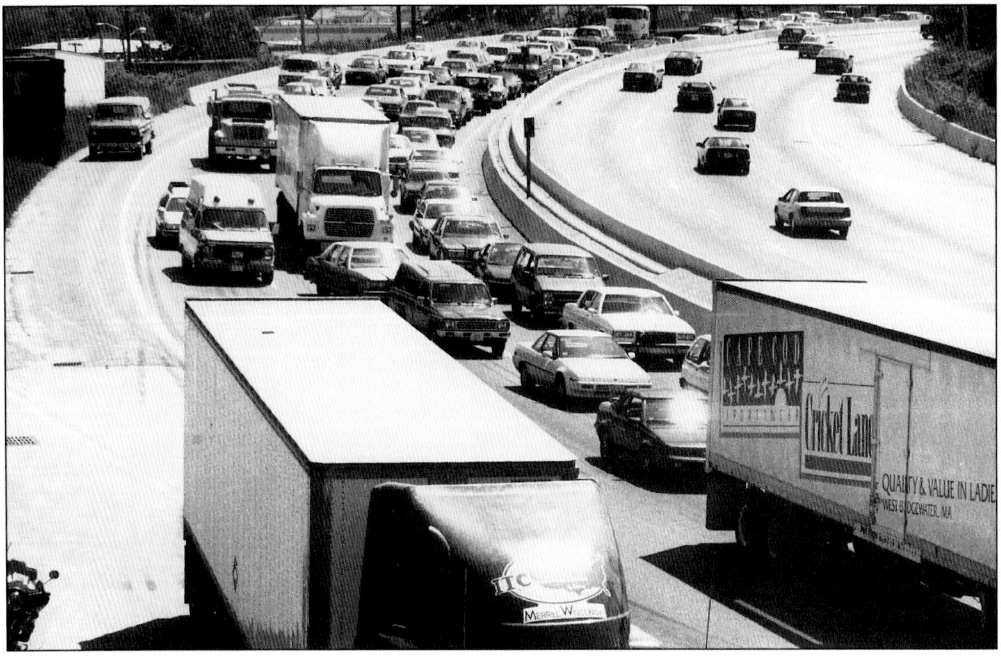

Going home! A northbound traffic jam on I-95 in the summer of 1991, with cars stalled back to Branch Avenue. This view is from the Walcott Street Bridge. (*Times*.)

ACKNOWLEDGMENTS

Many of the photographs and other illustrations in this book come from the collections of the Spaulding House Research Library and the Pawtucket Public Library. Where no credit line accompanies a picture, it should be inferred that the source is the Spaulding House Research Library collection. Pictures from the Pawtucket Public Library collection are designated accordingly.

The *Times* has generously allowed us to copy and use a number of their archive photographs. The pertinent pictures are credited accordingly. The *Times* photographers were Antoine Boulanger, C. Corrigan, Earl Dumin, Rich Dugas, and William Huntington.

We are appreciative to have been allowed to copy three photographs of import into our library for use in this book. We would like to thank: the Pawtucket Red Sox, for the picture on the bottom of p. 115; the Visiting Nurse Service of Pawtucket, Central Falls and Lincoln, for the picture on the bottom of p. 91; and the Providence Public Library, for the picture on pp. 52 and 53.

We are fortunate to have had gifts to our respective collections from many people. A number of these appear in this book. For these, we give appreciative thanks to: Peter and John Palagi, Hope B. Slocum, C. Louise Hague, Theresa E.P. McGeough, Deborah (Fleming) Charron, The Parker Luther Co., Wesley Yando Jr., Edith Dunbar, Edna (Hutchinson) Davis, Mrs. Roger Clapp, Mrs. Morris Russell, Miss Anna F. MacSwan, Alice E. Chace, The Robinson Green Beretta Corporation, Richard I. Buckley, Jim Caulfield, Kenneth Roberts, Charles H. Ross, and Alice Vincent.